The Book of Church Growth

History, Theology, and Principles

THE BOOK OF
CHURCH GROWTH

History, Theology, and Principles

THOM S. RAINER

BROADMAN
& HOLMAN
PUBLISHERS

Nashville, Tennessee

© Copyright 1993 Broadman Press
All Rights Reserved
4211-57
IBSN: 0-8054-1872-5
Dewey Decimal Classification: 262
Subject Heading: CHURCH GROWTH // CHURCH
Library of Congress Catalog Number: 92-29944
Printed in the United States of America

Unless otherwise noted, all Scripture quotations are taken from the Holy Bible, *New International Version*, ©1973, 1978, 1984 by International Bible Society.

The Chart of the Attributes of God—pp. 95-97, Chart of the Names of Satan—p. 125, and Chart of the Theories of the Atonement—p.137 were taken from *The Moody Handbook of Theology* by Paul Enns. © Copyright 1989, Moody Bible Institute of Chicago. Moody Press. Used by permission.

The illustration on p. 285 was taken from Gary McIntosh and Glen Martin, *Finding Them, Keeping Them: Effective Strategies For Evangelism and Assimilation in the Local Church* (Nashville: Broadman Press, 1992), 12. All rights reserved. Used by permission.

Library of Congress Cataloging-in-Publication Data
Rainer, Thom S.
    The book of church growth: history, theology, and principles / Thom S. Rainer.
        p. cm.
    Includes bibliographical references and indexes.
    ISBN 0-8054-1872-5
    1. Church growth. 2. Evangelicalism—History—20th century.
    I. Title.
    BV652.25.R35 1993
    254'.5— dc20   92-29944
                                                              CIP

To Jo
my wife
my best friend

Preface

Perhaps more than any other event to date, the publication of *The Book of Church Growth* signals the coming of age of the Church Growth Movement. Thom Rainer has accomplished what many of the veterans of church growth have been desiring for years—a true textbook for teaching church growth.

Donald McGavran's *Understanding Church Growth* (Eerdmans), now in a revised and updated third edition, will remain the foundational classic of the movement. No one will be able to claim professional expertise in the field without having read and digested that book. However, *Understanding Church Growth* has built-in limitations. As a pioneering work, it reflects what Thom Rainer calls "The McGavran Era," when one person's ideas were establishing a basic paradigm for others to follow, and thus the book is both limited and dated. Much has been added to the Church Growth Movement since 1970, when the book was first issued.

The second generation of church growth leaders, those who studied directly under McGavran in the 1960s and 1970s, had no inclination to write a comprehensive textbook. Rather, they chose to direct their research and writing toward more specific areas of church growth suggested either explicitly or implicitly by McGavran's writings. Through the contributions of the second generation the Church Growth Movement began to mature.

Thom Rainer is an outstanding representative of the third generation. He did not study under McGavran or Wagner. He has no degree from Fuller Seminary. He began his observation of the Church Growth Movement as a neutral practitioner in the field who had a deep desire to see souls won to Christ and churches multiplying. If, in his opinion, church growth principles could help accelerate the evangelization of his community and world, he would embrace them. If not, he would quickly look elsewhere for help.

As *The Book of Church Growth* clearly exhibits, Dr. Rainer liked what he saw. He liked it at least well enough to decide to dedicate two facets of his career to pursuing church growth. Thom Rainer is one of those rare combinations of a scholar and a practitioner. So he decided, first of all, to devote his Ph.D. research and writing to the subject. Second, he personally applied church growth principles to his pastoral ministry and saw churches grow as a result. As senior pastor of Green Valley Baptist Church, he has seen membership reach 1,700, and the church is still growing.

I mention this simply to say that I know no one better qualified to author the first true textbook of the Church Growth Movement. I feel privileged to know Thom personally and to sense the heart he has for God and His Kingdom. I am impressed with the breadth of his work. Rainer covers the field from Roland Allen to relevant books published only a couple of months before I read the manuscript.

This is a book not only for seminaries and Bible schools but for pastors and church leaders wherever they might be and whatever their denomination. If you want to get your church off dead center and moving vigorously forward for the glory of God, you will find no better resource than *The Book of Church Growth* you are about to read.

C. Peter Wagner
Fuller Theological Seminary
Pasadena, California

Acknowledgments

My students at Beeson Divinity School in Birmingham, Alabama, often heard me speak about the need for a general introductory work to the Church Growth Movement. Their encouragement and input played a major role in my writing "the Book," the name they later assigned to this project. I am indebted to all of my Beeson students, the most able and gifted students with whom I have ever been associated.

A special word of thanks is due to Broadman Press and the editor for this book, John Landers. *The Book of Church Growth* was my first publishing experience with Broadman, and I have not been disappointed. John Landers and the fine staff added clarity and organization to my book, while allowing me the freedom to express my thoughts and ideas.

I am blessed to be the senior pastor of Green Valley Baptist Church, a church that has caught the vision for many of the ideas expressed in this book. My gifted and joyful administrative secretary, Virginia Barksdale, has contributed to this book in numerous ways. She keeps me organized when my world would otherwise be in disarray. The entire wonderful staff of Green Valley Baptist deserves recognition for putting up with me and for allowing me to try my ideas and dreams. I express my deepest gratitude to all of the staff, especially the ministerial core group: Chuck Carter, Charles Dorris, Marion (Bubba) Eubank, Tim Miller, and Rhonda Freeman.

Without the support of two of my mentors, *The Book of Church Growth* would have never become a reality. Lewis A. Drummond, who is now the Billy Graham Professor of Evangelism and Church Growth at Beeson Divinity School, encouraged my pursuit of church growth research while I was a doctoral student at the Southern Baptist Theological Seminary. C. Peter Wagner, who honored me greatly by writing the foreword to this book, has given me countless hours of interviews and correspondence, and hundreds of pages of pertinent material. He is the primary reason I remain convinced that the best days of the Church Growth Movement are still ahead. The reader will see Dr. Wagner's influence throughout this book.

The Book of Church Growth, in many ways, has been a family project. My brother, Sam Rainer, Jr., gave generous technical support and loving encouragement to his little brother. Sam is truly the gifted writer of our family.

Peggy Dutton, better known as Peggy Sue, must be included in the Rainer family. Peggy Sue typed the entire manuscript, proofread the work, and retyped when necessary. On countless occasions, she welcomed my three sons into her home when their dad needed a few hours of writing time alone. May these fews words be a token of my deep gratitude to Peggy Sue.

In many ways we are products of our formative years. I thank God for my mother, Nan Rainer, who never stopped encouraging me, never stopped believing in me, never stopped praying for me, and never stopped loving me. She has been a constant source of encouragement for this book and for life. The memory of her husband and my father, Sam Rainer, Sr., has strengthened me in my weakest moments.

The lion's share of the credit for this book, however, goes to a beautiful lady named Nellie Jo Rainer, and three precious gifts from God named Sam Rainer, III, Art Rainer, and Jess Rainer. My three boys never fail to pray for their dad in all that I do. No father could possibly be as blessed as I am. A wife's love was my earthly motivation to keep writing as deadlines neared and pressures mounted. Jo not only was my primary proofreader, she also used her own abilities in church growth to significantly improve this book. Her keen eye for details and her ability to empathize with the prospective reader resulted in several improvements. I say thank you to Jo for the untold hours you put into this book. Above all, thank you for loving me and for being my supportive bride for over fifteen years.

One final word. Some twenty-five years ago in Union Springs, Alabama, a high school football coach named Joe Hendrickson introduced me to the Savior whose church I write about in this book. I never thanked my coach for the eternal difference he made in my life, and I do not know where he is today. Perhaps somehow these words will find you, coach. Thank you for caring enough about one hungry little kid to tell him about the Bread of Life.

May Christ build His church.

Introduction

It was an unusual beginning. I was a student in a seminary class dealing with contemporary issues in Christian missions. One of the course requirements was a research paper, and the topic had to be chosen from a list provided by the professor. Among the subjects on that list were two words: "church growth." I was curious. What did church growth have to do with missions? Why was that topic a "hot" contemporary issue? I decided to write on church growth.

That unusual beginning, however, took another turn when I asked the professor for a bibliography on the subject. Almost every book he recommended had a strong bias against church growth. It was my first taste of some of the strong emotions that have surfaced since the Church Growth Movement began in 1955.

Many pastors, church staff members, and laypersons have been exposed to some aspect of church growth. They have heard of such names as C. Peter Wagner, Donald McGavran, George Hunter, or Elmer Towns. They may have attended conferences dealing with critical issues like baby boomers, contemporary worship, CAMEO churches, or Sunday School growth. Yet perhaps many of those interested in church growth know little about the "big picture." What exactly is church growth? How did the movement start? Where is it headed? What are the theological beliefs of church growth? What are the major principles that the movement has advocated for nearly forty years?

The purpose of this book is to introduce readers to the "big picture" of church growth. The book is divided into three major sections: history, theology, and principles. Each section stands on its own while being integrally related to the others. Those with an interest in contemporary church history may delve first into the history of the Church Growth Movement. Theologians who read this book may begin in part two, which deals with the theology of church growth. Many of the criticisms directed against the movement have been theological, and it is certainly fair to ask if church growth has a solid theological foundation. Finally, pragmatists may decide to skip the first two sections to discover the principles of church growth. After all, the movement began by someone asking the question: "Why do some churches grow and other churches don't?" Church growth *is* a pragmatic movement, and its principles were written years before anyone wrote about its history or theology.

A book that attempts to be as comprehensive as this one will be lacking in detail. For example, chapter 19 deals with leadership and church growth, the subject of an entire book by C. Peter Wagner.[1] I hope that each chapter will provide a sufficient bibliography for those desiring to study an area in greater detail.

Though written by a church growth advocate, this book seeks to present an objective view of the movement. It will examine contributions as well as criticisms. Some of the criticisms reflect a superficial knowledge of church growth ("All they are interested in is numbers!"). Others perhaps had merit in the early years of the movement ("They don't seem to care about social concerns.").

What has impressed me most about the leaders of church growth, however, has been their open-mindedness and willingness to change. If a criticism was justified those leaders adjusted accordingly. It is perhaps this irenic spirit and receptive attitude that has won over many critics and led church growth to become a voice of credibility in late twentieth-century evangelicalism.

Several years ago, I asked C. Peter Wagner what he hoped ultimately would be the contribution of the Church Growth Movement. He unpretentiously responded that his ultimate goal would be that the movement glorify God. To a significant degree, I believe that goal has been realized. If this book in some small measure accomplishes that same goal, then I will rest with the assurance that my labor has not been in vain.

[1]C. Peter Wagner, *Leading Your Church to Growth* (Ventura, CA: Regal, 1984). This book is a classic in church growth literature. Pastors especially will appreciate the insight Wagner gives to their role in the growth of the church.

Contents

Part I The History of the Church Growth Movement

1. The History of the Church Growth Movement 19
2. Forerunners of Church Growth 27
3. A Movement Is Born, 1955-1970 33
4. A Movement Struggles and Grows, 1970-1981 41
5. The Wagner Era, 1981-1988 51
6. Toward the Twenty-First Century, 1988 to Future............................61

Part II A Theology of Church Growth

7. A Systematic Approach to Church Growth Theology 73
8. Bibliology and Church Growth 87
9. Theology Proper and Church Growth..93
10. Christology and Church Growth..101
11. Pneumatology and Church Growth 111
12. Angelology and Church Growth..121
13. Anthropology, Hamartiology, and Church Growth 129
14. Soteriology and Church Growth 135
15. Ecclesiology and Church Growth..145
16. Eschatology and Church Growth..161

Part III Principles of Church Growth

17. Principles of Church Growth 171
18. Prayer: The Power Behind the Principles 175
19. Leadership and Church Growth 185
20. Laity, Ministry, and Church Growth 195
21. Church Planting and Church Growth..205
22. Evangelism and Church Growth 215
23. Worship and Church Growth..225
24. Finding the People..239
25. Receptivity and Church Growth 249
26. Planning, Goal Setting, and Church Growth..265

27. Physical Facilities and Church Growth 271

28. Assimilation, Reclamation, and Church Growth..........................281

29. Small Groups and Church Growth..289

30. Signs and Wonders and Church Growth...301

Part IV Concluding Matters

31. The Church Growth Movement: A Postscript..................................317

Church Growth Bibiography 321

Name and Subject Index 335

Scripture Index 345

Part I

The History
of the
Church Growth Movement

1

The History of the Church Growth Movement

Students like Mark have become easy to spot. Mark came to the opening session of my church growth class at seminary and sat conspicuously on the back row. He took in every word I said. By the third class he was asking a plethora of debating questions. Mark was the classic church growth skeptic.

The reward for me as his professor came at the end of the semester. On an evaluation of the class, Mark wrote these words: "Dr. Rainer, I took your class to fulfill a requirement for graduation. I initially had no desire to study church growth. For various reasons my attitude about church growth was very negative. I realize now that my attitude was the result of a lot of misinformation. Though I am not 'sold' on everything about church growth, I do feel very positive about the contributions of the movement. Thanks for 'clearing the air.'"

In the pages that follow, I hope to "clear the air"— to provide information about one of the most exciting developments in twentieth-century Christianity. In this section we will see how the movement began and what precipitated its birth. We will see the distinct eras of church growth and the struggles and victories of each era. We will see a movement that has entered an era of maturity, gaining acceptance in the larger evangelical community. Before we begin the journey, it is necessary to introduce and define some basic terms and concepts.

What Is Church Growth?

Because the words "church growth" are such common names, confusion abounds about the precise meaning of the phrase. When the North American Society for Church Growth wrote its constitution, it included a lengthy definition of church growth:

> Church growth is that discipline which investigates the nature, expansion, planting, multiplication, function, and health of Christian churches as they relate to the effective implementation of God's commission to "make disciples of all peoples"(Matt. 28:18-20). Students of church growth strive to integrate the eternal theological principles of God's Word concerning the expansion of the church with the best insights of contemporary social and behaviorial sciences, employing as the initial framework of reference the foundational work done by Donald McGavran.[1]

This definition, though wordy, includes some of the basic tenets of church growth.

Church growth is a discipline.   A discipline is a field of study or a system with distinct characteristics. Church growth is accepted around the world as a discipline worthy of recognition. Classes in the field are taught at countless seminaries and Bible colleges and professorships of church growth are increasing in number. Conferences related to the discipline are offered almost every week in places around the world. Church growth consultation has become an established and respected profession. Books directly and indirectly related to church growth could fill a small library.

Church growth is interested in disciple-making.   It is not merely a number-counting emphasis. While evangelism, in the sense of making converts, is of vital interest, the heart of church growth is to see those new Christians develop into fruit-bearing disciples of Jesus Christ. Most church growth leaders consider "responsible church membership" to be a barometer for discipleship.[2]

Church growth is founded on God's Word.   Both implicitly and explicitly there is a high view of Scripture in the literature emanating from church growth writers. We will discuss this concept further in the chapter dealing with bibliology.

---

[1]C. Peter Wagner, *Strategies for Church Growth* (Ventura, CA: Regal Books, 1987), 114.

[2]See Wagner's discussion in *Strategies for Church Growth*, 53-54.

Church growth integrates social and behavioral sciences to help determine how churches grow. For example, demographic studies are one of many church growth tools. While demography is not necessarily a biblical concept, neither is it unbiblical. Any tool or method that is not contrary to the Bible can be used in understanding church growth.

Church growth, as a modern-day movement, began with the work of Donald McGavran in India. His book *The Bridges of God*, published in 1955, is the "birth certificate" of church growth. We will be studying this man and his vast contributions throughout this book.

Some attempts have been made to simplify the definition of church growth. Wagner, for example, said that "church growth means all that is involved in bringing men and women who do not have a personal relationship to Jesus Christ into fellowship with him and into responsible church membership."[3] While this definition provides a concise description, it fails to mention social and behavioral sciences and the movement's founder, Donald McGavran.

Perhaps, then, we can define church growth without all the verbiage of the first meaning, but with a bit more detail than Wagner's definition: *Church growth is that discipline which seeks to understand, through biblical, sociological, historical, and behaviorial study, why churches grow or decline. True church growth takes place when "Great Commission" disciples are added and are evidenced by responsible church membership. The discipline began with the foundational work of Donald McGavran.*

What Is "The Church Growth Movement"?

The next several chapters will provide a rather detailed history and summary of the Church Growth Movement. For now, a basic definition will introduce the term: *The Church Growth Movement includes all the resources of people, institutions, and publications dedicated to expounding the*

---

[3]C. Peter Wagner, *Your Church Can Grow*, rev. ed. (Ventura, CA: Regal Books, 1984), 14.

*concepts and practicing the principles of church growth,
beginning with the foundational work of Donald McGavran
in 1955.*

In the next chapter we will see several of the factors that
precipitated the birth of the movement. We will also look at
many of the key persons who influenced McGavran.

What Kind of Growth Is Church Growth?

A church may grow by one or a combination of three
sources. *Biological growth* takes place when babies are born
to church members. From a church growth perspective,
biological growth is the source of least interest because the
newborn is not a disciple of Christ, as evidenced by
responsible, fruit-bearing church membership.

Transfer growth occurs when one church grows at the
expense of another church. If a person was inactive in his or
her former church, or if that person had little opportunity
for spiritual growth, transfer growth would be positive by
church growth standards. Such a move could result in a
greater depth of discipleship for the new member. In
contrast many churches whose primary source of growth is
by transfer are the beneficiaries of "sheep swapping" that
rarely results in more deeply committed Christians.

Conversion growth takes place when a person makes a
commitment to Jesus Christ as Lord and Savior. That
commitment, when evidenced by responsible church membership,
is the chief concern of most church growth research and effort.

Wagner and other church growth proponents use other
popular typologies of evangelism and church growth in
describing the parameters of the movement. Evangelism and
church growth overlap is evident in some of their definitions.
One typology uses four different classifications according to
the persons who are being evangelized.

"E-O" or "evangelism-zero" takes place when people who are
already church members are evangelized. When these people
make a commitment to Jesus Christ, evangelism has taken
place but the church does not experience quantitative growth.

"E-1" or "evangelism one" is evangelism outside the local
church but within the same cultural group. Fewer barriers

must be overcome when the gospel is shared with someone of a like culture than in cross-cultural evangelism. Typically, the language, food, custom, and life experiences of the evangelist and the receiver of the gospel message are very similar.

"E-2" or "evangelism two" and "E-3" or "evangelism three" are types of cross-cultural evangelism. The one who evangelizes must reach people in a culture different from his or her own culture. Typically "E-2" evangelism is sharing the gospel in a culture that is different but similar. For example, Americans evangelizing persons from France would be considered "E-2," but Americans evangelizing the Chinese, a more distant culture, would fit the "E-3" category.

Church growth may also be classified into four distinct *types* of growth. *Internal growth* is the spiritual maturity of the members. As the individual members of the body mature spiritually through worship, Bible study, prayer, service, and manifestation of the fruit of the Spirit, the corporate body grows in strength. In the early years of the Church Growth Movement, quantitative growth was virtually synonymous with church growth. Now writers such as Wagner also include internal or spiritual growth as a church growth category.

Expansion growth is the numerical growth of a local congregation. The type of expansion growth most often mentioned by the Church Growth Movement is conversion growth. Believers move out into the world, win people to Christ, and bring them into church membership.

Extension growth is the church growth term synonymous with church planting. New converts of the same culture as the mother church are gathered into new congregations. "E-1" evangelism can result in extension growth.

Bridging growth is also a form of church planting, but the new converts are from a different culture than the culture of those who are evangelizing. Either "E-2" or "E-3" evangelism could result in bridging growth, depending on the cultural distance of the evangelized from those who are evangelizing.

What is the Difference Between Evangelism and Church Growth?

Depending upon one's understanding of evangelism, the definition of church growth could have significant overlap with evangelism. For example, Lewis Drummond defines evangelism as "a concerted effort to confront the unbeliever with the truth about and claims of Jesus Christ and to challenge him with the view of leading him into repentance toward God and faith in our Lord Jesus Christ and, thus, into the fellowship of the church."[4]

While "conversion growth," to use church growth terminology, is the primary goal of evangelism, Drummond's definition also includes "fellowship of the church" as the evidence that the evangelistic process is complete. If such a definition of evangelism is accepted, church growth and evangelism are very similar. Most definitions of evangelism are only concerned with the proclamation of the gospel with the desire to lead someone to Christ. In that sense, evangelism may or may not lead to church growth. The church will experience growth only if conversion takes place and if that conversion leads to fellowship in the church.

Church growth then, in the strictest sense of its definition, is more comprehensive than evangelism. A church may experience growth from evangelism, but it may also grow due to biological growth and to the influx of other Christians. As you listen to and read the materials of church growth advocates, however, you will note an obvious bias for church growth that is also kingdom growth. In that regard, evangelism and church growth are close relatives.[5]

Where Did the Concept of Church Growth Begin?

It is amazing to see how rapidly the concepts of church growth have spread in the last several years. Mainline denominations, once largely critical of the movement, are publishing materials and books promulgating church growth principles. Seminaries are creating professorships and

[4]Lewis A. Drummond, *Leading Your Church in Evangelism* (Nashville: Broadman, 1975), 21.

[5]For a more comprehensive discussion see C. Peter Wagner, "Evangelism and the Church Growth Movement" in Thom S. Rainer, ed., *Evangelism in the Twenty-First Century* (Wheaton, IL: Harold Shaw, 1989). Wagner discusses the aspects of organization, education, theology, social concerns, ecclesiology, and methodology of the two fields.

chairs singularly devoted to church growth. The movement has become so eagerly accepted at the local church level that church growth conferences and conventions are well attended.

We must acknowledge that the concepts advocated by the Church Growth Movement are as old as the early church in Acts. To cite 1955 as the "birth" of the movement neglects such major historical events as the spiritual awakenings of the seventeenth and eighteenth centuries; the evangelistic contributions of men like John Wesley, George Whitefield, and Charles Spurgeon; the methodological approach of Charles Finney; or the Sunday School movement embraced by the Southern Baptist Convention. These and other factors are significant influences on church growth today. This book, however, specifically focuses on the movement which began with the missionary work of Donald McGavran.

Where then did the movement begin? How did it grow so rapidly and where is the movement headed? In the next several chapters we will answer these and other questions. First, however, we will examine those factors that influenced and precipitated the modern Church Growth Movement.

Suggested Reading for Chapter 1

Rainer, Thom S., ed. *Evangelism in the Twenty-First Century*. Wheaton, IL: Harold Shaw, 1989. See especially chapter 3.

Wagner, C. Peter. *Leading Your Church to Growth*. Ventura, CA: Regal, 1987.

Wagner, C. Peter. *Strategies for Church Growth*. Ventura, CA: Regal, 1987.

Wagner, C. Peter. *Your Church Can Grow*. Rev. ed. Glendale, CA: Regal, 1984.

Wagner, C. Peter, ed., with Win Arn and Elmer Towns. *Church Growth: State of the Art*. Wheaton, IL: Tyndale, 1986.

2

Forerunners of Church Growth

Although 1955 is the accepted birth date of the Church Growth Movement, many factors precipitated and influenced the movement years before its official inception. How far back should we look to discover these factors? Historical movements in the Book of Acts directly influenced the movement, as evidenced by frequent references to Acts in church growth literature.

This chapter, however, will look at the direct influences of Donald McGavran, the founder of the movement. It should be remembered that McGavran was on the mission field in India when he wrote the founding book, *The Bridges of God*, in 1955. His understanding of what "mission" means greatly influenced him and, eventually, influenced the Church Growth Movement.

McGavran's Understanding of Christian Missions

What does it mean to be a missionary? What is the primary purpose of a Christian mission? Missiology is a field of study that examines these and other important questions about Christian missions. Some missiologists will place a heavy emphasis on good deeds: hospitals, aid to farmers, and assistance in building projects. Others see education and establishing schools as the major roles of missions. Most evangelical works on missiology give evangelism a prominent, if not priority, role in missions.

Evangelism, or an emphasis on converting non-Christians to Christ, is a major concern of missions that influenced Donald McGavran's approach to his calling in India. McGavran followed the path blazed by missionaries such as Henry Martyn and

William Carey who saw the saving of souls to be the priority of Christian missions. Likewise, the Student Volunteer Movement, whose influence could still be felt early in McGavran's missionary career, emphasized the conversion of individuals as the primary purpose of missions. Under the leadership of John Mott, Robert Speer, and Herman Rutgers, the movement mobilized thousands of American and European students to give their lives to missionary service, with the stated goal of "the evangelization of the world in this generation."

The concept of conversion as the primary task of missions is essential to church growth thought. Another important source of thought, however, is the concept of ecclesiocentricity, defined as a church-centered missionary strategy. This influence on McGavran is evident in many church growth writings today. These writings emphasize the importance of new converts becoming active in the fellowship of a local church. They stress that evangelism is not complete until local-church discipleship is evident.

Missionary leaders like Henry Venn in the eighteenth century and Rufus Anderson in the nineteenth century regarded the local church as central to missionary endeavors. While evangelism was still a central task, establishing indigeneous churches was also critical for developing new believers into Great Commission disciples. McGavran's understanding of Christian mission then is twofold: first, conversion of the lost; second, a church-centered strategy for discipleship.

Influences on McGavran
on the Mission Field

Donald McGavran saw the most important tasks of the missionary to be evangelizing the lost and concurrently establishing indigeneous churches in which disciples would grow. While serving in India, McGavran was moved to put his beliefs into action by three significant influences. The first two influences were men with whom he found a great affinity. The third significant influence was the particular mission situation in which he was serving.

Roland Allen.   Roland Allen was a missiologist with a single-minded purpose. His 1927 book, *The Spontaneous*

Expansion of the Church and the Causes Which Hinder It, contained the type of boldness and fierce pragmatism that typifies much of the church growth writing today. Allen boldly declared that the church in his day had forgotten the mission methods set forth in the New Testament. The church, he said, was neglecting the biblical principles necessary for church growth while following unbiblical traditions and methods. One of the traditions followed was establishing institutions for missionary activity. Allen believed that the institutions drained financial and personnel resources that could be better devoted to propagating the faith. Allen viewed with suspicion any principle that impeded church growth. How remarkably Allen's words resemble the future writing of McGavran and the Church Growth Movement!

J. Waskom Pickett. While Allen's boldness motivated McGavran, the research of Methodist Bishop J. Waskom Pickett moved the father of church growth to action. Pickett's survey showed that the 134 mission stations in mid-India (where McGavran then served) grew only 12 percent in ten years. Appalled at the slow growth and few conversions, McGavran began researching into church growth in his area, looking at statistics as far back as 1918.

When Pickett's research was published under the name *Christian Mass Movements in India* in 1933, McGavran became an enthusiastic disciple, learning how people become Christians through mass movements. Eventually the two men teamed with two other authors in 1936 to publish additional research in a book entitled *Church Growth and Group Conversion.* McGavran wrote the dedication. This book preceded the "birth" of the Church Growth Movement by almost two decades; yet the words seem as pragmatic and zealous as church growth writings today: "Dedicated to those men and women who labor for the growth of the Churches, discarding theories of church growth which do not work and learning and practicing productive patterns which actually disciple the peoples and increase the Household of God."[1]

---

[1]J. W. Pickett, A. L. Warnshuis, G. H. Singh, and D. A. McGavran, *Church Growth and Group Conversion*, 5th ed. (South Pasadena, CA: William Carey Library, 1973). The first edition was published in 1936.

Pickett's influence on McGavran can be felt in church growth today in at least three areas.

Pragmatic approach.   The pragmatic approach of Pickett to missions is proclaimed by church growth advocates today: if it is not unbiblical, and if it contributes to the growth of the church, then do it.

Mass Movements.   Pickett introduced McGavran to "mass movements" that McGavran later called "people movements," because mass movements implied "unthinking acceptance of Christ by great masses."[2] McGavran explained the specifics of the movement: "People become Christians as a wave of decisions for Christ sweeps through the group mind, involving many individual decisions but being far more than merely their sum. This may be called a chain reaction. Each decision sets off others and the sum total powerfully affects every individual. When conditions are right, not merely each sub-group, but the entire group concerned decides together."[3]

Receptivity.   Perhaps the clearest church growth principle that has emerged from Pickett to McGavran to modern church growth is the principle of receptivity. Receptive people are those who are most likely to hear the gospel message positively as a result of personal crisis, social dislocation, and/or the internal working of the Holy Spirit. Pickett and McGavran both emphasized that resources of people, money, and energy, in a world of limited resources, should be directed toward those who are most likely to hear and obey the gospel of Jesus Christ. Do not neglect unreceptive people, they said, but use the greatest level of resources to reach the greatest number likely to receive Christ.

McGavran's Mission Situation.   McGavran was greatly influenced by Allen and Pickett. He turned to these men as mentors beause of his great concern for his particular mission situation. Had it not been for the dismal outlook of his missionary work, the Church Growth Movement as we know it probably would not have been conceived. The discussion of his situation in India is thus vital in our

[2]Donald Anderson McGavran, *The Bridges of God* (New York:Friendship Press, 1955), 13.
[3]Ibid., 12-13.

understanding of the events that led to the 1955 birth date of church growth.

McGavran first became concerned about his particular mission situation in the 1930s, when he was executive secretary and treasurer of the United Christian Missionary Society in India. His responsibilities included the supervision of eighty missionaries, five hospitals, several high schools and primary schools, evangelistic efforts, and a leprosy home. Despite the massive amount of resources expended in his mission, McGavran was deeply disturbed that, through several decades of work, the mission had only twenty to thirty small churches, all of which were experiencing no growth.

McGavran left his administrative position and spent his next seventeen years planting churches and researching church growth. His interest was stirred by studying 145 mission stations in India. Of the 145 stations, only 11 were keeping pace with the general population of India! Even so, nine stations had doubled in just three years, mostly adult conversions. He asked again and again: "How do you account for growth and non-growth in identical situations where presumably missionaries have been equally faithful?"[4] Questions like these are behind most church growth research today.

McGavran's missionary situation and his realization that opportunities for evangelism were being lost daily gave him a sense of urgency in his task. It was this sense of urgency that led him out of administration and into church planting and research; his years of research ultimately led him to write *The Bridges of God*, the book which signaled the beginning of the Church Growth Movement. In the next chapter we will witness the birth of church growth and look at those first critical years under the leadership of Donald McGavran.

---

[4]A. R. Tippett, "Portrait of a Missiologist by His Colleague," in *God, Man, and Church Growth*, ed. A. R. Tippett (Grand Rapids, MI: Eerdmans, 1973), 21-22.

Suggested Reading for Chapter 2

Allen, Roland. *The Spontaneous Expansion of the Church and the Causes Which Hinder It.* 2nd ed. London: World Dominion, 1927.

McGavran, Donald A. *The Bridges of God.* New York: Friendship, 1955.

Pickett, J. Waskom, A. L. Warnshuis, G. H. Singh, and D. A. McGavran. *Church Growth and Group Conversion.* 5th ed. South Pasadena, CA: William Carey Library, 1973.

Tippett, Alan R., ed. *God, Man, and Church Growth.* Grand Rapids, MI: Eerdmans, 1973.

Verkuyl, J. *Contemporary Missiology: An Introduction.* Grand Rapids, MI: Baker, 1984.

Wagner, C. Peter, ed., with Win Arn and Elmer Towns. *Church Growth: State of the Art.* Wheaton, IL: Tyndale, 1986. See especially chapter 1.

3

A Movement Is Born, (1955-1970)

Donald Anderson McGavran was born in Damoh, India on December 15, 1897 to missionary parents John Grafton McGavran and Helen Anderson McGavran. His grandparents were also missionaries. McGavran came to America for college and post-graduate education. By 1923 he had earned three degrees, and he returned to the United States to earn a Doctor of Philosophy from Columbia University in 1936.

Following his ordination by the Disciples of Christ in 1923, McGavran returned to India as a missionary appointed by the United Christian Missionary Society. His first assignment was superintendent of the mission school system in Havda. This position was followed by the administrative assignment as director of Religious Education for the India Mission and, subsequently, as the secretary-treasurer. His experience in India included hospital administration, education, rural evangelism, church planting, and research. McGavran was also involved in translating the New Testament into the Chattisgarhee language. He also produced a motion picture portraying missionary life, entitled "Constrained by Love."

After twelve years of missionary service, McGavran began to inquire into the growth of churches. Influenced by the work of Pickett, the Mid-India Provincial Council asked McGavran to investigate the lack of growing Indian churches. Results of this study were published in 1936 under the title *Christian Missions in Mid-India*. The work was published under the new title *Church Growth and Group Conversion* in 1956, the third edition of the book. The fifth edition of the book was published in 1973.

Now McGavran's interest in church growth was developing into a passion. Between 1936 and 1953 he assembled a multitude of ideas and research about church growth. In 1953 McGavran's wife took over responsibility for the mission so that he could seclude himself in a jungle retreat. It was his desire to gather into a book nearly two decades of his church growth thinking. Little did McGavran know that he was writing a book that would mark the beginning of a new and major missiological movement.

The Bridges of God

After finishing his research, McGavran completed the manuscript in only one month. He submitted the work to Sir Kenneth Grubb of World Dominion Press, who called for several changes. The primary problem Grubb expressed was the new terminology in the book. "People movements," "perfecting," and "discipling" were terms that Grubb wanted to replace with more traditional language. McGavran refused to allow these changes and the first words of a new church growth vocabulary were coined. In 1955 *The Bridges of God* came off the press and the Church Growth Movement was born.

Reaction to the book was swift. Negative and positive reviews followed quickly on six continents. Some of the most well-known missiologists enthusiastically received it. Church and missiological historian Kenneth Scott Latourette wrote in the book's introduction: "To the thoughtful reader this book will come like a breath of fresh air, stimulating him to challenge inherited programmes and to venture forth courageously on untried paths. It is one of the most important books on missionary methods that has appeared in many years."[1] George F. Vicedom added his accolades: "This is in many respects a revolutionary book and the author is to be congratulated on his courage in writing it. Nobody can read it without being stimulated to re-think missionary policy in many lands."[2] Discussion and debate would continue for years.

[1]Kenneth Scott Latourette, "Introduction," in Donald Anderson McGavran, *The Bridges of God* (New York: Friendship, 1955), xiv.
[2]George F. Vicedom, "Revolution in Missionary Methods," *International Review of Missions*, 45 (1956), 331.

Wagner summarized the discussion of *The Bridges of God* into four principal areas: theological, ethical, missiological, and procedural.

Theological debate centered on McGavran's concept of evangelism. He saw evangelism as more than just proclaiming of the gospel; he insisted that evangelization is incomplete until the person becomes a responsible disciple of Christ. Later, church growth advocates such as C. Peter Wagner would look to active church membership as evidence of responsible discipleship. In other words, effective evangelism could be measured by numerical church growth.

The *ethical* issue concerned McGavran's pragmatism. He took Christ's command to make disciples seriously and literally. It was not enough to sow seeds and wait for God to produce results. *Accountability* was McGavran's watchword, and that accountability took place by evaluating numerical results. Critics charged that such pragmatism could result in high-pressured attempts to persuade people to make a decision for Christ. They feared that people would become little more than statistical victories.

The *missiological* issue would produce the greatest debate in missiology for the next three decades. The typical Western approach to evangelism was to preach an individualistic gospel and to expect decisions for Christ one by one. McGavran observed that the greatest number became Christians by making individual decisions collectively: families, extended families, villages, tribes, and so on. This process of conversion was called a "people movement." McGavran noted that the most effective evangelists were those who sought to win people of their own kind, persons from within their culture, class, tribe, or family. The controversy that erupted resulted from the *homogenous unit principle*. "Men like to become Christians without crossing social, linguistic, or class barriers."[3] This principle is a corollary to the people movement concept.

The final major issue in *The Bridges of God* was the *procedural* issue. McGavran said that the main task is discipling, bringing unbelievers to commitment to Christ

[3]Donald A. McGavran, *Understanding Church Growth*, rev. ed. (Grand Rapids, MI: Eerdmans, 1980), 198. C. Peter Wagner revised this book again in 1990.

and to active fellowship in the church. McGavran also said
that the discipling aspect of the Great Commission (Matt.
28:19) was a distinct, separate stage from the step of
"teaching them all things," which he called perfecting. When
perfecting took place, the community as a whole began to
live a thoroughly Christian way of life. McGavran's priority
of discipling over perfecting was criticized on procedural,
exegetical, and ethical grounds.

The Bridges of God had nevertheless made its impact.
McGavran soon became in demand as a speaker and
lecturer. He was invited as a visiting professor of missions to
seven different schools in a three-year period. The message
of church growth began to reach a wider audience.

The Movement Becomes an Institution

The longevity of the Church Growth Movement can be
attributed to a great extent to the beginning institutionalization
of the movement. While McGavran was traveling and
teaching, he dreamed of founding an institution that could be
the bearer of church growth principles. His dream became a
reality in 1960 when the Northwest Christian College in
Eugene, Oregon, invited him to locate his Institute of Church
Growth on its campus. The Institute began full operation in
1961. McGavran explained the guiding principles of the
institute.

> At this time, world mission faces a curious fact— knowledge
> of how churches grow is extremely limited. Instances of
> church growth occur, but are shut away in linguistic,
> geographic, and denominational compartments. Little
> knowledge of how churches grow is available. Few books are
> published on the subject. What are available have tiny
> circulations. Membership increase is a central function of
> mission, yet world mission has no clearing house for
> knowledge about it, no place dedicated to research
> concerning it, no centre at which missionaries and nationals
> can learn the many, many ways in which churches multiply,
> a distinct way for each particular population of mankind.
> This disastrous vacuum in knowledge and training
> handicaps the entire missionary enterprise.

> The Institute of Church Growth has been launched by
> Northwest Christian College, of Eugene, Oregon, USA,
> assisted by the United Christian Missionary Society of
> Indiana, as a pioneer effort to fill the vacuum.[4]

At the Institute of Church Growth, pioneers in the
movement began clarifying terminology and methods. The
Institute also provided the impetus for the movement to
begin publishing church growth concepts. At first McGavran
used the Lucknow Publishing House in India. Lucknow
published three church growth case studies. Soon, however,
William B. Eerdmans published two books that began the
Church Growth Series. The movement received more
attention when it began publishing the *Church Growth
Bulletin* (later called *Global Church Growth*). This periodical
was a bimonthly, sixteen-page publication edited by
McGavran and devoted to church growth concepts. The
response was so strong that it soon had more subscribers
than the well-known *International Review of Missions*.
These early publication ventures gave the Church Growth
Movement high visibility and influence and raised the
stature of the Institute of Church Growth.

The Iberville Consultation of 1963 also solidified the
influence of church growth during the Institute's years at
Eugene. This conference, sponsored by the World Council of
Churches in Canada, was a consultation on church growth.
Pickett, McGavran, and Tippett were invited to present the
movement's viewpoint. Many conference participants
enthusiastically endorsed church growth theory. The
Consultation as a body issued a formal statement endorsing
twelve points of church growth and approving the early
efforts of the Church Growth Movement.

Perhaps the single most important development in
holding the Church Growth Movement together transpired
in 1965. McGavran was invited to Fuller Theological
Seminary in Pasadena, California. There he reestablished
the Institute of Church Growth and became the founding
dean of Fuller's School of World Mission. Tippett

---

[4]Donald Anderson McGavran, "Institute of Church Growth," *International
Review of Missions*, 50 (1961), 431-432.

accompanied McGavran in this new endeavor, and the
School of World Mission and Institute of Church Growth
began to operate as a graduate institution in September,
1965.

Delos Miles affirms, "Nothing of greater importance has
happened to McGavran's church growth emphasis than his
move to the Fuller stronghold in Pasadena."[5] The Fuller
school became the hub around which many church growth
activities revolved. Included in the organizations and
services in the Pasadena area are the William Carey
Library, the largest publisher of church growth literature in
the world, founded in 1969 by Ralph D. Winter; a discount
outlet for church growth books, the Church Growth Book
Club, founded in 1970; the Institute for American Church
Growth, founded by Win Arn in 1973; the Charles E. Fuller
Institute for Evangelism and Church Growth, added in 1976;
the Missions Advanced Research and Communications
Center (MARC), a service of World Vision International's
Evangelism and Research Division; and the U.S. Center for
World Mission, founded in 1982 by Ralph Winter to help
reach the unreached peoples of the world.

The final significant development in the McGavran era of
the American Church Growth Movement was his writing of
Understanding Church Growth, which was published in
1970. Wagner has called this the *"Magna Carta* of the
Church Growth Movement."[6] *Understanding Church Growth*
spells out McGavran's mature thinking. The book discusses
and promotes the theology, sociology, and methodology of
church growth. Whereas *The Bridges of God* represented the
birth of the movement, *Understanding Church Growth*
brought the McGavran era to a fitting conclusion.

Although McGavran's influence in church growth
decreased after 1970, he continued to make significant
contributions. McGavran taught at Fuller until the age of
83; after retiring he maintained an active schedule of
writing, researching, traveling, and speaking until his death
in 1991. Saying that the McGavran era ended in 1970 with

[5]Delos Miles, *Church Growth: A Mighty River* (Nashville: Broadman, 1981), 12.
[6]C. Peter Wagner, *Your Church Can Grow* (Glendale, CA: Regal, 1976), 14.
This book was revised in 1980.

the publication of *Understanding Church Growth* does not mean that McGavran's influence on church growth ended. To the contrary, the influence of the father of the Church Growth Movement will be evident in missiology and evangelism for decades. However, since McGavran directed most of his attention in church growth to Third World nations and other areas outside the United States, church growth in America would be without clear leadership for approximately one decade.

McGavran was the pioneer of the Church Growth Movement, but a pioneering movement must eventually mature or die. For church growth, maturity did not come quickly. In the next decade debates, identity crises, and painful struggles would take place before the theological community accepted the Church Growth Movement and its many contributions. We will examine that era in the next chapter.

Suggested Reading for Chapter 3

McGavran, Donald A. *The Bridges of God*. Rev. ed. New York: Friendship, 1981.

McGavran, Donald A. *Understanding Church Growth*. 3rd edition revised by C. Peter Wagner. Grand Rapids, MI: Eerdmans, 1990.

Miles, Delos. *Church Growth: A Mighty River*. Nashville: Broadman, 1981.

Wagner, C. Peter, ed., with Win Arn ed., with and Elmer Towns. *Church Growth: State of the Art*. Wheaton, IL: Tyndale, 1986.

4

A Movement Struggles and Grows,
1970-1981

The 1970s was a time of both rapid growth and defensive retreat for the Church Growth Movement. This paradoxical situation resulted from some church growth advocates promoting their mission unapologetically while others used their works to defend church growth concepts which were being harshly criticized. With the exception of McGavran, no leader in this decade emerged as the primary spokesperson for the movement. McGavran himself did not write much about American church growth. Instead his writings focused on missions and church growth in other parts of the world.

The "Pasadena gang" was the group most clearly identified with church growth. This group includes those who were among the first faculty members at Fuller's School of World Mission: McGavran, Ralph Winter, Arthur Glasser, Charles Kraft, Allen Tippett, and C. Peter Wagner. To this group can be added Win Arn, who founded the Institute of American Church Growth in 1972, and John Wimber, who became founding director of the Department of Church Growth at Fuller Evangelistic Association (now known as the Charles E. Fuller Institute of Evangelism and Church Growth).

The 1970s produced some church growth advocates outside the Pasadena area as well. Kent R. Hunter founded the Church Growth Center in 1977 in Corunna, Indiana. Elmer Towns, now at Liberty University in Lynchburg, Virginia, made contributions specifically in the area of Sunday School growth. In Southern Baptist circles Charles Chaney and Ron Lewis co-authored the book *Design for Church Growth*.

Other developments also shaped church growth in the 1970s. Delos Miles notes seven factors that were shaping the Church Growth Movement.[1] The first such development was evangelical ecumenicity. This brand of ecumenism was exemplified best in the International Congress on World Evangelization in 1974 in Lausanne, Switzerland, and its predecessor, the World Congress on Evangelism held in Berlin in 1966. These meetings gave birth to numerous national congresses on evangelism and brought many evangelical leaders together for the first time. Lausanne drew evangelicals together, including church growth leaders, with the theological commitment set forth in the Lausanne Covenant.

Of particular importance to the Church Growth Movement in the new ecumenism was the easily accessible platform church growth leaders now had. Church growth leaders had high visibility, both at Lausanne and in the continuing Lausanne Committee for World Evangelization. The occasional papers published by the committee included some of the most widely discussed topics in church growth theory.

Second, the relationship between superchurches—large, aggressive, and growing churches—and church growth was also an influence in the movement. These numerically successful churches usually had highly visible pastors who gave strong leadership. This was realized as a principle of church growth in many books in the 1970s. The superchurches and their vigorous evangelism and outreach became models of church growth.

Third, the era of the 1970s coincided with the era of lay-witness training. Models for sharing the gospel emanated from such organizations as Evangelism Explosion III, the Billy Graham Evangelistic Association, and Campus Crusade for Christ. Southern Baptists developed WIN (Witness Involvement Now) and TELL (Training Evangelistic Lay Leadership). Evangelistic churches were receptive to witness training and to the precepts of the Church Growth Movement.

---

[1]See Delos Miles, *Church Growth: A Mighty River* (Nashville: Broadman, 1981), especially chapter 2.

The two forces complemented each other.

Fourth, church growth emphasized the role of equipping all believers to do the work of ministry. The lay renewal movement found an ally in the Church Growth Movement, since independent groups such as Faith at Work, Laity Lodge, the Yokefellows, and the Institute for Church Renewal joined various denominational groups in lay renewal emphases.

Fifth, the Neo-Pentecostal impact on church growth can be traced to this era. Not only was church growth touched positively by the charismatic movement in mainline denominations, the impact also came from such parachurch groups as the Full Gospel Business Men's Fellowship International, Women Aglow, PTL, and the 700 Club.

Sixth, Miles also makes a case for the influence of the Sunday School movement on church growth. Southern Baptists were especially noted for church growth through the Sunday School in the 1970s. There was a noticeable similarity between many tenets of church growth and Sunday School growth.

The final and seventh influence that affected church growth in the 1970s, said Miles, was the Keswick Movement. Keswick originated in England in the 1870s. While Keswick's primary focus is on internal and spiritual growth, "it has great potential for empowering Christians to turn outward in expansion, extension, and bridging growth,"[2] that is, it is also a type of church growth.

McGavran's influence on American church growth peaked in 1970 with the publication of *Understanding Church Growth*. He did, however, make two significant contributions in the 1970s that helped firmly establish church growth in America. First, in 1972, McGavran and Wagner taught an experimental course in church growth designed especially for a new generation of leaders in America. In the same year Paul Benjamin's *The Growing Congregation* was published. Wagner described Benjamin's book as "the first direct effort to apply church growth

[2]Ibid., 26.

principles to the American context by a denominational publishing house."[3]

McGavran's second major contribution to American church growth in the 1970s was the writing of *How to Grow a Church*, a book co-authored with Win Arn in 1973. The book was written as an easy-to-understand dialogue between McGavran and Arn. The highly technical language of earlier books was conspicuously absent, and many of the church growth principles were applied to the American scene.

Other events shaped church growth during this time. In 1972 Paul Benjamin founded the National Church Growth Research Center, an organization devoted to church growth in America. Also in 1972 the publication of *Why Conservative Churches Are Growing* generated much discussion and debate. The author was Dean Kelley, an executive with the National Council of Churches. His presentation of evidence that conservative churches were growing faster than liberal churches complemented church growth precepts, but it drew the criticism of many of his peers.

Despite the abundance of writings about and influences on church growth, the movement failed to establish a clear identity. Church growth material began to be published from so many different perspectives that it was difficult to answer the question: "Who speaks for church growth?"

Another critical factor adding to confusion in church growth circles was the manner in which the movement responded to criticism. McGavran was the aggressive protagonist of the movement. His writings were straightforward and unapologetic. The candid and sometimes polemical tone of McGavran's views set the pace by which church growth boldly asserted itself.

By the beginning of the 1970s, the critics of church growth began to gather momentum. Advances were being made in the Church Growth Movement, but a significant amount of the movement's time and resources were being devoted to responding to criticism. A sampling of the criticisms provides the general milieu in which church growth found itself in the 1970s.

[3]C. Peter Wagner, *Your Church Can Grow*, rev. ed. (Glendale, CA: Regal, 1980), 17.

Some critics showed disdain for the kind of evangelism inherent in church growth models. Commenting on the concept of the homogeneous unit, one critic concluded that church growth was "evangelism without the gospel."[4] Church growth, he said, has a theology of evangelism "which reduces initial Christian commitment to an inoffensive appeal avoiding the suggestion that to become a Christian one must turn from a social order that perpetuates injustice."[5] Archbishop William Temple's definition of evangelism had been a standard among evangelicals for years, but when McGavran affirmed the definition, he was criticized for having a "narrow description of . . . evangelism."[6]

Wagner received the brunt of the criticism after the fury over *Understanding Church Growth* subsided. Wagner's approach to church growth and development, said one critic, "is precariously deficient as a strategy for evangelism."[7] Kenneth L. Smith of Colgate Rochester-Bexley-Crozier found fault with Wagner's strategy of evangelism because it concentrated on evangelism "in the narrow sense of 'saving souls.'"[8] Smith further characterized Wagner's methodology as "a mixture of theological absolutism (i.e. the necessity for a born again experience) and sociological utilitarianism."[9]

The seventies were also the time that Wagner began receiving the theology of the rapidly growing Pentecostals more warmly. His views here did not escape the notice of the critics. After Wagner wrote *Look Out! The Pentecostals Are Coming*, one reviewer said that his "book tends to read like a propaganda piece."[10]

[4]Tom Nees, review of *Our Kind of People: The Ethical Dimensions of Church Growth* by C. Peter Wagner, *Sojourners*, 9 (February, 1980), 27. Nees examines particularly the sociological precepts of church growth.

[5]Ibid., 29.

[6]John H. Piet, review of *Understanding Church Growth* by Donald A. McGavran, *Reformed Review*, 25 (Fall, 1971), 30. Archbishop Temple's definition is: "Evangelism is the winning of men to acknowledge Christ as their Savior and King, so that they give themselves to His service in the fellowship of His Church."

[7]David L. Watson, review of *Our Kind of People: The Ethical Dimensions of Church Growth* by C. Peter Wagner, *Perkins Journal* 33 (Winter, 1979), 33.

[8]Kenneth L. Smith, review of *Our Kind of People; The Ethical Dimensions of Church Growth* by C. Peter Wagner, *Review of Religious Research*, 22 (September, 1980), 100.

[9]Ibid.

[10]James Patterson, review of *Look Out! The Pentecostals Are Coming* by C. Peter Wagner, *Christianity Today*, 18 (June 21, 1974), 30.

The definition of evangelism, still a point of debate between church growth proponents and others today, was debated as early as 1971, the publication date of Wagner's *Frontiers in Missionary Strategy*. Again, Wagner was the chief recipient of the criticisms, exemplified by one reviewer who claimed that theologically Wagner fell "dangerously close to Pelagianism."[11]

Another series of rapid-fire criticisms came from those who viewed church growth as a misguided theology and sociology with an overemphasis on numbers. Speaking in opposition to the concept that mission should emphasize "the actual number of souls gained," Sabbas J. Kilian retorted: "If one continues to look at church growth exclusively as saving souls and at theology as feeding the people with the one formula allowed, one can hardly speak of an understanding of church growth today. In a diaspora situation, numbers reveal nothing at all."[12]

While not every critic summarily rejected the importance of numerical increase in mission, Robert K. Hundnut wrote a book-length repudiation of the quantitative emphasis approach to mission.

> People are leaving the church. It could not be a better sign. Indeed, while they are leaving church income is growing. It was up 5.2 percent in 1973, according to the National Council of Churches. This proves that the more serious the membership, the more substantial the church . . . . Most churches could be two-thirds smaller and lose nothing in power. In most churches, the first third are committed, the second third are peripheral, and the third third are out.[13]

Some antagonists of church growth were not so much irritated at the quantitative emphasis of the movement as they were at the perception that church growth alone claimed exclusive rights to this emphasis. In a review of *Understanding Church Growth*, James Scherer wrote,

[11]Roger S. Greenway, review of *Frontiers in Missionary Strategy* by C. Peter Wagner, *The Westminster Theological Journal*, 35 (Fall, 1972 to Spring, 1973), 373.

[12]Sabbas J. Kilian, review of *Understanding Church Growth* by Donald A. McGavran, *Theological Studies*, 33 (1972), 182.

[13]Robert K. Hundnut, *Church Growth Is Not the Point* (New York: Harper & Row, 1975), xi. Hundnut rejects growth as the "point" of the church and offers fourteen alternative purposes.

"[McGavran] would have us believe that numerical increase is rejected by the majority of persons concerned with mission work—a view that many readers are not likely to accept—and that he alone remains faithful to the commission to disciple the nations, while others have gone whoring after the *Baalim* of social relevance, ecumenical relations, institutional witness, and so on."[14]

Still others totally rejected church growth as a legitimate missiological movement. Shortly after *Understanding Church Growth* appeared Kilian stated that he "disagree[d] with M[cGavran] on almost everything."[15] Alfred C. Krass questioned the legitimacy of church growth as a movement.

> They have lost the woods for the sake of trees which they did not need to climb. In trying to develop a psychology of mission, a sociology of mission, an ethnotheology of mission, they have had of necessity to start from scratch with each new synthesis. They have picked up the relevant secular discipline at a certain point and tried to mate it with a real mission-theological concern—and rarely do they seem to go back to that secular discipline again, but labor on, patiently shouldering an immense burden trying to develop a new science.[16]

Other critics in the 1970s attempted to accept the contributions of church growth; yet they found serious hermeneutical and theological problems. "One problem area with church growth theory," said Third World missiologist Orlando E. Costas, "is the fact that its theorists have not been able to come up with a sound hermeneutic for their theological endeavors."[17] Costas and other critics charged that the Church Growth Movement had "failed . . . to interpret the text in the light of the many situations of contemporary man."[18] The church growth approach to Scriptures was thus seen to be

[14]James A. Scherer, review of *Understanding Church Growth* by Donald A. McGavran, *International Review of Mission*, 60 (January, 1971), 127.

[15]Kilian, 182.

[16]Alfred C. Krass, review of *God, Man and Church Growth: A Festschrift in Honor of Donald Anderson McGavran*, ed. A. R. Tippett, *Missiology*, 3 (January, 1975), 118.

[17]Orlando E. Costas, *The Church and Its Mission: A Shattering Critique from the Third World* (Wheaton, IL: Tyndale, 1974), 131.

[18]Ibid., 132.

primarily, perhaps solely, concerned with correct strategies for best results. As a consequence, church growth advocates were accused of ignoring poverty, oppression, and social, economic, and political problems.

As a result of the shallow hermeneutic of church growth, the critics charged, the movement developed a concept of mission that was incomplete and unbiblical. They believed that advocates of church growth had a narrow missiology that so focused upon results and conversions that Christian social ministry was all but forgotten; propagation of the faith completely overshadowed the whole gospel of Jesus Christ.

Thus Rodger Bassham argued in 1979 that "church growth theology has some serious weaknesses. . . . the narrow conception of mission as evangelism."[19] He concluded that the Church Growth Movement "appears to have neglected a substantial discussion which has taken place over the past twenty-five years, in which the meaning of mission, evangelism, witness, service, and salvation have been explored and developed."[20]

Such was the milieu in which church growth struggled in the 1970s. Criticisms were hurled at the movement with greater frequency and intensity. The reactions of the church growth advocates were mixed. McGavran and Wagner continued to affirm boldly the basic tenets of the movement. Still others were involved in writing a mix of both defensive and affirmative statements about church growth.

Yet as one reads the church growth literature emanating from that period, one gets the impression that the movement was seeking a clear identity and a prominent spokesperson. While McGavran's name remained synonymous with the Church Growth Movement, he was increasingly viewed as its pioneer. Toward the end of the decade the movement was in great need of a person who would make McGavran's basic ideas acceptable to the missiological and theological community in general. Without a new leader, the movement

[19]Rodger C. Bassham, *Mission Theology: 1948-1975, Years of Worldwide Creative Tension: Ecumenical, Evangelical, and Roman Catholic* (Pasadena, CA: William Carey Library, 1979), 194-195.
[20]Ibid.

was in danger of fading away with its founder, becoming a footnote in the annals of church history.

Church growth did not fade away, however, nor is it any longer perceived as a missiological fad. Although many dynamics were at work, one principal factor in the movement's staying power has been the voice and writings of C. Peter Wagner. His leadership will be the subject of the next chapter.

Suggested Reading for Chapter 4

Costas, Orlando. *The Church and Its Mission: A Shattering Critique from the Third World.* Wheaton, IL: Tyndale, 1974.

Kelley, Dean M. *Why Conservative Churches Are Growing.* Rev. ed. Macon, GA: Mercer University, 1986. The first edition was published in 1972 by Harper & Row.

Miles, Delos. *Church Growth: A Mighty River.* Nashville: Broadman, 1981.

Wagner, C. Peter, ed., with Win Arn and Elmer Towns. *Church Growth: State of the Art.* Wheaton, IL: Tyndale, 1986.

Wagner, C. Peter. *Your Church Can Grow*, Rev. ed. Ventura, CA: Regal, 1984. The first edition was published in 1976.

5

The Wagner Era, 1981-1988

While the Church Growth Movement was struggling for identity and acceptance in the 1970s, one man was steadily rising to the top as the chief spokesperson for American church growth. C. Peter Wagner is now the Donald McGavran professor of church growth at Fuller Theological Seminary. Whereas Fuller Seminary gave the movement its institutional staying power, Wagner provided the personal leadership to keep church growth at the forefront of evangelical Christianity. His background and pilgrimage portray a most unlikely candidate to lead the Church Growth Movement toward a new century.

Biographical Sketch of C. Peter Wagner[1]

Charles Peter Wagner was born on August 15, 1930, in New York City to C. Graham Wagner and Mary Lewis Wagner. His home life was warm and loving, but it was not a Christian home. Religion was rarely discussed in the Wagner family.

Wagner spent his early years in St. Johnsville, in the Mohawk Valley of New York between Albany and Utica. His German ancestors came to America in 1710 and settled in the Mohawk Valley in 1735. Wagner, through his early twenties, continued the farming tradition of his family.

During the Depression, the Mueller family of Germany immigrated to America and bought farmland near the Wagner family farm in St. Johnsville. The seemingly

---

[1]I am grateful to Dr. Wagner for the hours of interviews, discussions, and letters he has provided me since 1987. Most of the biographical information came from our discussions.

inconsequential development of two families living near one
another would eventually prove to be a divine appointment
for both Wagner and the Church Growth Movement. Though
the Wagners would move frequently in the northeast, Peter
Wagner would eventually meet the Mueller family. He also
met their daughter Doris, who had just become a Christian a
week earlier.

That first meeting quickly became a steady relationship
that led to Wagner's proposal for marriage. Doris Mueller
responded that she had made two promises to God that she
would not break. First, she promised God that she would
only marry a Christian. Second, she pledged to God that she
would be a missionary to Africa. Wagner knew little about
Christianity and less about missionary work, but he soon
made commitments to Christ and the foreign mission field.
Both decisions were genuine, and both decisions were
critical in the history of the Church Growth Movement.

Wagner married Doris Mueller on October 15, 1950, and
finished his studies at Rutgers University where he earned
the Bachelor of Science degree and was elected to Phi Beta
Kappa. Immediately the Wagners left for California for
further training. Wagner enrolled in the institution he now
serves, Fuller Theological Seminary in Pasadena. Doris
pursued her missionary training at the Bible Institute of Los
Angeles (now Biola College in nearby La Mirada). In 1955
Wagner received the Master of Divinity degree from Fuller
Seminary. He was then ordained in the New Brunswick
Bible Church. Faithful to their promises to God and to each
other, the Wagners then embarked on a sixteen-year foreign
mission pilgrimage.

The Wagners would serve three terms in Bolivia. They
were appointed first by the South America Mission and then
by the Bolivian Indian Mission (which later changed its
name to the Andes Evangelical Mission, and thereafter
merged with the Sudan Interior Mission). During their first
term the Wagners worked in the tropical jungle of eastern
Bolivia, where they planted a church, started a Bible school,
trained indigeneous leaders, focused on general evangelistic
ministries, and conducted numerous works. During this first
term in the tropics, Wagner became aware of Donald

McGavran. With an insatiable appetite for reading (especially during the long afternoon tropical siestas), Wagner read a book that was creating a stir in missionary thought and practice in the late 1950s, *The Bridges of God* by Donald McGavran. Wagner's initial reaction is noteworthy:

> I read a review of *The Bridges of God* in *Practical Anthropology* magazine, where the book was recommended. So I ordered the book and read it. The more I read the book, the crazier I thought the author was. I thought he was a quack—really off the wall. None of what he was saying in that book was what I learned at Fuller Seminary in my mission classes. Everything was just the opposite. So I finished the book and put it on the shelf for cockroach food. I went on to some other books and forgot about it.

Wagner's second term was spent in the more congenial climate of Cochamba in the Andes mountains. He took advantage of furloughs to further his education. Between the first and second term, from 1960 to 1962, Wagner returned to the United States to Princeton Seminary where he earned the Master of Theology degree.

Upon returning to Bolivia from Princeton Seminary, Wagner began to hear from Fuller Seminary alumni that McGavran had been invited to become the founding dean of a new School of World Mission. Wagner's response was less than placid. "They had invited this fellow McGavran, the crazy one, to become the founding dean—the fellow whose book was cockroach food. I thought, 'What is going on here?' So I decided that on my second furlough which was in 1967 and 1968, to enroll in the new School of World Mission and to see what this McGavran had to say."

Wagner thus pursued his third masters degree. His opinion of McGavran quickly changed. He was impressed with his mentor-to-be almost from the first day of classes. McGavran was equally impressed with Wagner. After Wagner earned the Master of Arts in Missiology in 1968, McGavran invited him to join the faculty of Fuller rather than returning to Bolivia. Wagner, however, felt an obligation to go back to Bolivia, where he had become the director of the mission. Nevertheless, Wagner visited Fuller in 1968, 1969, and 1970 as an adjunct professor in the School of World Mission. Finally, in 1971, Wagner felt free to answer God's call to become a full-time faculty member at Fuller Seminary, where he has remained to the present. In 1977, while he was teaching at Fuller, Wagner completed the Doctor of Philosophy degree in Social Ethics from the University of Southern California. He focused his studies there on the much-debated homogeneous unit principle.

The Rise of Wagner in the Church Growth Movement

C. Peter Wagner was one of many who followed the teachings of Donald McGavran in the seventies. By 1981, however, with the publication of *Church Growth and the Whole Gospel*, Wagner began to be identified as the leading spokesperson for the Church Growth Movement. The publication of this book alone did not raise him to the level of prominence he now holds in the movement.

Wagner and McGavran were mutual admirers from the first day they met. When Wagner speaks of his mentor, he expresses a devotion that is like the devotion of a loving son for his father. McGavran's writings reflect similar feelings toward Wagner, and he was glad he had recruited Wagner to teach at Fuller Seminary.

A bond of friendship existed between the two men, but the professional admiration of McGavran for Wagner did even more to move the student toward the point of becoming successor to his teacher. Wagner excelled in his studies under McGavran, and McGavran's enthusiasm for church growth principles caught the attention of his mentor. Beginning in 1971 the two were colleagues on the faculty for over a decade. McGavran had founded the School of World Mission to train students who were serving in Third World nations. The scope of the studies broadened, however, when Wagner joined the faculty in 1971. Under Wagner's leadership, the field of American church growth began to gain prominence. The first course in church growth for American pastors was added in the fall of 1972. McGavran and Wagner co-taught the experimental course, which became a prototype for future courses in American church growth. When Wagner was named the Donald A. McGavran professor of church growth at Fuller Theological Seminary in 1984, few people expressed surprise.

His relationship to McGavran was not the sole factor in Wagner's rise to prominence in the Church Growth Movement. In many ways Wagner has been a most influential promotional agent for church growth. He has promoted the church growth message through a broad-based teaching ministry, by maintaining a high visibility in many theological, missiological, and denominational circles, and by a prolific writing ministry.

Each year hundreds of students study church growth at Fuller Theological Seminary under Wagner. A full-time professor at Fuller teaches a minimum of twenty-four units annually. Wagner typically teaches sixty-two units, all in the field of church growth.

In 1975 the Fuller School of Theology began a new Doctor of Ministry program, and Wagner was asked to teach one church growth course. A second course was added to the curriculum shortly thereafter. Students can now do up to eighty percent of the Doctor of Ministry work in church growth. All seminars last two weeks; the program requires three seminars and a dissertation.[2]

Hundreds of students, pastors, and denominational leaders are thus exposed to church growth training in Fuller Seminary's Doctor of Ministry program. Though he is assisted in the teaching load, Wagner is the main force in the church growth aspect of the training. About two thousand students have studied under Wagner alone in this program. Many of these students have become active and visible proponents of church growth. In addition, each Doctor of Ministry student must submit two papers for publication before graduating. Thus the message of the Church Growth Movement is multiplied each year.

Wagner's teaching ministry goes beyond the Pasadena campus of Fuller Seminary. Of the four Doctor of Ministry seminars he teaches annually, one is offered in a location away from the California coast. Because of the increasing

[2]See C. Peter Wagner, ed. with Win Arn and Elmer Towns, *Church Growth: State of the Art* (Wheaton, IL: Tyndale, 1986), 272.

popularity of church growth, students come from all locations to study under Wagner. An off-campus location for one seminar a year makes the program more attractive for students who do not live near the West Coast.

Another important facet of Wagner's teaching ministry is his service through the Charles E. Fuller Institute of Evangelism and Church Growth in Pasadena. This seminar ministry began when he became executive director of the Fuller Evangelistic Association in addition to his professorship at Fuller Seminary in 1971. In 1975 Wagner asked John Wimber to become the founding director of the Fuller Institute in order to have an institution for professional church growth consultation. Wimber later left the Institute to become the founding pastor of Vineyard Christian Fellowship and Vineyard Ministries International. Carl George succeeded Wimber and continues to lead a wide array of ministries through the Institute today. Wagner remains connected to the Institute as Senior Consultant. He leads church growth seminars that are in turn producing a new generation of church growth disciples.

Wagner keeps the church growth message alive giving seminars, conferences, committees, and meetings around the world. He typically plans at least two overseas trips yearly, in addition to his extensive travels in the United States.

Peter Wagner has served in many positions as a proponent for church growth. He was one of fifty charter members of the Lausanne Committee for World Evangelization when it was formed in 1974. He was subsequently elected to the Executive Committee, on which he served for six years. Because of his prominent role at Lausanne, he was founding chairperson of the Lausanne Strategy Working Group which sought to discover unreached peoples as part of the strategy for world evangelization. As a result of this effort, Wagner initiated the *Unreached Peoples* annuals and co-edited the first three volumes with Edward Dayton, who succeeded him as chairperson of the Strategy Working Group.[3] The initial

[3]See C. Peter Wagner and Edward R. Dayton, eds., *Unreached People '79* (Elgin, IL: David C. Cook, 1978); C. Peter Wagner and Edward R. Dayton, eds., *Unreached Peoples '80* (Elgin, IL: David C. Cook, 1980); and C. Peter Wagner and Edward R. Dayton, eds., *Unreached Peoples '81* (Elgin, IL: David C. Cook, 1981).

Lausanne gathering was a milestone in the rising influence of modern evangelicalism. Primarily because of the work of Wagner, church growth played a major role at Lausanne.

Wagner was also instrumental in founding the North American Society for Church Growth, serving as its first president in 1984. He remains active in the organization today. Another organization, the Institute for American Church Growth in Pasadena, has the mark of Wagner's influence as well. The Institute was conceived by Win Arn after Arn had studied in an experimental course under Wagner and McGavran in the fall of 1972. Immediately after the course Arn established the Institute, and Wagner and McGavran were made members of the founding board of directors. The Institute for American Church Growth is one of the most influential communicators of church growth principles in North America.

Although McGavran was the pioneer of the Church Growth Movement, C. Peter Wagner has been its best salesperson, teaching, speaking, serving in key positions, and traveling worldwide. His most important work, however, has been his writing. He began his writing ministry in 1956, and published his first book in 1966. Wagner has published over seven hundred works since 1956, including almost forty full-length books.

During the 1970s Wagner wrote several books explaining the practical application of church growth theories. His major contribution in this area was that the books were written for American pastors and churchgoers. *Your Church Can Grow* sold over 100,000 copies. *Your Spiritual Gifts Can Help Your Church Grow* was likewise successful. These books brought home church growth from the mission fields abroad to America.

Perhaps Wagner's most significant books were not his better-selling works. A book-length treatment of the homogeneous unit principle, *Our Kind of People: The Ethical Dimensions of Church Growth in America*, was published in 1979. Despite harsh criticisms from many sectors, *Our Kind of People* was foundational in discussing church growth's most controversial principle.

Despite Wagner's increasing prominence in the Church Growth Movement, the 1970s continued to be a time of crisis and confusion. Criticism pounded the movement relentlessly, while no definitive defense of church growth principles appeared. That predicament ended in 1981 with the publication of *Church Growth and the Whole Gospel: A Biblical Mandate*. As author of this book, C. Peter Wagner rose to the top of the movement and became clearly identified as the heir to McGavran's place of leadership in church growth. The publication of the book marks the beginning of the Wagner era of church growth.

In *Church Growth and the Whole Gospel* Wagner responded to the years of criticisms of the movement. The tone of this book was much less polemical than most earlier church growth writings. Openness to criticisms and new input marked the book. Speaking on his view of social concern, Wagner said:

> I feel like a candidate for the "how my mind has changed" series. Not that I have taken a complete 180 degree turn. In fact I am reasonably sure that some readers of this new book will say that the leopard has not changed his spots. But today I could no longer argue as I did that "one searches the Scriptures in vain to find a commandment that would have Christians move into the world with a mission designed to create peace and order, justice, and liberty, dignity and community."[4]

Wagner also demonstrated on openness to future developments and changes: "I realize that I am still not free from theological contradictions, although I hope to show before the first chapter is finished that I have resolved some of the old ones. Some new inconsistencies that I am not yet aware of undoubtedly crept in, and I would hope I recognize them within ten more years."[5]

What marks this book as a watershed in the Church Growth Movement is its defense of critical issues in church growth. Wagner responded to the critics who had hounded

---

[4]C. Peter Wagner, *Church Growth and the Whole Gospel: A Biblical Mandate* (San Francisco: Harper & Row, 1981), xii.
[5]Ibid., xiii.

him for years. He even acknowledged a debt of gratitude to many of them. Then he set forth an apologia for church growth. While Wagner realized that *Church Growth and the Whole Gospel* would not satisfy all the critics, he was pleased to see objections to the movement rapidly diminish. Virtually all of the criticisms raised since 1981 have been a rehash of earlier objections.

The Wagner era of the Church Growth Movement thus began with the publication of a book in 1981 that addressed concerns and criticisms. His church growth books since 1981 have demonstrated his growing influence and increasing contributions to church growth. In 1986 Wagner was the primary editor of *Church Growth: State of the Art*, a mini-encyclopedia and reference book about the Church Growth Movement. In 1987 he wrote a brief theological treatment of the movement in his book *Strategies for Church Growth*. This book includes discussions of the definition-of-evangelism debate and the unique hermeneutic of the movement.

C. Peter Wagner is still recognized as the leading spokesperson for the Church Growth Movement today. Largely because of his influence in other areas, however, a new era is taking shape. We will examine the modern era of the movement in the next chapter.

What has transpired in church growth since Wagner became the movement's leader? Church growth is increasingly recognized as a legitimate academic discipline in colleges and seminaries worldwide. Scholarly works are being produced in the form of theses and dissertations. Dozens of practical books on church growth appear each year. Professorships in church growth are being funded around the nation. Now almost forty years old, the Church Growth Movement has moved into a mature and modern era. To that period we now turn.

Suggested Reading for Chapter 5

Rainer, Thom S., ed. *Evangelism in the Twenty-First Century*. Wheaton, IL: Harold Shaw, 1989. See C. Peter Wagner's chapter on church growth and evangelism.

Rainer, Thom S. "An Assessment of C. Peter Wagner's Contributions to the Theology of Church Growth." Unpublished Ph.D. dissertation, The Southern Baptist Theological Seminary, 1988.

Wagner, C. Peter. *Church Growth and the Whole Gospel: A Biblical Mandate*. San Francisco: Harper & Row, 1981.

Wagner, C. Peter. *Our Kind of People: The Ethical Dimensions of Church Growth in America*. Atlanta: John Knox, 1979.

Wagner, C. Peter. *Your Church Can Be Healthy*. Nashville: Abingdon, 1979.

Wagner, C. Peter. *Your Church Can Grow*. Rev. ed. Glendale, CA: Regal Books, 1979.

Wagner, C. Peter. *Your Spiritual Gifts Can Help Your Church Grow*. Glendale, CA: Regal, 1979.

Wagner, C. Peter, ed., with Win Arn and Elmer Towns. *Church Growth: State of the Art*. Wheaton, IL: Tyndale, 1986.

6

Toward the Twenty-First Century, 1988 to the Future

When I finished my doctoral studies and my dissertation on C. Peter Wagner and church growth in 1988, I was uncertain about the future of the movement. Wagner was such a dominant voice that I wondered whether the movement could sustain its momentum beyond his lifetime. Several recent events, however, suggest that the Church Growth Movement will continue to grow well into the twenty-first century.

Wagner's Signs-and-Wonders Pilgrimage

The modern era of the Church Growth Movement began in 1988 when Wagner published a book that demonstrated his focus on one facet of church growth: signs-and-wonders church growth or power evangelism. The book carried the somewhat humorous title of *How to Have a Healing Ministry without Making Your Church Sick.* This book explained that God displays His supernatural powers to attract people to the gospel. The central focus of power evangelism is divine healing, though the display of God's supernatural powers has included tongues speaking, discerning of spirits, exorcising evil powers, and other extraordinary acts.

Wagner's venture into this arena of church growth brought criticism from two major groups. The first group critical of this facet of church growth argued that the "sign gifts" (tongues, interpretation, and healings) ceased with the apostolic era. Any manifestation of those gifts should be considered false or even demonic.

Another group critical of Wagner did not rule out the legitimate manifestation of sign gifts, but believed that Wagner's focus was a venture into the extreme. "He's gone charismatic!" some lamented. Others worried that he had left the mainstream of church growth thought and practice. We will look at this entire issue in chapter 30. For now, let us see how Wagner came to this new paradigm and how his view has affected the modern Church Growth Movement.

Wagner's early Christian years were certainly not times of openness to Pentecostal movements. He reflected on his early beliefs: "I used the Scofield Bible in both English and Spanish where the editor's footnote to 1 Corinthians 13:8 affirmed that the 'sign' gifts such as tongues, healings and miracles went out of use after the age of the apostles. I believed that miracles were useful in spreading the gospel before the New Testament was written, but once the canonical Scriptures were available, they rendered miracles absolute."[1]

In fact, Wagner readily admits that he was anti-Pentecostal. He felt that most of "Pentecostalism was at best a delusion and at worst a fraud."[2] Several events transpired, however, that moved him to a new understanding of some Pentecostal teachings.

First, Wagner was healed of a dangerous problem resulting from neck surgery to remove a cyst. The healing took place overnight after Wagner had attended a healing service in Bolivia out of curiosity. Second, the rapid growth of Pentecostalism led the ever-pragmatic Wagner to examine some Pentecostal and charismatic churches. His attitude changed dramatically. Third, Donald McGavran himself became more open to Pentecostalism. Said Wagner, "This, for me, was like a papal *imprimatur*. If it was all right for Donald McGavran, it was all right for me."[3]

Fourth, the influence of John Wimber was a major factor in Wagner's paradigm shift. Wimber, the founding director of the Charles E. Fuller Institute of Evangelism and Church Growth, eventually left the Institute to lead the rapidly growing Vineyard Christian Fellowship in Anaheim. One of the major influences of Vineyard was its healing ministry.

[1]C. Peter Wagner, *How to Have a Healing Ministry without Making Your Church Sick: Your Church and the Third Wave* (Ventura, CA: Regal, 1988), 33.
[2]Ibid.
[3]C. Peter Wagner, "MC510: Genesis of a Concept," in *Signs & Wonders Today*, ed. C. Peter Wagner (Altamonte Springs, FL: Creation House, 1987), 44.

Wagner was once again influenced by a close friend who held to signs-and-wonders church growth.

The final, and most controversial factor, was a new class offered at Fuller Theological Seminary: "MC510: Signs, Wonders and Church Growth." Wagner was the professor of record, but Wimber did most of the teaching. The lecture time was uneventful on the surface. After each class, however, students were invited to remain for a "ministry time" including prayers for healings. Although the additional session was strictly voluntary, rarely did students leave before the ministry time. Each week many participants in the class requested prayer for healings, and many testified to physical healings.

The course attracted national attention and controversy. Supporters of the seminary worried that the school was "going charismatic." Students and observers attended in droves. Many of the Fuller faculty feared that the course was damaging Fuller's reputation. MC510 was finally withdrawn from the curriculum in 1985. A task force worked for eight months, sorting through the various issues of the controversy. In the spring of 1987, a new course was offered, "MC550 — The Ministry of Healing and World Evangelization." The controversy died and order returned to the seminary.

Wagner would write about his theological shift and favorable attitude toward some aspects of Pentecostalism for several years. Finally, with the publication of *How to Have a Healing Ministry without Making Your Church Sick*, Wagner urged that the Church Growth Movement consider a paradigm shift. It is still too early to discern the direction of the movement as a whole in this regard. In the meantime, Wagner's focus in this area has opened the door for other church growth leaders to focus on mainstream topics about which he had previously written. Wagner has ironically helped the movement become stronger and more wide-based by delving into a controversial area.

The Era of Practioners

Some of the new church growth leaders, unlike Wagner, are practioners or pastors testing and proving church growth principles on the field. Pastoral leaders such as Bill Hybels, Rick Warren, John Maxwell, Doug Murren, and Ed Young have grown churches that have become models of church growth. They have written books, led conferences, and taught seminars to eager audiences desiring to hear and see how church growth works in practice. Undoubtedly, the Church Growth Movement, with a generation of applied growth principles in operation, will turn to practioners to learn how the principles might work in other settings.

Sociologists and Demographers

The Church Growth Movement has depended on research to understand its potential field from the very earliest days of the movement. The modern era of church growth, however, has witnessed an explosion of information coming from sociologists and demographers. Some of the information has emanated from a Christian perspective, from the studies of researchers like George Gallup and George Barna. Barna and his research team have become favorites of church growth conferences around the nation, and his books are among the best sellers on church growth bookshelves.

Church growth advocates, however, are not limiting themselves to books written strictly by Christians or from a Christian perspective. Any research that helps one understand the people who need to be reached for Christ is considered valuable to the movement. Generational books dealing with "baby boomers," "baby busters," and other groups of people have become popular reading material for church growth proponents.

Consultants and Consultation

Though church growth consultation is not a new concept its greatest growth apparently is still ahead. The number of consultants is growing rapidly. Lyle Schaller, the dean of church consultants, has focused much of his work on church growth, though he still does not identify himself with the Church Growth Movement. Carl F. George, the director of the Charles E. Fuller Institute of Evangelism and Church Growth, provides growth consultations to churches and denominations all over the United States.

Ron Lewis is probably the most well-known consultant among Southern Baptists. Church Growth Visions is a consulting firm established by Chuck Carter and me in 1991. As the message of church growth continues to grow, the demand for consultations and consultants will undoubtedly expand.

Publications and Other Media

The modern era of church growth has witnessed an explosion of printed, audio, and video materials on various church growth topics. My personal library of church growth books is now larger than my entire library of a few years earlier. Some recent books deal with general church growth principles (for example, *Church Growth Principles* by C. Kirk Hadaway[4]). Others have focused on a specific aspect of church growth, such as George Barna's book on the need for vision for growth, *Without a Vision the People Perish*.[5] Still others are closely related to church growth, such as those dealing with demographic or sociological trends. Again, Barna provides a good example of this type book in *The Frog in the Kettle*.[6]

Newsletters, magazines, and demographic news and trends are examples of print media offered in church growth. One of my personal favorites is *Growing Churches* magazine, published by the Sunday School Board of the Southern Baptist Convention.

Audio and video materials are also available. The Fuller Institute provides an excellent monthly audio cassette called *The Pastor's Update*. Video presentations on church growth precepts can bring a model church into the viewing of interested individuals at a reasonable cost. Willow Creek Community Church and senior pastor Bill Hybels offer videos on such subjects as worship and philosophy of ministry.

[4]C. Kirk Hadaway, *Church Growth Principles* (Nashville: Broadman, 1991).

[5]George Barna, *Without a Vision the People Perish* (Glendale, CA: Barna Research Group, 1992).

[6]George Barna, *The Frog in the Kettle* (Ventura, CA: Regal, 1990).

The number of media resources on church growth is thus a defining mark of the modern era. With new concepts being explored each year, there is no indication that the flow of materials will slow down.

A New Ecumenism

When the International Congress of World Evangelization met in Lausanne, Switzerland in 1974, a new ecumenical movement gained momentum. The movement was evangelical and evangelistic. The Church Growth Movement, well represented at Lausanne, has carried forth that same spirit two decades later. The movement claims supporters from virtually all denominations and bodies of believers, especially in North America. It is not unusual to see pastors and other church staff members use limited budget dollars for church growth and related conferences, funds which in the past would have gone to denominational conferences or conventions. The modern era of church growth has unified believers from diverse Christian backgrounds whose priorities are evangelizing and growing churches by adding "Great Commission disciples."

The Changing Shape of the Church

Perhaps the most visible impact of church growth in the modern era is the challenge it has brought to the customs and traditions of local churches. Because of its influence and its search to reach most effectively the lost and the unchurched, church growth is challenging the idea of "We've always done it that way before!"

The new or revitalized emphasis on lay ministry is causing many churches to transfer ministry responsibilities from clergy to laity. The traditional, though unbiblical, concept of the clergy's doing most of the ministry is slowly changing in many churches, though the influence of church growth is accelerating the process.

Worship changes are taking place at different rates in different churches in this new period of church growth. Such adjectives as "user-friendly," "contemporary," and "experiential" are associated with this new worship, much to the delight of some generations and much to the chagrin of others.

The very structure of the church is being challenged by some church growth advocates. The committee system, traditional staffing, the influence of denominations and seminaries, and the monthly business meeting are often seen as impediments to growth. Some leaders within the movement are insisting that "business as usual" must change if the lost are to be reached. One of the best books on the reasons behind these rapid changes in churches is Lyle Schaller's *The Seven-Day-a-Week Church*.[7] Schaller examines theological and sociological factors that have precipitated changes in churches. He explains the rise of megachurches, specialty churches, and the not-so-bright future of traditional Sunday-morning churches.

Perhaps no period since the Reformation has brought such changes and challenges to the church. The next two decades may be the most critical in the modern history of Christianity. While the Church Growth Movement did not cause the changes (as Schaller notes, a myriad of sociological and theological factors were at work), the movement has been among the first to respond to the changing world. What are some of the major challenges that church growth faces in the near future? A few examples will illustrate the dramatic pace with which the world is changing.

1. The aging of the boomer generation and the demands upon a church faced with an aging congregation.

2. The unbelievable pace of the information age. Will the church be left behind?

3. A new definition of "family." What are the implications for a church seeking to grow and to minister?

4. Social acceptance of lifestyles that are explicitly prohibited by Scripture.

5. The declining level of charitable and church contributions.

---

[7]Lyle Schaller, *The Seven-Day-a-Week Church* (Nashville: Abingdon, 1992).

6. A syncretistic nation: Christian, Jewish, Muslim, Morman, Hindu, Buddhist, Jehovah's Witnesses, New Age, or the cult-of-the-month.

7. Old and new world views: humanism, naturalism, scientism, mysticism, or Judeo-Christian theism.

8. The changing roles and conflicting views of women in ministry.

9. The one-campus, neighborhood church with one Sunday morning worship service: antique of older generations?

Can churches respond to this fast-pace change without losing their theological, historical, and confessional moorings? That chapter of church history is yet to be written.

The Church Growth Movement: Growing Acceptance

For many years church growth was perceived as a movement on the fringe of evangelical Christianity. Thirty years after its birth, the movement has found widespread denominational, practical, and theological acceptance.

Many denominations have embraced some church growth precepts. In my own Southern Baptist denomination, the Sunday School growth principles preceded and influenced the Church Growth Movement. Today the Sunday School Board of the Southern Baptist Convention publishes *Growing Churches,* a periodical mentioned earlier. The Home Mission Board conducts and sponsors church growth conferences. Most of the six convention seminaries offer church growth courses and the seminary at New Orleans recently opened a church growth center.

Other denominations also bear the impact of church growth principles. Even some mainline denominations, once wary of the movement, have accepted many church growth teachings.

On a practical level, tens of thousands of American churches have applied church growth principles with differing degrees of satisfaction and success. The movement's practical impact evidenced at the local church level is beyond measurement.

Theological acceptance of church growth is increasing, but questions about the movement still persist. The most significant challenge of church growth is to answer these theological questions, to define clearly the theological parameters of the movement. Because of church growth's desire to reach people for Christ, "relevancy" has been a watchword. In its enthusiasm to be culturally relevant, is the movement in danger of becoming biblically irrelevant? Has church growth compromised the doctrine of grace by insisting that the "evidence" of salvation be "responsible church membership"? Is the message of the "whole gospel" distorted by an overemphasis on evangelism?

Though the movement did not begin with a neatly defined set of theological principles, church growth, contrary to the opinion of some critics, is not "atheological." We must now examine the theology of the Church Growth Movement. We will not answer all theological questions in this modest attempt to systematize church growth theology, but perhaps we will put them in clearer focus.

Suggested Reading for Chapter 6

Barna, George. *The Frog in the Kettle*. Ventura, CA: Regal, 1990.

Barna, George. *User-Friendly Churches*. Ventura, CA: Regal, 1991.

Barna, George. *Without a Vision, the People Perish*. Glendale, CA: Barna Research Group, 1992.

Hadaway, C. Kirk. *Church Growth Principles: Fact or Fiction?* Nashville: Broadman, 1991.

Murren, Doug. *The Baby Boomerang*. Ventura, CA: Regal, 1990.

Schaller, Lyle. *The Seven-Day-a-Week Church*. Nashville: Abingdon, 1992.

Towns, Elmer. *Ten of Today's Most Innovative Churches*. Ventura, CA: Regal, 1991.

Wagner, C. Peter. *How to Have a Healing Ministry without Making Your Church Sick*. Ventura, CA: Regal, 1988.

Wagner, C. Peter. *Signs & Wonders Today*. Altamonte Springs, FL: Creation House, 1987.

Wimber, John with Kevin Springer. *Power Evangelism*. San Francisco: Harper & Row, 1986.

Part II

A Theology
of Church Growth

7

A Systematic Approach to Church Growth Theology

One's approach to theology can come from several different perspectives. Biblical theology examines each book or group of books in the Bible within their historical context to discern doctrines and God's progressive revelation from Genesis to Revelation. Historical theology studies the doctrines of the Christian faith as they have been articulated and debated for nearly two thousand years. Contemporary theology is the study of unique doctrines developed by Christian groups in recent years. Systematic theology studies the major teachings of the Christian faith, seeking especially to determine their meaning for the living church.

I have chosen to look at church growth theology in the context of each major doctrinal theme of the Bible. Although I realize that systematizing church growth theology may prove awkward at times, I see the need to view the movement's teaching in light of the major theological issues of the Bible.

Defining Systematic Theology

The word *theology* is the English combination of two Greek words, *theos*, meaning "God," and *logos*, most often defined as "word." The literal meaning of theology is "word about God," but, because we typically understand the *logos* suffix to mean "study of," we can simply understand theology to be "the study of God."

"Systematic" also has a Greek origin in the verb *sunistano*, which means "to stand together" or "to organize." Systematic theology then is the organization of facts about

God and His Word. The process of organization is usually by major biblical doctrines.

Earlier Church Growth Theology

This modest attempt to organize church growth theology builds upon several statements previously articulated. For example, C. Peter Wagner cited seven foundational theological precepts for church growth:[1]

1. The glory of God as the chief end of humans.

2. The sovereignty of God and human responsibility.

3. The exclusiveness of salvation through Christ.

4. The lordship of Christ.

5. The authority of Scripture.

6. The present and eschatological realities of sin, salvation, and eternal death.

7. The present and future reality of the kingdom of God.

No contemporary body of literature has shaped church growth's theology so much as the literature that emerged from the International Congress of World Evangelization in Lausanne in 1974. Because the Lausanne material is so important in understanding the framework of church growth theology, the entire Lausanne Covenant of 1974 is included in this chapter. Church growth, primarily through the work of Wagner in the Theology Working Group of Lausanne, influenced the Lausanne theology, which in turn has affected profoundly church growth theology.

Rather than examine Wagner's theological assumptions or the Lausanne Covenant in this chapter, the basic tenets will be considered in the following chapters in the context of their respective Christian doctrines. Other works making

---

[1]Two good summaries of Wagner's general theological assumptions appear in his books *Church Growth and the Whole Gospel: A Biblical Mandate* (San Francisco: Harper & Row, 1981), xiii-xiv, and *Strategies for Church Growth* (Ventura, CA: Regal, 1987), 39-40.

substantial theological contributions to church growth include *I Believe in Church Growth* by Eddie Gibbs[2]; *Contemporary Theologies of Mission* by Donald McGavran and Arthur Glasser[3]; *Balanced Church Growth* by Ebbie Smith[4]; and *Foundations of Church Growth* by Kent Hunter.[5]

As we examine church growth theology systematically, most of the basic tenets will be synonymous with mainstream evangelical thought. What sets church growth theology apart, however, is its unique hermeneutical approach. It is critical, then, that we understand how church growth theology approaches and interprets Scripture. That is the task of the next chapter dealing with bibliology.

Addendum
The Lausanne Covenant

Introduction

We, members of the Church of Jesus Christ, from more than 150 nations, participants in the International Congress on World Evangelization at Lausanne, praise God for his great salvation and rejoice in the fellowship he has given us with himself and with each other. We are deeply stirred by what God is doing in our day, moved to penitence by our failures and challenged by the unfinished task of evangelization. We believe the gospel is God's good news for the whole world, and we are determined by his grace to obey Christ's commission to proclaim it to all mankind and to make disciples of every nation. We desire, therefore, to affirm our faith and our resolve, and to make public our covenant.

Lausanne Covenant was reprinted with permission of the International Congress of World Evangelization, Lausanne, Switzerland, July 1974.

[2]Eddie Gibbs, *I Believe in Church Growth* (London: Hodder & Stoughton, 1985).

[3]Donald A. McGavran and Arthur F. Glasser, *Contemporary Theologies of Mission* (Grand Rapids, MI: Baker, 1983).

[4]Ebbie C. Smith, *Balanced Church Growth* (Nashville: Broadman, 1984).

[5]Kent R. Hunter, *Foundations of Church Growth* (New Haven, MO: Leader, 1983).

1. The Purpose of God

We affirm our belief in the one-eternal God, Creator and Lord of the world, Father, Son and Holy Spirit, who governs all things according to the purpose of his will. He has been calling out from the world a people for himself, and sending his people back into the world to be his servants and his witnesses, for the extension of his kingdom, the building up of Christ's body, and the glory of his name. We confess with shame that we have often denied our calling and failed in our mission, by becoming conformed to the world or by withdrawing from it. Yet we rejoice that even when borne by earthen vessels the gospel is still a precious treasure. To the task of making that treasure known in the power of the Holy Spirit we desire to dedicate ourselves anew.

(Isa. 40:28; Matt. 28:19; Eph. 1:11; Acts 15:14; John 17:6,18; Eph. 4:12; 1 Cor. 5:10; Rom. 12:2; 2 Cor. 4:7)

2. The Authority and Power of the Bible

We affirm the divine inspiration, truthfulness and authority of both Old and New Testament Scriptures in their entirety as the only written Word of God, without error in all that it affirms, and the only infallible rule of faith and practice. We also affirm the power of God's Word to accomplish his purpose of salvation. The message of the Bible is addressed to all mankind. For God's revelation in Christ and in Scripture is unchangeable. Through it the Holy Spirit still speaks today. He illumines the mind of God's people in every culture to perceive its truth freshly through their own eyes and thus discloses to the whole church even more of the many-colored wisdom of God.

(2 Tim. 3:16; 2 Pet. 1:21; John 10:35; Isa. 55:11; 1 Cor. 1:21; Rom. 1:16; Matt. 5:17,18; Jude 3; Eph. 1:17,18; 3:10,18)

3. The Uniqueness and Universality of Christ

We affirm that there is only one Saviour and only one gospel, although there is a wide diversity of evangelistic approaches. We recognize that all men have some knowledge of God through his general revelation in nature. But we deny that this can save, for men suppress the truth by their unrighteousness. We also reject as derogatory to Christ and the gospel every kind of syncretism and dialogue which implies that Christ speaks equally through all religions and ideologies. Jesus Christ, being himself the only God-man, who gave himself as the only ransom for sinners, is the only mediator between God and man. There is no other name by which we must be saved. All men are perishing because of sin, but God loves all men, not wishing that any should perish but that all should repent. Yet those who reject Christ repudiate the joy of salvation and condemn themselves to eternal separation from God. To proclaim Jesus as "the Saviour of the world" is not to affirm that all men are either automatically or ultimately saved, still less to affirm that all religions offer salvation in Christ. Rather it is to proclaim God's love for a world of sinners and to invite all men to respond to him as Saviour and Lord in the wholehearted personal commitment of repentance and faith. Jesus Christ has been exalted above every other name; we long for the day when every knee shall bow to him and every tongue shall confess him Lord.

(Gal. 1:6-9; Rom. 1:18-32; 1 Tim. 2:5,6; Acts 4:12; John 3:16-19; 2 Pet. 3:9; 2 Thess. 1:7-9; John 4:42; Matt. 11:28; Eph. 1:20,21; Phil. 2:9-11)

4. The Nature of Evangelism

To evangelize is to spread the good news that Jesus Christ died for our sins and was raised from the dead according to the Scriptures, and that as the reigning Lord he now offers the forgiveness of sins and the liberating gift of the Spirit to all who repent and believe. Our Christian presence in the world is indispensable to evangelism, and so is that kind of dialogue whose purpose is to listen sensitively in order to understand. But evangelism itself is the proclamation of the historical, biblical Christ as Saviour and Lord, with a view to persuading people to come to him personally and so be reconciled to God. In issuing the gospel invitation we have no liberty to conceal the cost of discipleship. Jesus still calls all who would follow him to deny themselves with his new community. The results of evangelism include obedience to Christ, incorporation into his church and responsible service in the world.

(1 Cor. 15:3,4; Acts 2:32-39; John 20:21; 1 Cor. 1:23; 2 Cor. 4:5; 5:11,20; Luke 14:25-33; Mark 8:34; Acts 2:40,47; Mark 10:43-45)

5. Christian Social Responsibility

We affirm that God is both the Creator and the Judge of all men. We therefore should share his concern for justice and reconciliation throughout human society and for the liberation of men from every kind of oppression. Because mankind is made in the image of God, every person, regardless of race, religion, colour, culture, class, sex or age, has an intrinsic dignity because of which he should be respected and served, not exploited. Here too we express penitence both for our neglect and for having sometimes regarded evangelism and social concern as mutually exclusive. Although reconciliation with man is not reconciliation with God, nor is social action evangelism, nor is political liberation salvation, nevertheless we affirm that evangelism and sociopolitical involvement are both part of our Christian duty. For both are necessary expressions of our doctrines of God and man, our love for our neighbor and our obedience to Jesus Christ. The message of salvation implies also a message of judgment upon every form of alienation, oppression and discrimination, and we should not be afraid to denounce evil and injustice wherever they exist. When people receive Christ they are born again into his kingdom and must seek not only to exhibit but also to spread its righteousness in the midst of an unrighteous world. The salvation we claim should be transforming us in the totality of our personal and social responsibilities. Faith without works is dead.

(Acts 17:26,31; Gen. 18:25; Isa. 1:17; Ps. 45:7; Gen. 1:26,27; Jas. 3:9; Lev. 19:18; Luke 6:27,35; Jas. 2:14-26; John 3:3,5; Matt. 5:20; 6:33; 2 Cor. 3:18; Jas. 2:20)

6. The Church and Evangelism

We affirm that Christ sends his redeemed people into the world as the Father sent him, and that this calls for a similar deep and costly penetration of the world. We need to break out of our ecclesiastical ghettos and permeate non-Christian society. In the church's mission of sacrificial service evangelism is primary. World evangelization requires that the whole church take the whole gospel to the whole world. The church is at the very centre of God's cosmic purpose and is his appointed means of spreading the gospel. But a church which preaches the cross must itself be marked by the cross. It becomes a stumbling block to evangelism when it betrays the gospel or lacks a living faith in God, a genuine love for the people, or scrupulous honesty in all things including promotion and finance. The church is the community of God's people rather than an institution, and must not be identified with any particular culture, social or political system, or human ideology.

(John 17:18; 20:21; Matt. 28:19,20; Acts 1:8; 20:27; Eph. 1:9,10; 3:9-11; Gal. 6:14,17; 2 Cor. 6:3,4; 2 Tim. 2:19-21; Phil. 1:27)

7. Cooperation in Evangelism

We affirm that the church's visible truth is God's purpose. Evangelism also summons us to unity, because our oneness strengthens our witness, just as our disunity undermines our gospel of reconciliation. We recognize, however, that organizational unity may take many forms and does not necessarily forward evangelism. Yet we who share the same biblical faith should be closely united in fellowship, work and witness. We confess that our testimony has sometimes been marred by sinful individualism and needless duplication. We pledge ourselves to seek a deeper unity in truth, worship, holiness and mission. We urge the development of regional and functional cooperation for the furtherance of the church's mission, for strategic planning, for mutual encouragement, and for the sharing of resources and experience.

(John 17:21,23; Eph. 4:3,4; John 13:35; Phil. 1:27; John 17:11-23)

8. Churches in Evangelistic Partnership

We rejoice that a new missionary era has dawned. The dominant role of western missions is fast disappearing. God is raising up from the younger churches a great new resource for world evangelization, and is thus demonstrating that the responsibility to evangelize belongs to the whole body of Christ. All churches should therefore be asking God and themselves what they should be doing both to reach their own areas and to send missionaries to other parts of the world. A re-evaluation of our missionary responsibility and role should be continuous. Thus a growing partnership of churches will develop and the universal character of Christ's church will be more clearly exhibited. We also thank God for agencies which labor in Bible translation, theological education, the mass media, Christian literature, evangelism, missions, church renewal and other specialist fields. They too should engage in constant self-examination to evaluate their effectiveness as part of the church's mission.

(Rom. 1:8; Phil. 1:5; 4:15; Acts 13:1-3; 1 Thess. 1:6-8)

9. The Urgency of the Evangelistic Task

More than 2,700 million people, which is more than two-thirds of mankind, have yet to be evangelised. We are ashamed that so many have been neglected; it is a standing rebuke to us and to the whole church. There is now, however, in many parts of the world an unprecedented receptivity to the Lord Jesus Christ. We are convinced that this is the time for churches and para-church agencies to pray earnestly for the salvation of the unreached and to launch new efforts to achieve world evangelization. A reduction of foreign missionaries and money in an evangelised country may sometimes be necessary to facilitate the national church's growth in self-reliance and to release resources for unevangelised areas. Missionaries should flow ever more freely from and to all six continents in a spirit of humble service. The goal should be, by all available means and at the earliest possible time, that every person will have the opportunity to hear, understand, and receive the good news. We cannot hope to attain this goal without sacrifice. All of us are shocked by the poverty of millions and disturbed by the injustices which cause it. Those of us who live in affluent circumstances accept our duty to develop a simple life-style in order to contribute more generously to both relief and evangelism.

(John 9:4; Matt. 9:35-38; Rom. 9:1-3; 1 Cor. 9:19-23; Mark 16:15; Isa. 58:6,7; Jas. 1:27; 2:1-9; Matt. 25:31-46; Acts 2:44,45; 4:34,35)

10. Evangelism and Culture

The development of strategies for world evangelization calls for imaginative pioneering methods. Under God, the result will be the rise of churches deeply rooted in Christ and closely related to their culture. Culture must always be tested and judged by Scripture. Because man is God's creature, some of his culture is rich in beauty and goodness. Because he is fallen, all of it is tainted with sin and some of it is demonic. The gospel does not presuppose the superiority of any culture to another, but evaluates all cultures according to its own criteria of truth and righteousness, and insists on moral absolutes in every culture. Missions have all too frequently exported with the gospel an alien culture, and churches have sometimes been in bondage to culture rather than to the Scripture. Christ's evangelists must humbly seek to empty themselves of all but their personal authenticity in order to become the servants of others, and churches must seek to transform and enrich culture, all for the glory of God.

(Mark 7:8,9,13; Gen. 4:21,22; 1 Cor. 9:19-23; Phil. 2:5-7; 2 Cor. 4:5)

11. Education and Leadership

We confess that we have sometimes pursued church growth at the expense of church depth, and divorced evangelism from Christian nurture. We also acknowledge that some of our missions have been too slow to equip and encourage national leaders to assume their rightful responsibilities. Yet we are committed to indigenous principles, and long that every church will have national leaders who manifest a Christian style of leadership in terms not of denomination but of service. We recognize that there is a great need to improve theological education, especially for church leaders. In every nation and culture there should be an effective training program for pastors and laymen in doctrine, discipleship, evangelism, nurture and service. Such training programs should not rely on any stereotyped methodology but should be developed by creative local initiatives according to biblical standards.

(Col. 1:27,28; Acts 14:23; Titus 1:5,9; Mark 10:42-45; Eph. 4:11,12)

12. Spiritual Conflict

We believe that we are engaged in constant spiritual warfare with the principalities and powers of evil, who are seeking to overthrow the church and frustrate its task of world evangelization. We know our need to equip ourselves with God's armor and to fight this battle with the spiritual weapons of truth and prayer. For we detect the activity of our enemy, not only in false ideologies outside the church, but also inside it in false gospels which twist Scripture and put man in the place of God. We need both watchfulness and discernment to safeguard the biblical gospel. We acknowledge that we ourselves are not immune to worldliness of thought and action, that is, to a surrender to secularism. For example, although careful studies of church growth, both numerical and spiritual, are right and valuable, we have sometimes neglected them. At other times, desirous to ensure a response to the gospel, we have compromised our message, manipulated our hearers through pressure techniques, and become unduly preoccupied with statistics or even dishonest in our use of them. All this is worldly. The church must be in the world; the world must not be in the church.

(Eph. 6:12; 2 Cor. 4:3,4; Eph. 6:11,13-18; 2 Cor. 10:3-5; 1 John 2:18-26; 4:1-3; Gal. 1:6-9; 2 Cor. 2:17; 4:2; John 17:15)

13. Freedom and Persecution

It is the God-appointed duty of every government to secure conditions of peace, justice and liberty in which the church may obey God, serve the Lord Christ, and preach the gospel without interference. We therefore pray for the leaders of the nations and call upon them to guarantee freedom of thought and conscience, and freedom to practice and propagate religion in accordance with the will of God as set forth in The Universal Declaration of Human Rights. We also express our deep concern for all who have been unjustly imprisoned, and especially for our brethren who are suffering for their testimony to the Lord Jesus. We promise to pray and work for their freedom. At the same time we refuse to be intimidated by their fate. God helping us, we too will seek to stand against injustice and to remain faithful to the gospel, whatever the cost. We do not forget the warnings of Jesus that persecution is inevitable.

(1 Tim. 1:1-4; Acts 4:19; 5:29; Col. 3:24; Heb. 13:1-3; Luke 4:18; Gal. 5:11; 6:12; Matt. 5:10-12; John 15:18-21)

14. The Power of the Holy Spirit

We believe in the power of the Holy Spirit. The Father sent his Spirit to bear witness to his Son; without his witness ours is futile. Conviction of sin, faith in Christ, new birth and Christian growth are all his work. Further, the Holy Spirit is a missionary spirit; thus evangelism should arise spontaneously from a Spirit-filled church. A church that is not a missionary church is contradicting itself and quenching the Spirit. World-wide evangelization will become a realistic possibility only when the Spirit renews the church in truth and wisdom, faith, holiness, love and power. We therefore call upon all Christians to pray for such a visitation of the sovereign Spirit of God that all his fruit may appear in all his people and that all his gifts may enrich the body of Christ. Only then will the whole church become a fit instrument in his hands, that the whole earth may hear his voice.

(1 Cor. 2:4; John 15:26,27; 16:8-11; 1 Cor. 12:3; John 3:6-8; 2 Cor. 3:18; John 7:37-39; 1 Thess. 5:19; Acts 1:8; Ps. 85:4-7; 67:1-3; Gal. 5:22,23; 1 Cor. 12:4-31; Rom. 12:3-8)

15. The Return of Christ

We believe that Jesus Christ will return personally and visibly, in power and glory, to consummate his salvation and his judgment. This promise of his coming is a further spur to our evangelism, for we remember his words that the gospel must first be preached to all nations. We believe that the interim period between Christ's ascension and return is to be filled with the mission of the people of God, who have no liberty to stop before the End. We also remember his warning that false Christs and false prophets will arise as precursors of the final Antichrist. We therefore reject as a proud, self-confident dream the notion that man can ever build a utopia on earth. Our Christian confidence is that God will perfect his kingdom, and we look forward with eager anticipation to that day, and to the new heaven and earth in which righteousness will dwell and God will reign forever. Meanwhile, we rededicate ourselves to the service of Christ and of men in joyful submission to his authority over the whole of our lives.

(Mark 14:62; Heb. 9:28; Mark 13:10; Acts 1:8-11; Matt. 28:20; Mark 13:21-23; John 2:18; 4:1-3; Luke 12:32; Rev. 21:1-5; 2 Pet. 3:13; Matt. 28:18)

Conclusion

Therefore, in the light of this our faith and our resolve, we enter into a solemn covenant with God and with each other, to pray, to plan, and to work together for the evangelization of the whole world. We call upon others to join us. May God help us by his grace and for his glory to be faithful to this our covenant! Amen, Alleluia!

Suggested Reading for Chapter 7

Enns, Paul. *The Moody Handbook of Theology.* Chicago: Moody, 1989.

Erickson, Millard J. *Christian Theology.* Grand Rapids, MI: Baker, 1983.

Rainer, Thom S. "An Assessment of C. Peter Wagner's Contributions to the Theology of Church Growth." Unpublished Ph.D. dissertation, The Southern Baptist Theological Seminary, 1988.

Wagner, C. Peter. *Church Growth and the Whole Gospel: A Biblical Mandate.* San Francisco: Harper & Row, 1981.

Wagner, C. Peter. *Leading Your Church to Growth.* Ventura, CA: Regal, 1987.

8

Bibliology and Church Growth

In bibliology, the doctrine of the Bible, two words are used often. The first word is the English word "bible" which has its origin in the Greek *biblion*, commonly translated "book" or "roll." The papyrus plant that grew along the Nile was called *byblos*, from which scrolls for writing were made.

A second word is "scripture," which is the English translation of the Greek *graphe*, which literally means "writing." When the verb *grapho* or the noun *graphe* is used, it almost always refers to the Scriptures. These Scriptures, specifically stated in 2 Timothy 3:16 to be "God-breathed," are divine in origin and revelation, completely authoritative, and without error in all that they teach.

Church growth admittedly draws from sources other than the Bible. Many of its principles come from the social and behaviorial sciences. Although church growth will continue to use these sources, the framework and foundation of the movement must be God's Word. A potential danger of the enthusiasm and pragmatism of church growth is the elucidating of principles without scriptural foundation. Though it is rare to hear of unbiblical church growth principles, the danger of an unbalanced hermeneutic does exist. We will examine that potential pitfall after reviewing some basic affirmations of the Bible.

The Divine Nature of the Bible

The Lausanne Covenant affirms "the *divine* inspiration, truthfulness, and authority of . . . . Scriptures" (emphasis added). The Bible claims for itself divine origin nearly four thousand times when it declares that "God said" or "the Lord said" (e.g. Lev. 4:1, Isa. 1:10, Jer.1:11). Paul and the other New Testament writers also affirmed the God-given origin of Scriptures (1 Cor. 14:37; 2 Pet. 1:16-21).

Because the Bible is viewed as divine in origin, it must also be seen as a unique revelation from God. While revelation can be general, for example, God's disclosure of Himself in history and nature, the Bible is a special revelation only for those who trust it and hold it as authoritative. The Bible then is God-breathed (2 Tim. 3:16), yet written by persons whose words were superintended by the Holy Spirit (2 Pet. 1:21). As a consequence, the written Word (Heb. 4:12) reveals accurately and without error our understanding of Jesus Christ, the incarnate Word (John 1:1, 14). The essence of church growth is to communicate to a lost world the living Word so that God's church may grow. Only a divinely given Bible could give us without error the written story of Jesus Christ and His commands, including His Great Commission to "make disciples of all nations" (Matt. 28:19).

The Inspiration of the Bible

Paul Enns defines inspiration as "the Holy Spirit's superintending over the writers so that while writing according to their own styles and personalities, the result was God's Word written—authoritative, trustworthy, and free from error in the original autographs."[1]

Such inspiration applies to the whole of Scripture and to its parts. While 2 Timothy 3:15 or 2 Peter 1:21 could be used to defend the inspiration of Scripture, the view of Scripture by Christ Himself is consistent with this perspective. Jesus affirmed the inspiration of the *whole* of the Old Testament (Matt. 5:17-18); yet He quoted frequently the *parts* of the Old Testament with equal authority (e.g. Matt. 4:4, 7, 10; Matt 21:42; Matt. 22:44; John 10:34, etc.). This view of inspiration is sometimes called *verbal plenary* because it affirms the inspiration of the parts or actual words (verbal) *and* the entire Bible (plenary).

---

[1]Paul Enns, *The Moody Handbook of Theology* (Chicago: Moody, 1989), 160.

The Power of the Bible

Because the Bible is God-given and God-inspired, it is able to accomplish God's purpose of salvation (see the Lausanne Covenant at the conclusion of the previous chapter, section 2). The writer of Hebrews articulates clearly the power of God's Word: "For the Word of God is living and active. Sharper than any double-edged sword, it penetrates even to dividing soul and spirit, joints and marrow; it judges the thoughts and attitudes of the heart" (Heb. 4:12). The reading and proclamation of that powerful Word reaches the lost; through it God saves those who believe (1 Cor. 1:2). Church growth proclaims a Savior who is known through the written Word. The written Word itself is powerful, penetrating hearts that may be added to God's kingdom and His church.

The Authority of Scripture over All Other Sources

Our definition[2] states that church growth is a "discipline which seeks to understand, through biblical, sociological, historical, and behavioral study, why churches grow or decline." History, sociology, and other behaviorial sciences must be viewed as tools rather than sources of authority for church growth. The Bible is the movement's source of authority.

When Martin Luther nailed his Ninety-Five Theses on the door at Wittenberg in 1517, he outlined his opposition to the abuses of the Catholic church. Luther emphasized *sola scriptura*—Scriptures alone are authoritative. Neither the church nor the councils could speak above the authority of God's Word.

When the tools of the social sciences are used to discern ways to reach more people, those tools must not be the authority, but rather instruments that are subject to the authority of Scripture. Leaders of the Reformation viewed neither the church nor the councils as inherently evil, but these organizations became evil when they abandoned the parameters of Scripture. The tools of church growth are not

[2]See above, p. 21.

inherently evil; but those tools must always be within the bounds of Scripture and subject to biblical authority.

To my knowledge, church growth theologians and practioners would affirm that which has been said thus far about the authority of Scripture. Critics do not debate the movement's high regard for the Bible. Questions arise, however, over its interpretation of Scripture.

The Hermeneutic of Church Growth

Bernard Ramm defined hermeneutics as "the science and art of Biblical interpretation. It is a science because it is guided by rules within a system; and it is an art because the application of the rules is by skill, not by mechanical imitation."[3] The process of biblical interpretation involves the interpreter as a whole person, including his or her predjudices. An honest hermeutical approach must consider potential biases. Although we will examine potential hermeneutical biases of church growth in the chapters in this section, it is appropriate to look at an interpretation grid that represents a potential hazard for the movement.

C. Peter Wagner refers to the hermeneutic of church growth as phenomenological: "Church growth leans toward a phenomenological approach which holds theological conclusions somewhat more tentatively and is open to revise them when necessary in the light of what is learned through experience."[4] Perhaps a better description of the hermeneutic is one that is directed by growth pragmatism: those beliefs that receive the greatest attention are those that are directly related to enhancing the growth of the church.

The best example of this hermeneutic can be found in church growth's keen interest in sociology, demography, and marketing. The movement is using every possible tool to reach its culture on a "user-friendly" basis. The biblical justification for this approach is from 1 Corinthians 9:22b:

---

[3]Bernard Ramm, *Protestant Biblical Interpretation*, 3rd ed. (Grand Rapids, MI: Baker, 1970), 1.

[4]Peter Wagner, *Strategies for Church Growth* (Ventura, CA: Regal, 1987), 38.

"I have become all things to all men so that by all possible means I might save some."

Paul's "adaptation" to culture has become somewhat of a rally cry in some church growth circles. "We must do whatever is necessary to win an audience so that we may share Christ!" The potential hermeneutical deficiency is not that the Corinthians' passage is misinterpreted. The possible problem is that the bulk of church growth principles could be based on just one portion of Scripture.

Paul would say later to the Corinthian church that, though we live in the world, we live differently from the world (2 Cor. 10:4). Jesus would tell His followers to be different from the world, to be salt and light (Matt. 5:13-14).

Church growth, then, must affirm a hermeneutic that captures the tension of being in the world but not of the world. A hermeneutic that attempts to isolate the text from modern culture will not speak to the world. The Bible simply will not be relevant. However a hermeneutic constantly seeking the favor of culture, even if numerical church growth results, may gain relevancy while losing true disciples. We may "win" this world but make few cross-bearing disciples. The cost of discipleship must remain in tension with a culturally-relevant message.

It is ironic that the greatest theological danger of church growth, a conservative, evangelical movement, is the same danger to which liberalism succumbed earlier in this century. The "tools" of culture are not inherently evil, but a hermeneutic that flirts with the enticements of modernity must always be cautious that the gospel essence is never compromised. Earlier in the century liberalism reduced Christianity to a social gospel. The Church Growth Movement must beware not to reduce the good news of the twenty-first century to a mere sociological gospel.

Suggested Reading for Chapter 8

Gibbs, Eddie. *I Believe in Church Growth*. London: Hodder & Stoughton, 1985.

Geisler, Norman L., ed. *Inerrancy*. Grand Rapids: Zondervan, 1980.

Henry, Carl F. H. "Bible, Inspiration of." In Walter A. Elwell,
    ed., *Evangelical Dictionary of Theology.* Grand Rapids,
    MI: Baker, 1984. 145-149.
Henry, Carl F. H. "Revelation, Special." In Walter A. Elwell,
    ed., *Evangelical Dictionary of Theology.* Grand Rapids,
    MI: Baker, 1984. 945-948.
Ramm, Bernard. *Protestant Biblical Interpretation.*, 3rd ed.
    Grand Rapids, MI: Eerdmans, 1970.
Smith, Ebbie C. *Balanced Church Growth.* Nashville:
    Broadman, 1984.

9

Theology Proper and Church Growth

In chapter 7 we defined *theology* as the study of God, recognizing that the word is generally understood in a broader sense, covering the entire field of Christian belief. To distinguish the general study of all Christian belief from the more specific study of God the Father, the term *theology proper* is used to designate the doctrine of God.

In one concise statement the Lausanne Covenant affirms the "belief in the one-eternal God, Creator and Lord of the world, Father, Son, and Holy Spirit, who governs all things according to the purpose of his will," (see chap. 7). The sentence affirms some basic beliefs about God with little elaboration.

Existence of God

Though many volumes have been written about the existence of God, church growth affirms *a priori* that God is. While theologians may argue for the existence of God cosmologically, teleologically, morally, ontologically, or anthropologically, church growth's presupposition of an infallible Scripture accepts without question the God who said "I am" (Ex. 3:14).

The anthropological argument for the existence of God, as one example, speaks directly about a God who created humans from a motive of total love. The word *anthropology* comes from the Greek word *anthropos* which means "man." Chafer states the anthropological argument in this manner: "There are philosophial and moral features in man's constitution which may be traced back to find their origin in God. . . . A blind force . . . could never produce a man with intellect, sensibility, will, conscience, and inherent belief in a Creator."[1]

Men and women, therefore, were created in the image of God (Gen. 1:27) to have perfect fellowship with their Creator. While the anthropological argument points to the existence of God, it also points to a God who desires to bring His creation from the death of sin and the tarnished image of humanity (Gen. 9:6) back into full fellowship with Him. Such discussion is beyond the scope of this section, but it does provide a foundation upon which church growth theology builds. The God-who-is is also the God seeking to draw His creation to Him and to build His church.

Revelation of God

Revelation comes from the Greek word *apokalupsis*, literally meaning "to disclose" or "to unveil." Revelation is God's disclosure of Himself to humankind. Typically, revelation is seen in two broad categories, general and special.

General revelation causes men and women to be aware of God's existence by the majesty of His creation (Ps. 19:1-6; Rom. 1:18-21.) This type of revelation alone causes humankind to be accountable to God, to be "without excuse" in responding to Him (Rom. 1:20).

Special revelation is God's more direct and specific self-disclosure. Though this type of revelation could include audible voices, visible manifestations (theophonies), dreams, or visions, special revelation usually refers to Scriptures and to Jesus Christ. The Scriptures were written by men who were carried along by the Holy Spirit so that the written testimony might be perfect or inerrant. The scriptural testimony also reveals the living Word, Jesus Christ, who in turn revealed God the Father to humankind. The emphasis of church growth is proclaiming the written Word so that people may become disciples of the living Word, Jesus Christ.

[1]Lewis Sperry Chafer, *Systematic Theology,* 8 vols. (Dallas: Dallas Seminary, 1947) 1:155, 157.

The Trinity of God

Theology proper recognizes that God has been revealed as three united persons who are one God. The three persons are the Father, Son, and Holy Spirit. The unique relationships of the Son and the Holy Spirit will be discussed in the next two chapters. In this chapter we focus upon God the Father.

Attributes of God

The distinguishing characteristics of God are often called *attributes* of God. There are many varities of classification and categories of God's attributes. Paul Enns developed the following chart which looks at some of the classifications by different theologians. Of all the attributes of God, none has

The Attributes of God:
Varieties of Categorization

Theologians	Categories	Attributes
Henry C. Thiessen Vernon D. Doerksen	Non-moral	Omnipresence Omniscience Omnipotence Immutability
	Moral	Holiness Righteousness and Justice Goodness and Mercy Truth
A. H. Strong	Absolute/Immanent	Spirituality: life, personality Infinity: self-existence, immutability, unity Perfection: truth, love, holiness
	Relative/Transitive	Related to time and space: eternity, immensity Related to creation: omnipresence, omniscience, omnipotence Related to moral beings: truth and faithfulness, mercy and goodness (transitive love), justice and righteousness (transitive holiness)

(continued next page)

The Attributes of God: Varieties of Categorization
(continued)

Theologians	Categories	Attributes
Millard J. Erickson	Greatness	Spirituality Personality Life Infinity Constancy

	Goodness	Moral Purity
		  holiness
		  righteousness
		  justice
		Integrity
		  genuineness
		  veracity
		  faithfulness
		Love
		  benevolence
		  grace
		  mercy
		  persistence

Gordon R. Lewis	Metaphysically	Self-existent Eternal Unchanging
	Intellectually	Omniscient Faithful Wise
	Ethically	Holy Righteous Loving
	Emotionally	Detests evil Long-suffering Compassionate
	Existentially	Free Authentic Omnipotent

	Relationally	Transcendent in being
		Immanent universally in
		  providential activity
		Immanent with His people in
		  redemptive activity

The Attributes of God: Varieties of Categorization
(continued)

Theologians	Categories	Attributes
William G. T. Shedd Charles Hodge Louis Berkhof Herman Bavinck	Incommunicable	Shedd/Hodge: self-existence, simplicity, infinity, eternity, immutability Berkhof: self-existence, immutability, unity, infinity (perfection, eternity, immensity) Bavinck: independence, self-sufficiency, immutability, infinity: eternity, immensity (omnipresence); oneness (numerical, qualitative)

	Communicable	Shedd/Hodge: wisdom, benevolence, holiness, justice, compassion, truth
		Berkhof:
		  spirituality
		  intellectual
		    knowledge
		    wisdom
		    veracity
		  moral
		    goodness (love, grace, mercy, longsuffering)
		    holiness
		  righteousness
		    remunerative justice
		    retributive justice
		  sovereign power
		Bavinck:
		  Life and Spirit
		    spirituality
		    invisibility
		  Perfect in self-consciousness
		    knowledge, omniscience
		    wisdom
		    veracity
		  Ethical nature
		    goodness
		    righteousness
		    holiness
		  Lord, King, Sovereign
		    will
		    freedom
		    omnipotence
		  Absolute Blessedness
		    perfection
		    blessedness
		    glory

been discussed more in church growth circles than the attribute of God's sovereignty.

The Sovereignty of God

A missionary to South America wrote an article several years ago about church growth methods that he felt compromised his Reformed faith. The anonymous writer said that he "saw a spirit of deadness come over a mission as Dr. Donald McGavran's 'church growth theory' was experimented with." He said that church growth theology "applies sociology to the realm of church planting and endeavors to discover by means of statistics, graphs, charts, and even computers, where ripe fields are." He was frustrated because church growth methods determined "where mission personnel should be placed" and established "an unhealthy emphasis on goal setting." The writer's foundational concern was that church growth theology "leaves no room for the sovereignty of God and the spontaneity of the Spirit's work."[2]

Sovereignty of God means that He is in absolute control, that whatever He ordains always comes to pass, and that His divine purpose is always accomplished (Eph. 1:11). Does church growth methodology ignore or deny this attribute? As the movement uses such "human-made" tools as sociology and demography is it denying that God will draw to Himself the elect?

In His sovereignty God decides how He wants lost men and women to be brought into the kingdom, those chosen for salvation before the foundation of the world (Eph. 1:4-5; 2 Tim. 1:9). An omnipotent (all-powerful) God could devise any means to bring the lost to himself. Human instrumentality is not necessary for God to carry forth His plan, but God nevertheless has chosen humans as His intermediaries. The mystery of the human and divine means of spreading the gospel and growing the church are in harmony according to God's sovereign will.

[2]Anonymous, "The Dilemma of the Reformed Missionary Today," *Reformation Today*, (May-June 1974), 21, cited in C. Peter Wagner, *Strategies for Church Growth* (Ventura, CA: Regal, 1987), 17-18.

God's sovereign decree does not violate humankind's free will nor does it make it unnecessary to seek methods that best communicate the gospel so that God's church may grow. Any objection as such takes place because of the antinomy in the human mind. Paul proclaimed the predestination of his people to salvation (Eph. 1:5-11) and taught the doctrine of election (Rom. 1:1; 8:30; 9:11). With equal conviction and assertion, Paul urged the necessity of human intervention and preaching in order that people might be saved and that the church might grow (Acts 16:13; Rom. 10:14-15; 1 Cor. 9:16). Church growth theology is not only compatible with the attribute of God's sovereignty, but the methods that emanate from the theology are obedient to the sovereign Lord in the spreading of the gospel of Jesus Christ.

Suggested Reading for Chapter 9

Elwell, Walter, ed. *Evangelical Dictionary of Theology.* Grand Rapids, MI: Baker, 1984.

Enns, Paul. *The Moody Handbook of Theology.* Chicago: Moody, 1989. See especially chapter 9 dealing with theology proper.

Wagner, C. Peter. *Strategies for Church Growth.* Ventura, CA: Regal, 1987. Chapter 2 includes a brief but good discussion on the sovereignty of God in church growth theology.

10

Christology and Church Growth

Christology is the study of Jesus Christ. The definition of church growth given in chapter 1 stated that church growth seeks to make "Great Commission" disciples (Matt. 28:19). It was Christ Himself who mandated the Great Commission. For that reason and others, the doctrine of Christ is a central doctrine of the Church Growth Movement. Several basic affirmations of Christology must be a part of the church growth message. We will examine the necessary components of the message in each subheading.

Exclusiveness of Salvation Through Christ

Jesus said that "on this rock I will build *my* church" (Matt. 16:18, emphasis added). Church growth is concerned only with the growth of Christ's church. Any belief system that gives other claims to the church must be rejected. The Lausanne Covenant rejects "as derogatory to Christ and the gospel every kind of syncretism and dialogue which implies that Christ speaks equally through all religions and ideologies. Jesus Christ, being himself the only God-man, who gave himself as the only ransom for sinners, is the only mediator between God and man."[1] "There is no other name . . . . by which we must be saved" (Acts 4:12). Jesus Himself would state explicitly that no one could come to the Father except through Him (Christ) (John 14:6).

Because of the clear, biblical claims of the exclusiveness of salvation through Christ, church growth must not be tempted to open the door of salvation any wider than through the Person of Jesus Christ. In its pragmatic zeal, the movement may find

[1]Lausanne Covenant, article 3.

numerical growth easier if a broader definition of salvation is offered. Many in our society today are offended by such a narrow-minded religion; but any growth that does not come through the narrow way of Christ is not true church growth.

Eternality of Christ

To accept the deity of Christ is to accept the eternality of Christ. John referred to Jesus as "the Word" and affirmed the continuous existence of Christ (John 1:1). In another passage in John, Jesus referred to His eternal state by declaring "before Abraham was born, I am!" (John 8:58). The writer of Hebrews declared that the throne of Christ "will last for ever and ever" (Heb. 1:8). Paul likewise affirmed the eternity and pre-existence of Christ when he said: "He is before all things, and in him all things hold together" (Col. 1:17).

Fulfillment of Prophecy

As the Church Growth Movement seeks to fulfill the Great Commission, it is imperative that the message of the person of Christ be communicated clearly. When C. H. Dodd wrote *The Apostolic Preaching and Its Development*, he focused on the New Testament word *kerygma*. Dodd emphasized that certain christological truths must be communicated about the Person of Jesus Christ. Although the *kerygma*, or content of the gospel message, was probably not so rigid as Dodd implied, his focus is worthy lest church growth enthusiasts miss the true meaning of the gospel. Among the specific truths to be communicated about Christ, Dodd consistently identified fulfillment of prophecy as a central christological doctrine.

The Old Testament is replete with detailed and specific passages pointing to Christ. In God's sovereign plan, He determined that the incarnate Son would have an earthly birth, life, ministry, and death and then be brought to victorious resurrection. In the context of the old covenant, God prepared His people for their Messiah.

The lineage of Jesus, for example, was prophesied to include the line of Abraham (Gen. 12:2), Judah (49:10), and

David (2 Sam. 7:12-16). The first chapter of Matthew depicts the fulfillment of this lineage (cf. Matt. 1:1 and 1:2), as well as the virgin birth of Christ (Matt. 1:23) prophesied in Isaiah 7:14. Even the specific birthplace of Jesus, Bethlehem (cf. Matt. 2:6), is foretold in Micah 5:2.

The threefold office of Christ, King (Matt. 21:5), Prophet (Acts 3:22-23), and Priest (Heb. 5:6-10), is depicted in the Old Testament with precision (cf. Num. 24:17; Ps. 2:6; Deut. 18:15-18; Ps. 110:4). Jesus' forerunner, John the Baptist (Matt. 3:3), is the fulfillment of the prophecies in Isaiah 40:3 and Malachi 3:1.

Psalm 22:1 prophesies the cry of Jesus on the cross when He bore the sins of the world (Matt. 27:46; Mark 15:34). Psalm 22:7-8 describes the ridicule Christ endured while on the cross (Matt. 27:39). Psalm 22:8 even prophesies the precise words of those insulting Him (Matt. 27:43).

The violent death of Christ is foretold in Psalm 22, which describes the piercing of the hands and feet (Ps. 22:16, fulfilled in John 20:25) and indicates that none of Jesus' bones would be broken (Ps. 22:17, fulfilled in John 19:33-36). Psalm 22:48 prophesies the gambling for Christ's clothes by the soldiers (John 19:24). Psalm 22:24 prophesies Christ's prayer to the Father as His death draws near (Matt. 26:39; Heb. 5:7).

The disfiguring of Christ is described in Isaiah 52:14 and fulfilled in John 19:1. The painful scourging and death of Jesus is prophesied in Isaiah 53:5 and fulfilled in John 19:1 and John 19:18. Peter applies David's hope of Psalm 16:10 to the resurrection of Christ (Acts 2:27-28). And, finally, Psalm 68:18 prophesies the ascension and the end of Jesus' earthly life (Luke 24:50-53; Acts 1:9-11).

Incarnation and Humanity of Christ

Another essential component of the *kerygma,* according to Dodd, was that Jesus was "born of the seed of David."[2] In other words, the eternal Son of God not only is divine, but He also took upon Himself the nature of humanity. "The result is that Christ remains forever unblemished deity, which He has from

[2]C. H. Dodd, *The Apostolic Preaching and Its Development* (Grand Rapids, MI: Baker, 1980), 17.

eternity past; but He also possesses true, sinless humanity in one Person forever (cf. John 1:14; Phil. 2:7-8; 1 Tim. 3:6)."[3]

The doctrine of the humanity of Christ is a critical part of the gospel message communicated by church growth proponents. Though Christ did not have our sinful and fallen nature, He was fully human so that He might die for us on the cross (cf. 1 John 3:5; 4:2). That the body of Jesus was painfully human was evident when the scourging took place (John 19:1), when nails pierced His body (John 19:18), and when Jesus thirsted on the cross (John 19:28).

Luke focused on the humanity of Jesus in the early chapters of his gospel. Jesus was born to an earthly mother, grew up as a child, and developed in each stage of life (cf. Luke 2:52). Further examples of the humanity of Jesus are found in His hunger (Matt. 4:2), His weariness (John 4:6), and His expression of human emotions (Matt. 9:36; Matt. 23:37; Luke 19:14; John 11:34-35).

The Virgin Birth

The doctrine of the virgin birth provides the bridge between the essential christological doctrines of the humanity of Christ and the deity of Christ. Both Matthew and Luke emphasize the role of the Holy Spirit in Mary's conception. Jesus the man would be born of a human mother and a divine Father (cf. Matt. 1:20; Luke 1:35). Though Christ as a person exists for all eternity, the human nature of Christ began at the moment of Mary's conception. The human nature of Christ, though sinless, would experience the limitations of humanity and the sacrificial sufferings in our sins.

Deity of Christ

The great christological heresies of church history have centered on the denials of either the humanity of Christ or the deity of Christ. Though church growth will continue to seek innovative ways to reach people for Christ, the

---

[3]Paul Enns, *The Moody Handbook of Theology* (Chicago: Moody, 1989), 222.

essential message that Christ was fully human and fully God must be communicated clearly. The Docetists of early church history denied the humanity of Christ while affirming His deity. The Ebionites, to the contrary, denied both the virgin birth and deity of Christ, but emphasized that Jesus was a human prophet. One legacy given to liberal theology today is the teaching in some circles that denies the deity of Christ. Enns says, "An attack on the deity of Jesus Christ is an attack on the bedrock of Christianity. At the heart of orthodox belief is the recognition that Christ died a substitutionary death to provide salvation for a lost humanity. If Jesus were only a man he could not have died to save the world, but because of his deity, his death had infinite value whereby he could die for the entire world."[4]

A sampling of Scripture demonstrates the clear biblical teaching of the deity of Christ. Jesus is called "Lord and God" (John 20:28); "Savior and God" (Titus 2:13); "Lord" (Matt. 22:44; Rom. 10:9); and "Son of God" (John 5:25). Furthermore the Bible affirms attributes and works of Christ that can only be ascribed to God. John 1:1 points to the eternality of Christ. The promise of Christ's indwelling of all believers demonstrates omnipresence (cf. Eph. 3:17; Col. 1:27). Jesus had complete knowledge that was demonstrated repeatedly in Scripture. His disciples marveled in His omniscience (John 16:30), and Jesus spoke of His complete knowledge in pointing to His death (cf. Matt. 20:18-19; 26:1-2).

The deity of Christ is also affirmed in His omnipotence (Matt. 28:15) and immutability (Heb. 13:8). Only He who is God could forgive sins (Mark 2:1-12) and perform miracles (cf. Matt. 8:23-27; Matt. 9:18-20; Matt. 9:27-31; Matt. 14:15-21; Matt. 14:26; Luke 5:1-11; John 2:1-11; John 4:46-54; John 5:1-18; John 11:1-44). Jesus Christ is fully God, and one day every person will acknowledge His deity. The Lausanne Covenant affirms that "Jesus Christ has been exalted above every other name; we long for the day when every knee shall bow to him, and every tongue shall confess him Lord"[5] (Phil. 2:9-11).

[4]Ibid., 225.
[5]Lausanne Covenant, article 3.

Death of Christ

The Pauline *kerygma,* said Dodd, included that essential element that Christ "died according to Scriptures, to deliver us out of the present evil age."[6] A number of theories have emerged concerning the death or atonement of Christ: the example theory, the commercial theory, the dramatic theory, the ethical theory, and the ransom theory. The emphasis in the New Testament, however, is that Christ died as a substitute for and on behalf of sinners. His death was vicarious or, in place of, another. The words in 1 Peter 2:24 emphasize the substitutionary nature of Christ's death: "He himself bore our sins in his body on the tree, so that we might die to sins and live for righteousness; by his wounds you have been healed."

Further truths emerge as a result of the death of Christ. The idea that redemption is purchased with a price (2 Cor. 6:20) demonstrates the cost of Christ's work to deliver us from the bondage of sin (1 Cor. 7:23; Gal. 3:13; Gal. 4:5). The joy of reconciliation, God's restoration of fellowship between humanity and Himself, is a result of the cross (2 Cor. 5:18-20). Jesus' death also satisfied the demands of a righteous God; this is often called propitiation (cf. Rom. 3:25). Finally, justification took place on the cross. God, in His law, declared the sinner who believes in Christ to be righteous (Rom. 5:1).

Resurrection of Christ

Paul declared that the resurrection was the central doctrine of the Christian faith: "And if Christ has not been raised, your faith is futile; you are still in your sins" (1 Cor. 15:17). In his comparison of the Jerusalem *kerygma* (Acts 2:16ff.) with the Pauline *kerygma,* Dodd emphasizes that both contained the essential element of the resurrection.

Not only did the resurrection affirm the truth of the Christian faith, it also demonstrated that the work of the cross was complete and that many of the prophecies of the

[6]Dodd, 17.

Old Testament (e.g. Ps. 16:10) were fulfilled because of the resurrection. Christ's death and resurrection were also a part of God's plan to send the Holy Spirit as His advocate in the lives of believers (cf. John 16:7).

Ascension of Christ

While the ascension is not explicit in all of the gospel messages in the New Testament, it is an important element in christology and the message that church growth must convey. The ascension of Christ is found in two gospels: Mark 16:19 and Luke 24:51. Further descriptions of the ascension are in Acts 1:9, Ephesians 4:8, Hebrews 4:14, and 1 Peter 3:22.

The ascension marks the end of Christ's earthly ministry and the beginning of His intercessory ministry in His glorified state. Because of the ascension, Christ could send the Holy Spirit (John 16:17) to dwell in and among believers.

Present Ministry of Christ

As the Head of the body of Christ (Col. 1:18), Christ is presently building the church and giving it direction. He is the source of spiritual gifts that the Holy Spirit is administering (Eph. 4:8, 11-13) for the building of the church.

Christ also intercedes for believers before the Father (Rom. 8:34; Heb. 7:25). When Christians sin, fellowship with the Father is broken. Christ acts as our *parakletos*, or advocate (1 John 2:1), in order that the fellowship may be restored.

Future Ministry of Christ

The Lausanne Covenant affirms "that Jesus Christ will return personally and visibly, in power and glory, to consummate his salvation and his judgment. The promise of his coming is a further spur to our evangelism, for we remember his words that the gospel must first be preached to all nations. We believe that the interim period between Christ's ascension and return is to be filled with the mission of the people of God, who have no liberty to stop before the

End."[7] The anticipation of the return of Christ (1 Cor. 15:51-58; 1 Thess. 4:13-18) is further impetus for church growth to seek obedience to the Great Commission so that people will be reached for Christ and made disciples before the evangelistic opportunity is no longer available.

The Importance of Christology to Church Growth

Let us now examine some of the components of church growth theology to see the critical importance of christology.

Church Growth Theology and Christological Truths:

1. God created humans in His own image (Gen. 1:26-27). *Christological truth*: In His eternality (John 1:1), Jesus Christ was the second Person of the Triune God who created humans.
2. Humans fell into sin (Gen. 3). *Christological truth*: As a consequence of sin, judgment fell on creation (Rom. 8:19-21) and humanity (Rom. 5:12). A perfect reconciler was necessary to pay the price for humanity's sin. That reconciler is, of course, Jesus Christ.
3. God became a man to bring salvation to the world (Matt. 1:20; Luke 1:35). *Christological truth:* Jesus Christ took upon Himself the nature of humanity for the sake of sinful humanity (Phil. 2:7-8).
4. God's only Son died on the cross to redeem (purchase) the sins of humanity (1 Cor. 6:20). *Christological truth:* Christ was humanity's substitute on the cross (1 Pet. 2:24).
5. Because He who was our perfect sacrifice rose from the dead, victory over death for humanity is made possible. *Christological truth*: Jesus Christ rose from the dead to take away the sins of humanity and to give victory over death (1 Cor. 15: 56-57).
6. Salvation is available only through Christ and His sacrifice. No one can come to the Father except through Jesus. *Christological truth:* Jesus Christ is the only way of salvation (John 14:6).

---

[7]Lausanne Covenant, article 15.

7. The sharing of the message of the exclusiveness of salvation through Christ is mandated by Jesus Himself. *Christological truth*: Jesus commands His followers to go and make disciples of all nations (Matt. 28:19). Such is the central tenet of church growth.

8. Christ will return to establish His kingdom. *Christological truth:* The task of church growth and evangelism is made even more urgent by the anticipated return of Christ (1 Thess. 5:4-10).

Suggested Reading for Chapter 10

Dodd, C. H. *The Apostolic Preaching and Its Development.* Grand Rapids, MI: Baker, 1980.

Drummond, Lewis A. *Leading Your Church in Evangelism.* Nashville: Broadman, 1974.

Enns, Paul. *The Moody Handbook of Theology.* Chicago: Moody, 1989. Enns' chapter on Christology is one of his best.

Erikson, Millard J. *Christian Theology.* Grand Rapids, MI: Baker, 1983.

11

Pneumatology and Church Growth

Pneumatology is the study of the Holy Spirit. The word has its origin in the Greek word *pneuma*, which means spirit. The Holy Spirit is the third Person of the Trinity. Needless to say, pneumatology is a critical component in our understanding of church growth theology.

The Person of the Holy Spirit

For reasons too extensive to discuss in this overview, the third Person of the Trinity is sometimes perceived as an "it" rather than a "he." One of the early heresies of the Christian church was the denial of personhood to the Holy Spirit. Arius, who was condemned at the Council of Nicea in A.D. 325, described the Holy Spirit as a force or influence emanating from God the Father. Modern-day teachings of Jehovah's Witnesses and Unitarianism continue the Arian influence into the twenty-first century.

The Bible is replete with teachings that affirm the personhood of the Holy Spirit. He is a decision-maker, exercising His will on God's people. Paul and his companions attempted to enter Bithynia, "but the Spirit of Jesus would not allow them to" (Acts 16:7). The Holy Spirit, according to Ephesians 4:30, is grieved by the contemptuous actions of believers. Furthermore, the Holy Spirit is a knowledgeable Person, understanding fully the mind of God (1 Cor. 2:11). Thus the Holy Spirit demonstrates personality in His attributes of will, emotions, and knowledge.

The actions of the Holy Spirit further exhibit the characteristics of a person. The Spirit teaches (John 14:26), testifies (John 15:26), and guides (John 16:13). He performs some actions that demonstrate a divine personality. The Holy Spirit convicts (Gk. *elegcho*) or acts as a divine prosecutor; regenerates and gives us new life (Titus 3:5); intercedes on behalf of the believer (Rom. 8:26); and gives commands (Acts 13:2).

The Ministry of the Holy Spirit

The Holy Spirit has performed and continues to perform many unique ministries in His place in the Godhead. Already in the second verse of the Bible (Gen. 1:2), we see the Spirit of God involved in the work of creation. This work, along with many others, demonstrates the deity of the Holy Spirit.

The Spirit has been involved in two unique historical events that have been pivotal to the Christian faith. In the earthly birth of Jesus Christ, Mary "was found to be with child through the Holy Spirit" (Matt 1:18). The living Word (John 1:1), Jesus, was thus brought to human conception through the overshadowing of Mary by the Holy Spirit. The written Word also involved the ministry of the Holy Spirit. He superintended the human writers of Scripture in order to keep the Bible perfect or inerrant and inspired by God (2 Pet. 1:21).

The Holy Spirit's ministry includes His baptism that unites believers with Christ and with other believers (1 Cor. 12:13). The Church Growth Movement focuses on the union of all believers in the body of Christ. The evangelistic thrust of church growth practice is never complete until a person demonstrates responsible participation in the body of Christ. While church growth recognizes that the Holy Spirit dwells in carnal Christians (1 Cor. 6:19), the movement nevertheless *assumes* the lostness of a person until fruit-bearing behavior is evident within the body.

This discussion leads to another obvious ministry of the Holy Spirit, which is the *indwelling* of all believers. This indwelling is a gift to those who have faith in Christ (John 7:37-39). It is an irrevocable or permanent gift (John 14:16) given at salvation (Eph. 1:13). Anyone not possessing the Holy Spirit is an unbeliever (Rom. 8:9).

A few New Testament passages (cf. 2 Cor 1:22; Eph. 1:13) refer to *sealing* with the Holy Spirit, which demonstrates God's ownership of the believer. Again, this is an action or ministry of the Holy Spirit rather than something done by the believer. The seal was given to us (2 Cor. 1:22) as a sign of ownership and security; it was not something earned or merited.

Another aspect of the ministry of the Holy Spirit that has been the subject of much church growth discussion is the *gifts* of the Holy Spirit. Because of its emphasis in church growth literature, we will examine this area in the following section.

Gifts of the Holy Spirit

The Church Growth Movement has focused extensively on the gifts of the Holy Spirit because of their relationship to unleashing all the laity for ministry.[1] If Christians discover their spiritual gifts and use them for building the body of Christ (1 Cor. 12:1ff), then the church will grow naturally. C. Peter Wagner puts it this way: "I do not think there is any dimension of the Christian life that more effectively joins the teachings of Scripture with the day-to-day activities of the people of God than spiritual gifts." Wagner then explains the relationship of gifts to church growth: "It is with their spiritual gifts that Christian people minister. Therefore, if a pastor is leading a church to growth one of the essential goals of that leadership is to make sure every member of the church discovers, develops, and is using his or her spiritual gift or gifts."[2]

Spiritual gifts are gifts of grace given to the believer by the Holy Spirit. They are "a divine endowment of a special

---

[1]In his book *Your Spiritual Gifts Can Help Your Church Grow,* Wagner identifies twenty-seven spiritual gifts instead of the usual nineteen listed by most writers of spiritual gifts. This book was the first complete monograph on the subject relating the gifts specifically to church growth. Many church growth/spiritual gifts books have been written since.

[2]C. Peter Wagner, *Leading Your Church to Growth* (Ventura, CA: Regal, 1984), 131-132.

ability for service upon a member of the body of Christ."[3]
Debate continues about the giving and manifestation of
what some call "sign gifts." Dispensational theologians often
regard the gifts of prophecy, miracles, healings, tongues,
interpretation of tongues, discerning spirits, and knowledge
as gifts given and manifested only during the apostolic age.[4]
Citing Paul's words that "when perfection comes, the
imperfect disappears" (1 Cor. 13:10) and Paul's prophesy
that prophecies, tongues, and knowledge will pass away (1
Cor. 13:8), dispensationalists conclude that "because the
foundation of the church has been laid and the canon of
Scripture is complete [i.e. "perfection" has come] there is no
need for the gift(s)."[5]

Some church growth advocates would fit in a category best
described as "practical dispensationalists." While their
theology may disagree with the dispensational hermeneutic
of 1 Corinthians 13:8-10, their writings and practice make
little or no room for the "sign gifts" mentioned in the
previous paragraph.

A third group of church growth followers not only affirm
the giving and manifestation of *all* gifts, but advocate that
such gifts should be manifested on a regular basis in their
churches. In fact prophecy, miracles, healings, tongues,
interpretation of tongues, discerning of spirits, and
knowledge may be at the center of their worship and church
life. This group is often called the "signs and wonders" wing
of the Church Growth Movement. This debate and
controversy will be examined in chapter 30.

While realizing that theologians may differ on the number
of spiritual gifts, the following gifts are those nineteen
typically mentioned in most spiritual-gifts literature. These
gifts are bestowed on individuals (1 Cor. 12:11) for the
building up of the entire church (Eph. 4:12).

Apostle.   The word apostle comes from two Greek words:
apo, which means "from," and *stello*, which means "to send."

---

[3]William McRae, *The Dynamics of Spiritual Gifts* (Grand Rapids, MI:
Zondervan, 1976), 18.
[4]See for example, Paul Enns, *The Moody Handbook of Theology* (Chicago:
Moody, 1989), 270-277.
[5]Ibid., 271.

An apostle is one, therefore, who is "sent from." In chapter 21, we will examine the tremendous impact of church planting on church growth. God may very well be sending Christians with the gift of the apostle to start new works. The gift of the apostle is mentioned twice, both times by Paul, in 1 Corinthians 12:28 and Ephesians 4:11. The gift of the apostle is different from the office of the apostle.

Prophecy. The gift of prophecy is mentioned in three of Paul's letters: Romans 12:6, 1 Corinthians 12:10, and Ephesians 4:11. A prophet in Scripture received a direct revelation from God and gave that revelation to his or her peers. The prophecy may have been future-oriented, or it may have been a present-day word of edification, instruction, encouragement, or comfort (cf. 1 Cor. 14:3). Since we have direct revelation from God today in Scripture, it would seem that those with the gift of prophecy today would apply biblical truths to contemporary society.

Miracles. The gift of miracles (1 Cor. 12:10, 28) seems to be a gift used to authenticate the gospel message. It is a broader gift than the gift of healing. The performing of miracles by individuals in the Bible was often described in conjunction with the phrase "signs and wonders" (cf. Acts 5:12). Often because of the miracles, many people believed in the Lord (cf. Acts 5:14). Such is the emphasis of the signs-and-wonders movement today, which we will examine in a later chapter.

Healing. The gift of healing (1 Cor. 12:9, 28, 30) served the same biblical purpose as the gift of miracles, to authenticate the gospel message and point to the Savior. It is probably the most prominent gift displayed in the signs-and-wonders movement.

Tongues. Another authenticating gift in Scriptures is tongues (1 Cor. 12:10). Paul affirmed that he spoke in tongues (1 Cor. 14:18), but he considered it the lesser gift (1 Cor. 12:28). Nevertheless, said Paul, tongues were a "sign" for unbelievers (1 Cor. 14:22) that many might be drawn to Christ.

Interpretation of tongues. Accompanying the gift of tongues is the necessary gift of interpretation. Worship must be orderly, declared Paul. Someone must interpret whenever tongues are spoken (1 Cor. 14:28-29). The gift of interpretation (1 Cor. 12:30), then, can only be exercised alongside tongues.

Distinguishing spirits. The person with the gift of distinguishing spirits (1 Cor. 12:10) has the God-given ability to determine if something or someone is of Christ or not. The exhortation by John to "test the spirits" (1 John 4:1) obviously has a relationship here. Those with this gift would have an extraordinary ability to discern if a spirit is from God or is the spirit of the antichrist (1 John 4:3).

Knowledge. The gift of knowledge (1 Cor. 12:8) is a supernatural revelation of some truths. Many in the signs-and-wonders movement see this gift exercised through "words of knowledge" given directly by God.

Evangelism. Since all believers are mandated to evangelize (2 Tim. 4:5), this gift (Eph. 4:11) most likely provides some believers with the unique ability to proclaim the good news so that people respond in conversion and discipleship. Those with the gift of evangelism will have a burden for the lost, the ability to present Christ with clarity, and the joy of seeing people come to Christ. Wagner estimates that about one Christian in ten has the gift of the evangelist,[6] but everyone should be involved in obeying Christ's command to fulfill the Great Commission (Matt. 28:19-20).

Pastor-Teacher. The one who has the gift of pastor-teacher (Eph. 4:11) exercises that gift by caring for and instructing a group of Christians. The word "pastor" comes from the Greek *poimenas* which literally means shepherd. The word is not only used to refer to a gift, but it also is used to refer to Christ as the shepherd of the entire church (John 10:11, 14, 16; Heb. 13:20; 1 Pet. 2:25).

Teacher. "This gift is clearly evidenced in a person who has the ability to take profound biblical and theological truths and communicate them in a lucid way so ordinary people can readily grasp them. That is the gift of teaching. The gift was emphasized considerably in the local churches in the New Testament because of its importance in bringing believers to maturity (cf. Acts 2:42; 4:2; 5:42; 11:26; 13:1;

[6]C. Peter Wagner, personal interview, July 1987.

15:35; 18:11, etc.).")[7] The gift of teaching is found in Romans 12:7 and 1 Corinthians 12:28.

Service.   One of the most common words in the New Testament is "service" (Gk. *diakonia*). While the word refers to looking after the needs of others in general, it is also a gift evidenced by those who have an extraordinary burden to put others before themselves (Rom. 12:7). The very nature of the word indicates a role of voluntary subservience.

Helps.   Because this word (Gk. *antilempsis*) has such a similiar meaning as service, some view the two gifts as identical. While there are similarities, the gift of service seems to focus on those helps that necessitate a subservient role. Helps (1 Cor. 12:28) then would have a broader scope. I know one man in my church who definitely has the gift of helps. He is constantly seeing that the needs of others are met, but because of his very busy schedule, he is unable to serve each need personally. Those he gets to serve others personally could have the gift of service.

Faith.   Like many of the other gifts, the gift of faith (1 Cor. 12:9) is an extraordinary measure of something all Christians should exercise. All believers have saving faith (Eph. 2:8); all believers should have a daily walk of trust; but only faith-gifted believers have the capacity to see God's possibility in an otherwise impossible situation.

Exhortation.   The person with the gift of exhortation (Rom. 12:8) has the unusual ability to affect a person's will with the will of God. The gift is manifested when someone urges others to make a specific decision, or demonstrates consolation for someone else who has experienced difficulties.[8]

Mercy.   As our church has helped believers discover their spiritual gifts, we have seen significant growth because many of our members exercise the gift of mercy (Rom. 12:8). Showing mercy is a ministry greatly needed in the body, especially today. The number of people hurting, sick, and troubled seems to be increasing daily. The good news for those with the gift of mercy is that their ministry is one of

[7]Enns, 275.
[8]McRae, 49-50.

joy despite the joyless circumstances in which they find themselves.

Administration/leadership. Though they are different words in the New Testament, administration (Gk. *kubernesis,* 1 Cor. 12:28) and leadership (Gk. *prohistimi,* Rom. 12:8) are synonyms. Those who most effectively lead people and organizations exercise the gift of administration or leadership.

Giving. Giving appears to be another "subset" gift as healing is to miracles and service is to helps. The gift of giving (Rom. 12:8) is a specific function of the gift of faith. Those who give beyond what others dream possible have the eyes of faith in sharing their material goods with others. Giving and faith are not synonyms. One who has the gift of giving may not have the gift of faith beyond this scope; and one who has the gift of faith may manifest it in ways other than giving.

Wisdom. The gift of wisdom (1 Cor. 12:8) is a supernatural gift of understanding that unifies the body of Christ. A person with the gift of wisdom is able to see God's design in a situation that is beyond the understanding of other believers. Paul showed this gift in seeking to unite the Corinthian church (1 Cor. 2:6ff.).

Filling with the Spirit

The apostle Paul wrote to the church at Ephesus: "Do not get drunk on wine, which leads to debauchery. Instead, be filled with the Spirit" (Eph. 5:18). The verb, in the present active imperative tense, is first a command for all believers. Simply put, we are to be filled (Gk. *plerousthe*) or controlled by the Spirit by daily submission to Him in regular confession of sins (1 John 1:9). Second, it is a continuous, repeated event. We are not filled by the Spirit in a once-and-for-all event; rather, in our daily submission to Christ and dying to sins, we allow the Holy Spirit to fill us again and again.

The implications of the filling with the Holy Spirit for church growth are many. Those filled with the Spirit will manifest the fruit of the Spirit: love, joy, peace, patience, kindness, goodness, faithfulness, gentleness, and self control (Gal. 5:22-23). Such fruit-bearing will draw people to Christ and, like the people in the early church, believers will "enjoy" the favor of all the people (Acts 2:47). When Christians are filled with the Spirit, their behavior becomes exemplary, their churches become unified, and their excitement becomes contagious. It was no wonder that in the Jerusalem church, "The Lord added to their number daily those who were being saved" (Acts 2:47).

Furthermore, Christians who are filled with the Spirit are obedient Christians. All of the imperatives of Scripture become a joyful opportunity. Disciple-making (Matt. 28:19) becomes a way of life as many are won to Christ and the church grows daily.

Suggested Reading for Chapter 11

McRae, William. *The Dynamics of Spiritual Gifts*. Grand Rapids, MI: Zondervan, 1976.

Stott, John R. W. *The Spirit, the Church, and the World*. Downers Grove, IL: InterVarsity, 1990

Wagner, C. Peter. *Leading Your Church to Growth*. Ventura, CA: Regal, 1983.

Wagner, C. Peter. *Spiritual Power and Church Growth*. Altamonte Springs, FL: Creation, 1986.

Wagner, C. Peter. *Your Spiritual Gifts Can Help Your Church Grow*. Glendale, CA: Regal, 1979.

12

Angelology and Church Growth

In both the Old Testament and the New Testament, the word "angel" means "messenger." The Hebrew word *malak* refers both to angelic messengers and to human messengers. In the New Testament, however, the word *angelos* almost exclusively refers to the heavenly creatures who occupy both heaven and earth.[1]

A decade ago angelology and church growth could hardly be discussed together. Today, however, church growth literature on spiritual warfare, unfallen angels, fallen angels (demons), and Satan is growing monthly. C. Peter Wagner once again is at the forefront of this movement.[2] While one may not be in full agreement with some of the tenets of church growth angelology, the movement certainly can no longer be perceived as an instrument of human devices and calculation.

Angelology, of course, refers to the study of angels. We will first examine unfallen angels, followed by demons or fallen angels, and conclude with a study of the chief fallen angel, Satan.

Angels and Church Growth

Thirty-four of the sixty-six books of the Bible refer to angels.[3] By the command of the Lord, angels were created (Ps. 148:2-5) as beings whose primary purpose is to serve Christ (Col. 1:16). Though angels are a higher order than humankind

---

[1]The Greek word *angelos* occurs in the New Testament 175 times; it is used to refer to human messengers only 6 times.

[2]Recent books by Wagner on the subject include: C. Peter Wagner, *Warfare Prayer* (Ventura, CA: Regal, 1991); C. Peter Wagner, ed., *Engaging the Enemy* (Ventura, CA: Regal, 1991); and C. Peter Wagner and F. Douglas Pennoyer, eds., *Wrestling with Dark Angels* (Ventura, CA: Regal, 1990).

[3]Paul Enns, *Moody Handbook of Theology* (Chicago: Moody, 1989), 288.

now (Heb. 2:7), at the end of the age, humankind will be exalted above the angels (1 Cor. 6:3).

These thousands of angels (Heb. 12:22) apparently are ranked in some type of order. Ephesians 6:12 seems to give a ranking of evil angels, while verse 9 in the book of Jude refers to the unfallen angel Michael as an archangel. Daniel 10:13 also speaks of "chief princes," and Ephesians 3:10 mentions "rulers and authorities in the heavenly realms." Furthermore, the cherubim (Gen. 3:24; Ezek. 1) and seraphim (Isa. 6:2-3) seem to hold some position as attendants and givers of praise to God.

While some angels such as the cherubim and seraphim have a direct ministry to God, other angels have had and will have a ministry to Christ. Angels ministered to Christ in His birth (Luke 1:26-38), His infancy (Matt. 2:13), His temptation (Matt. 4:11), His emotional needs (Luke 22:43), His resurrection (Matt. 28:5-7; Mark 16:6-7; Luke 24:4-7; John 20:12-13), and His ascension (Acts 1:10). Angels will also accompany Jesus at His second coming (Matt. 25:31).

Do angels have a role in the growth of the church? Is there any relation between the activity of angels and the expansion of God's kingdom as people accept Christ and become disciples in the church? The Epistle to the Hebrews states that all angels minister to believers: "Are not all angels ministering spirits sent to serve those who will inherit salvation?" (Heb. 1:14). Since angels are directly responsible for believers as they seek to fulfill Christ's Great Commission, we must conclude that the "ministering spirits" have a role in the growth of the church.

The guardian and ministering responsibility of the angels includes physical protection (e.g. Ps. 34:7; Acts 5:19; Acts 12:7-11) and physical provision (1 Kings 19:5-7). In the instance of Peter's release from prison (Acts 12:7-11), the church was praying for Peter's release (Acts 12:5). God then sent an angel to answer the prayer and to be the instrument for the apostle's freedom. How often, perhaps unknown to believers, do angels become God's instruments to answer our prayers, even the prayer for the fulfilllment of the Great Commission?

Angels may also minister to believers by encouragement (Acts 10:3-6). In many of these acts, then, is it not likely that the ministry of angels encouraged believers to a more dynamic obedience to make disciples?

Church growth literature now includes spiritual warfare, which is so clearly discussed in Scripture (e.g. Eph. 6:10-18). The focus thus far in church growth literature has been on fallen angels (which we will see in the paragraphs that follow). The relationship between church growth and the unfallen angels is ripe for discussion in the years ahead.

Fallen Angels (Demons) and Church Growth

Fallen angels, also called demons, probably followed Lucifer or Satan in rebelling against God. Satan is sometimes called the dragon; Revelation 12:7 speaks of "the dragon and his angels." Jesus Himself speaks of the fallen angels and their leader as "the devil and his angels" (Matt. 25:41).

Because demonic activity is prevalent in much of Scripture, we can surmise that many demons have a great deal of freedom, and that this freedom will continue until all rebellious creatures are thrown into the lake of fire (Rev. 20:15). Some demons, however, are restricted or bound from activity, presumably because of the enormity of their sin or their potential power to inflict damage (Luke 8:31; 2 Pet. 2:4; Rev. 9:2). Some scholars believe that Revelation 9:3-11 describes the release of these most horrendous demons during the great tribulation.

Demons are of the same make-up as their unfallen counterparts, angels. They are spirit creatures (Matt. 8:16; Luke 10:17) who are limited in their power and intelligence. Only God is omnipresent, ominscient, and omnipotent. Though demons have great power, they can not be like God or do the works of God (John 10:21).

The activity of demons can be detrimental to church growth. The Church Growth Movement, led by C. Peter Wagner, has published several works recently that focus upon this spiritual warfare as a major topic in church growth.[4] This focus represents a significant shift for a movement often accused of being overly humanistic and methodical.

[4]See note 2.

What, then, can demons do to inhibit the growth of the church? They can deceive both believers and unbelievers. Unbelievers can be deceived and blinded from receiving the gift of salvation through Jesus Christ: "The god of this age has blinded the minds of unbelievers, so that they cannot see the light of the gospel of the glory of Christ, who is the image of God" (2 Cor. 4:4). A believer can also be distracted from Great-Commission obedience and single-minded devotion to Christ (2 Cor. 11:3). The apostle Paul, concerned that the church of the Thessalonians might have lost zeal for spreading the gospel, wrote that the people might be aware of demonic discouragement: "For this reason, when I could stand it no longer, I sent to find out about your faith. I was afraid that in some way the tempter might have tempted you and our efforts might have been useless" (1 Thess. 3:5).

Sometimes demons will go beyond merely influencing people by invading or possessing someone. Demon possession is common in the gospels and Acts (cf. Matt. 4:24; 8:16, 28, 33; 12:22; 15:22; Mark 1:32; 5:15, 16, 18; Luke 8:36; John 10:21; Acts 19:13-16). The role of demons, whether influence or possession, is to keep unbelievers away from salvation in Christ and to render believers ineffective in their quest for obedience to Christ.

Satan and Church Growth

The leader of the fallen angels is Satan who is also known by a number of other names (see chart). Enns, in the *Moody Handbook of Theology,* says "The New Testament evidence for Satan's existence is extensive. Every New Testament writer and nineteen of the books make reference to him (cf. Matt. 4:10; 12:26; Mark 1:13; 3:23, 26; 4:15; Luke 11:18; 22:3; John 13:27, etc.). Christ Himself makes reference to Satan twenty-five times. The fact of Satan's existence finds ultimate support in the veracity of Christ's words." [5]

The characteristics of demons described earlier would apply to Satan. It would seem, however, that Satan would manifest the greatest power, the greatest deception, and the

[5]Enns, p. 292.

greatest evil. Any demonic activity of Satan would be of the greatest intensity. Until his fall, Satan was the greatest of the angels: "You were the model of perfection, full of wisdom and perfect in beauty . . . You were blameless in your ways from the day you were created till wickedness was found in you" (Ezek. 28:12, 15).

Satan, therefore, leads his demonic hordes to oppose the church and to thwart its growth. Any true church growth strategy must first be aware of the spiritual battles that must transpire.

NAMES OF SATAN

Name	Meaning	Citation
Satan	Adversary	Matthew 4:10
Devil	Slanderer	Matthew 4:1
Evil one	Intrinsically evil	John 17:15
Great red dragon	Destructive creature	Revelation 12:3,7,9
Serpent of old	Deceiver in Eden	Revelation 12:9
Abaddon	Destruction	Revelation 9:11
Apollyon	Destroyer	Revelation 9:11
Adversary	Opponent	1 Peter 5:8
Beelzebul	Lord of the fly (Baalzebub)	Matthew 12:24
Belial	Worthless (Beliar)	2 Corinthians 6:15
God of this world	Controls philosophy of world	2 Corinthians 4:4
Ruler of this world	Rules in world system	John 12:31
Prince of the power of the air	Control of unbelievers	Ephesians 2:2
Enemy	Opponent	Matthew 13:28
Tempter	Solicits people to sin	Matthew 4:3
Murderer	Leads people to eternal death	John 8:44
Liar	Perverts the truth	John 8:44
Accuser	Opposes believers before God	Revelation 12:10

Church Growth and Spiritual Warfare

The Church Growth Movement could have once been described as sociological analysis, demographic study, methodological innovation, theological contextualization, leadership guidance, and strategic application. However, C. Peter Wagner has recognized the deficiency of these tools used alone: "Now that these pieces are in place as they never have been before, they appear to many as a rocket on the launching pad ready to take us to new dimensions of effectiveness in advancing the kingdom of God." Yet Wagner realizes that church growth must be more than man-made methodologies: "But at the same time there has been a growing awareness that the rocket itself, with all of its state-of-the-art technology, will go nowhere without the fuel."[6]

The "fuel" is the Holy Spirit and the battle is spiritual. "For our struggle is not against flesh and blood, but against the rulers, against the authorities, against the powers of this dark world and against the spiritual forces of evil in the heavenly realms" (Eph. 6:12). With this perspective in mind, says Wagner, church growth strategies are seen in a very different light. "If the real battle for the advancement of the kingdom of God is spiritual, we need to learn as much as we can about the rules of the war, the battle plans, the nature of our enemy, the resources at our disposal and the best tactics for employing them."[7]

Paul gives us an outline of these warfare tactics in Ephesians 6. He calls these tactics "the full armor of God" (Eph. 6:13). The full armor first includes a godly and obedient lifestyle ("righteousness . . . readiness . . . faith," Eph. 6:14-16). Second, it means a knowledge of, commitment to, and obedience to the Word of God (" . . . the sword of the Spirit, which is the Word of God," Eph. 6:17). Finally, the full armor includes prayer (Eph. 6:18). We will examine in more detail prayer and church growth in chapter 18. Prayer may very well prove to be the key to unlock the door to church growth worldwide as never known before.

---

[6]"Introduction," by C. Peter Wagner *Wrestling with Dark Angels*, C. Peter Wagner and F. Douglas Pennoyer, eds. (Ventura, CA: Regal, Books 1990), 9.
[7]Ibid., 10.

Suggested Reading for Chapter 12

Dickason, C. Fred. *Angels: Elect and Evil*. Chicago: Moody, 1975.

Dickason, C. Fred. *Demon Possession and the Christian: A New Perspective*. Chicago: Moody, 1987.

Unger, Merrill F. "Satan." In Walter A. Elwell, ed., *Evangelical Dictionary of Theology*. Grand Rapids, MI: Baker, 1985. 972-973.

Wagner, C. Peter, ed. *Engaging the Enemy*. Ventura, CA: Regal, 1991.

Wagner, C. Peter. *How to Have a Healing Ministry without Making Your Church Sick*. Ventura, CA: Regal, 1987.

Wagner, C. Peter. *Warfare Prayer*. Ventura, CA: Regal, 1992.

Wagner, C. Peter and F. Douglas Pennoyer, eds. *Wrestling with Dark Angels*. Ventura, CA: Regal, 1990.

13

Anthropology, Hamartiology, and Church Growth

Two closely related branches of theology are anthropology and hamartiology. Anthropology comes from the Greek word *anthropos* which means "man." Hamartiology has its origin in the Greek *hamartia*, the noun for sin. We will thus discuss the fall and sin of humanity as we study the two fields of anthropology and hamartiology.

Church Growth and Anthropology

The beginning of the study of humanity must ask the question of human origin. Non-Christians, particularly those who do not hold to a theistic point of view, usually see humans' beginnings as evolutionary. Atheistic evolution denies any supernatural involvement in the creation of men and women. Some theists believe in an evolution of humankind that allows for God's supervision in the gradual process of creation.

Progressive creationism, sometimes called the day-age theory, states that the days of creation are not literal twenty-four-hour days, but are eras or ages. Another creation theory, the gap theory, allows for a prolonged creation period by placing a period of time between Genesis 1:1 and 1:2. The problem with both progressive creationism and the gap theory is that they are, at best, an argument from biblical silence. A growing number of biblical scholars in fact believe that the theories are "not built on exegesis but (are) rather an attempt to reconcile the Bible with the views of science."[1]

[1]Paul Enns, *The Moody Handbook of Theology* (Chicago: Moody, 1989), 303. Henry M. Morris has probably been the most influential voice on re-examining science in light of the literal scriptural testimony. See two of his books: *Evolution and the Modern Christian* (Grand Rapids, MI: Baker, 1967) and *The Biblical Basis for Modern Science* (Grand Rapids, MI: Baker, 1984).

Fiat creation is the view that God created in literal twenty-four-hour days. This perspective sees creation as instantaneous. It rejects any form of human evolution since evolution would negate the uniqueness of men and women, made in the image of God (Gen. 1:26).

Church growth and anthropology intersect when the Scripture speaks of the fall (Gen. 3). Adam and Eve were sinless persons created in perfect fellowship with God. They had complete freedom in the garden except for the prohibition of eating from the tree of knowledge of good and evil (Gen. 2:16-17). The result of Adam's and Eve's disobedience was judgment not only upon woman (Gen. 3:16), man (Gen. 3:17-19), and creation (Gen. 3:17-18), but also judgment on the entire human race (Rom. 5:12). Contrary to the serpent's lie that Adam and Eve would not die, disobedience and sin did indeed subject all of humanity to death.

Church growth focuses on a reconciliation between God and humanity. The human effort to spread the good news of Christ, that He can conquer sin and death, is called evangelism. The efforts of evangelism and the process of making fruit-bearing disciples of new converts who can then spread the good news is a priority of church growth (Matt. 28:19).

Church Growth and Hamartiology

Hamartiology, or the doctrine of sin, is a critical doctrine of theology in general and church growth in particular. Sin is disobedience to the law of God which, unless forgiven, creates an unbridgeable chasm between God and humankind. The very nature of God who is love cries out for the reconciliation of God and humankind through the forgiveness of sins. God made this forgiveness possible through His love by sending His Son Jesus Christ (John 3:16).

The Greek *hamartia* literally means "missing the mark." This word family is by far the most frequently used for sin in the New Testament, with nearly three hundred occurrences. The New Testament concept of *hamartia* is not that of merely a mistake, but a deliberate, conscious, and culpable act. The sin is always against God since it is His standard of righteousness that we fail to meet.

Millard Erickson notes three natural human desires "which, while good in and of themselves, are potential areas for temptation and sin."[2] The first of these is the desire to enjoy things. God has implanted within us the desire of certain things, some of which are essential. Food, drink, sex, and leisure activities are but some of the desires most people have. Legitimately pursued within the boundaries of Scripture, God delights in providing the desires of His children (Matt. 7:7-11). However, beyond the boundaries of Scripture, the meeting of these desires can become excessive and, thus, sinful. Gluttony, drunkenness, adultery, fornication, and slothfulness are sins resulting from the violation of clearly established biblical guidelines.

A second human desire is the desire to obtain things. We are to have dominion over the world (Gen. 1:28), and material possessions are legitimate incentives toward industriousness. "When, however, the desire to acquire worldly goods becomes so compelling that it is satisfied at any cost, even by exploiting or stealing from others, then it has degenerated into 'the lust of the eyes' (1 John 2:16)."[3]

The desire to achieve is a third potential area for temptation and sin. The stewardship parables of Jesus (e.g. Matt. 25:14-30) illustrate the worthiness of achievement in God's eyes. "When, however, this urge transgresses proper limitations and is pursued at the expense of other humans, it has degenerated into 'the pride of life' (1 John 2:16)."[4]

The Christian finds the struggle with sin arising from three areas. The first of these areas is termed "world," or *kosmos* in the Greek. When world is used in this context, it refers to everything that opposes God and His will. Christians are told to love neither the world nor the things in the world (1 John 2:15).

The flesh is a second area of struggle for the Christian. In fact Paul told the Romans that unbelievers, "those who live according to the sinful nature," are controlled by the flesh

[2]Millard J. Erickson, *Christian Theology* (Grand Rapids, MI: Baker, 1983, 1984, 1985), 597. The three desires Erickson discusses are paraphrased by me.
[3]Ibid.
[4]Ibid.

(Rom. 8:5-6). Believers struggle also between control by the Spirit and control by the flesh. Paul experienced and articulated this struggle well: "So I find this law at work: When I want to do good, evil is right there with me. For in my inner being I delight in God's law; but I see another law at work in the members of my body, waging war against the law of my mind and making me a prisoner of the law of sin at work within my members. What a wretched man I am! Who will rescue me from this body of death? Thanks be to God—through Jesus Christ our Lord!" (Rom. 7:21-25).

Finally, the Christian struggles with Satan and his demonic following. In our struggle with sin we are called to resist the devil (Jas 4:7) by putting on the full armor of God (Eph. 6:10-18).

Sin is not to be taken lightly. Church growth theology must not avoid this topic in its efforts to encourage churches to be "user friendly." While the teaching and preaching of church growth churches should avoid judgmental and pharisaic attitudes, they must also include a healthy and balanced teaching about sin.

If the doctrine of sin is not taught, neither believers nor unbelievers will comprehend the consequences of sin. For the unbeliever, unforgiven sin results in eternal damnation and death. Sin has consequences in addition to eternal death. Erickson has categorized these consequences into our relationships with God, ourselves, and other humans.[5]

In our relationship with other humans, sin can lead to unhealthy competitiveness (perhaps among churches and pastors) and, on a larger scale, it can even lead to war. Sin can also affect our ability to empathize. "Being concerned about our own personal desires, reputation, and opinions, we see only our own perspective. Because what we want is so important to us, we can not step into shoes of others and see their needs as well, or see how they might understand a situation in a somewhat different way."[6] In other words, we do not look out for the interests of others because we do not

---

[5]Ibid, 601-619. I have summarized chapter 28 of Erickson's book in these next few paragraphs.
[6]Ibid., 619.

have the mind of Christ (Phil. 2:3-5). Perhaps the ultimate consequence of sin in our relationship with others is an inability to love. One of the greatest freedoms that comes from Christ indwelling in us is the freedom to put others before us instead of "looking out for number one." There is an abundance of joy and release in no longer worrying about our own needs, but rather focusing on the needs of others as we learn to love one another (1 John 4:7).

Sin has devastating effects on the sinner as well. One of the effects is an enslaving power leading to habits and addictions. Paul urged the Romans to be slaves to righteousness rather than slaves to sin (Rom. 5:17-18). Living in sin can result in flight from reality, denial, self-deceit (cf. Matt. 7:3), insensitivity (cf. 1 Tim. 4:2), self-centeredness, and restlessness. Certainly the effects of sin in the lives of sinners has the opposite effect of "the peace of God, which transcends all understanding" (Phil. 4:7).

Sin ultimately affects our relationship with God. His hatred of sin is evident throughout Scripture (e.g. Prov. 6:16-17; Zech. 8:17). Unforgiven and unrepentant sin for the unbeliever results in eternal death (Matt. 25:41-46). Physical death or human mortality is also a result of sin (Gen. 2:17; Rom. 6:23). The believer not only is subject to physical death like the unbeliever, but a Christian can also experience broken fellowship with God if he or she continues in unrepentant sin (cf. 1 John 1:5-10).

Sin is a critical doctrine in theology in general and in church growth theology in particular. It is because of sin we need a Savior, therefore God elected to send His Son as that Savior in an act of pure love (John 3:16). Such is the heart of Christian theology and the Church Growth Movement: a loving God seeking to reconcile with rebellious humanity by sending His Son Jesus Christ who then commanded all believers to make disciples (Matt. 28:19). We now turn to the doctrine that focuses on the reconciling act of Jesus Christ for our salvation, the doctrine of soteriology.

Suggested Reading for Chapter 13

Demarest, B. A. "Fall of Man." In Walter A. Elwell, ed. *Evangelical Dictionary of Theology*. Grand Rapids, MI: Baker, 1984. 403-405.

Erickson, Millard J. *Christian Theology*. Grand Rapids, MI: Baker, 1983, 1984, 1985. Outstanding evangelical theological work. Erickson's chapters on sin (part six) are especially good. See particularly chapters 26 and 28.

Morris, Henry M. *The Biblical Basis for Modern Science*. Grand Rapids, MI: Baker, 1984. See especially chapters 4 and 5 dealing with evolution and creation respectively.

Morris, Henry M. *Evolution and the Modern Christian*. Grand Rapids, MI: Baker, 1967.

Pun, P. P. T. "Evolution" In Walter A. Elwell, ed. *Evangelical Dictionary of Theology*. Grand Rapids, MI: Baker, 1984. 388-397.

Ross, Hugh. *The Fingerprint of God*. 2nd ed. Orange, CA: Promise, 1991.

14

Soteriology and Church Growth

The word "soteriology" has its origin in the Greek word *soterion*, which means salvation; hence soteriology is the study of the doctrine of salvation. Salvation is God's rescuing of humanity from the power and effects of sin. Salvation then comes from God and is effected by God. We can do nothing to win back the favor of God. "In Jesus' openness and friendship toward sinners, the loving welcome of God found perfect expression. Nothing was needed to win back God's favor. It waited eagerly for man's return (Luke 15:11-24). The one indispensable preliminary was the change in man from rebelliousness to childlike trust and willingness to obey."[1]

The Death of Christ and Soteriology

Our sin causes the chasm between God and us. Without the removal of that sin, there is no reconciliation and no salvation. Since Christ voluntarily submitted Himself to death on the cross (Phil. 2:8) to bring forgiveness to humanity and reconciliation between God and humanity, the death of Christ becomes a key element in our understanding of soteriology.

Various theories have been set forth to explain the death of Christ. A summary of those theories is given in the chart developed by Paul Enns on the following page. Each of these theories has significant weaknesses to the extent that no individual proposal could be characterized as the correct view of the atonement. That is not to say, however, that

[1] R. E. O. White, "Salvation," in *Evangelical Dictionary of Theology*, Walter A. Elwell, ed. (Grand Rapids, MI: Baker, 1984), 968.

there is no value or contribution in some of the views. For example, the Socinian understanding of the atonement, usually called the example theory, is heretical in its rejection of any idea of vicarious satisfaction. Yet some thread of truth can be found in the focus of Jesus' death as an example of total love for God and as an inspiration to followers since. The governmental theory is scripturally weak in that "it is possible for God to relax the law so that he need not exact a specific punishment or penalty for each violation."[2] The governmental theory, however, emphasizes the seriousness of sin and the need for dealing with that sin.

Despite the strengths of some of the atonement views, the most accurate understanding of Christ's death is the idea of substitution. Jesus died in the place of sinners, a death that is called vicarious, which means "one in place of another." This view can best be explained by several terms related to the death of Christ.

The first of these terms is the word *substitution* itself. "There are many passages that emphasize Christ's substitutionary atonement in the place of mankind. Christ was a substitute in being made sin for others (2 Cor. 5:21); He bore the sins of others in His body on the cross (1 Pet. 2:24); He suffered once to bear the sins of others (Heb. 9:28); He experienced horrible suffering, scourging, and death in place of sinners (Isa. 53:4-6)."[3]

Propitiation is another word related to the substitutionary death of Christ. It literally means "a covering for sin." This covering was necessary to satisfy the righteous demands of a wrathful God. Jesus' substitutionary death satisfied the requirements for the appeasement of God (cf. Lev. 4:35). By receiving Christ's gift of salvation, the believer can be spared from the wrath of God. "For this reason he had to be made like his brothers in every way, in order that he might become a merciful and faithful high priest in service to God, and that he might make atonement for [propitiation] the sins of the people" (Heb. 2:17).[4]

[2]Millard Erickson, *Christian Theology* (Grand Rapids, MI: Baker, 1983, 1984, 1985), 789.

[3]Paul Enns, *The Moody Handbook of Theology* (Chicago: Moody, 1989), 323.

[4]The NIV offers an alternative translation in its notes: " . . . and that he might turn aside God's wrath, taking away the sins of the people."

THEORIES OF THE ATONEMENT

Theory	Original Exponents	Main Idea	Weakness	Recent Exponents
Ransom to Satan	Origen (A.D. 184–254)	Ransom paid to Satan because people held captive by him.	God's holiness offended through sin; cross was judgment on Satan, not ransom to Satan.	No known current advocates.
Recapitulation	Irenaeus (A.D. 130–200)	Christ experienced all Adam did, including sin.	Contradicts Christ's sinlessness. (1 John 3:5)	None known.
Commercial (Satisfaction)	Anselm (1033–1109)	Sin robbed God of honor; Christ's death honored God enabling Him to forgive sinners.	Elevates God's honor above other attributes; ignores vicarious atonement.	None known.
Moral Influence	Abelard (1079–1142)	Christ's death unnecessary to atone for sin; His death softens sinners hearts to cause them to repent.	Basis of Christ's death is God's love, not holiness. Atonement viewed as unnecessary.	Friedrich Schleiermacher Albrecht Ritschl Horace Bushnell
Example	Socinius (1583–1604)	Christ's death unnecessary to atone for sin; His death was example of obedience to inspire reform.	Views Christ only as a man; atonement viewed as unnecessary.	Thomas Altizer Unitarians
Governmental	Grotius (1583–1645)	Christ upheld government in God's law; His death was a token payment; enables God to set law aside and forgive people.	God is subject to change; His law is set aside; God forgives without payment for sin.	Daniel Whitby Samuel Clarke Richard Watson J. McLeod Campbell H. R. Mackintosh
Accident	A. Schweitzer (1875–1965)	Christ became enamored with a Messiah complex and was mistakenly crushed under it in the process.	Views Christ's death as a mistake; denies substitutionary atonement.	None known.

Redemption (Gk. *agorazo*) means "to purchase." The word was used often in the context of purchasing slaves in the marketplace. The New Testament writers used the word to refer to the effect of Christ's substitutionary death in setting people free from the slavery or bondage of sin. The redemption price was the death of Christ (1 Cor. 6:20; 7:23; Rev. 5:9).

The most common biblical word for *forgiveness* is *aphiemi,* which literally means "to send away." Jesus' death on the cross released or sent away our sins. "In him we have redemption through his blood, the forgiveness [sending away] of sins, in accordance with the riches of God's grace" (Eph. 1:7).

The writer of Hebrews focuses upon the death of Christ as *sacrifice* (Heb. 9—10). Christ is the high priest who entered into the Holy Place to make the once-and-for-all sacrifice, negating the need to make "the same sacrifices repeated endlessly year after year" (Heb. 10:1). "So Christ was sacrificed once to take away the sins of many people; and he will appear a second time, not to bear sin, but to bring salvation to those who are waiting for him" (Heb. 9:28).

Reconciliation (Gk. *katalasso*) means "to effect a change, to reconcile."[5] Because of our sin an estrangement exists between God and humanity. Christ's death on the cross demonstrates God's initiative in restoring the relationship. Reconciliation is available to everyone, but it is not effective unless one receives by faith Christ who made possible the restoration of the relationship.

A final term is that of *justification.* Justification is a legal act, based on the death of Christ (Rom. 5:9), whereby God declares righteous those who have faith in Jesus Christ. The gift of justification (Rom. 3:24) involves the pardon and removal of all the sins of the believer and salvation from the wrath of God (Rom. 5:9). Our righteousness is not from ourselves but is a gift from God to all those who believe (Rom. 3:22).

The Implications of Substitutionary Atonement

Because of the rich implications of Christ's substitutionary death on the cross, this understanding will be studied in

[5]Enns, 324.

greater detail. Millard Erickson has written a summary of the issue.

> The substitutionary theory of the atoning death of Christ, when grasped in all its complexity, is a rich and meaningful truth. It carries several major implications for our understanding of salvation:
>
> 1. The penal-substitution theory confirms the biblical teaching of the total depravity of all humans. God would not have gone so far as to put his precious Son to death if it had not been absolutely necessary. Man is totally unable to meet his need.
> 2. God's nature is not one-sided, nor is there any tension between its different aspects. He is not merely righteous and demanding, nor merely loving and giving. He is righteous, so much so that sacrifice for sin had to be provided. He is loving, so much so that he provided that sacrifice himself.
> 3. There is no other way of salvation but by grace, and specifically, the death of Christ. It has an infinite value and thus covers the sins of all mankind for all time. A finite sacrifice, by contrast, cannot even fully cover the sins of the individual offering it.
> 4. There is security for the believer in his or her relationship to God. For the basis of the relationship, Christ's sacrificial death, is complete and permanent. Although our feelings might change, the ground of our relationship to God remains unshaken.
> 5. We must never take lightly the salvation which we have. Although it is free, it is also costly, for it cost God the ultimate sacrifice. We must therefore always be grateful for what he has done; we must love him in return and emulate his giving character.
>
> "This is love: not that we loved God, but that he loved us and sent his Son as an atoning sacrifice for our sins" (1 John 4:10).[6]

Other Considerations of Soteriology

Before we examine the implications of soteriology for church growth theology, we need to focus on six other biblical words

[6]Erickson, 822-823. Used by permission.

related to salvation. *Election* and *predestination* are two terms that often cause a level of discomfort because of the perception that they take away our responsibility to respond. The emphasis of Scripture, however, is that anyone who is lost forfeits salvation because of their own disobedience, not because of election or predestination. Similarly, the responsibility of believers to evangelize remains a mandate. We must admit that a tension exists between humanity's free will (John 3:16-18) and God's sovereign choice (Eph. 1:4). Such tension exists not because of contradiction in Scripture but because of our finite understanding.

"Election is a sovereign, eternal decree of God."[7] The decree involves the choice of people to be the recipients of grace and salvation (Eph. 1:4). "The word *predestination* comes from the Greek *proorizo,* which means 'to mark out beforehand,' and occurs six times in the New Testament (Acts 4:28; Rom. 8:29-30; 1 Cor. 2:7; Eph. 1:5, 11)."[8] Both election and predestination are necessary characteristics of a sovereign God; but neither absolve humanity of the clear mandate to receive Christ, and then to make disciples. (Matt. 28:19).

Adoption comes from the Greek term *huiothesia,* which is used to describe a Christian's new position and status in Christ—a child of God. By joining the family of God and enjoying the status of child (Gal. 4:5), believers are removed from their old life and brought into a new life with all the benefits and privileges made available to a fully legitimate child of the Father.

Sanctification, from the Greek word *hagiasmos,* means "to make holy," or "to set apart." When we refer to the believer's standing before God, we are speaking of positional sanctification. Because of Christ's death on the cross, the believer is holy or set apart or a saint before God (cf. 1 Cor. 1:2; 2 Cor. 1:1; and Eph. 1:1). Even the church at Corinth, with its abounding carnality, was addressed by Paul as "those sanctified in Christ Jesus" (1 Cor. 1:2).[9]

[7]F. H. Klooster, "Elect, Election," in *Evangelical Dictionary of Theology,* Walter A. Elwell, ed. (Grand Rapids, MI: Baker, 1984), 349.

[8]Enns, 328.

[9]Ibid., 329-330.

The believer is always a "saint" in his or her standing before God, but the experiential sanctification of the believer varies in relation to one's dedication to God. Thus Peter could command believers to be sanctified or to be holy: "But just as he who called you is holy, so be holy in all you do" (1 Pet. 1:15). Final or ultimate sanctification takes place when believers will be made into the likeness of Christ, "holy and blameless" (Eph. 5:27).[10]

Grace is another important term in understanding salvation. A general definition of grace is "the provision of God's unmerited favor." Specific connotations of grace, however, must be understood in order to receive the full impact of the term.

Common grace refers to God's favor granted to all of humanity. It includes the provisions of creation: sunshine, rain, food, clothing, beauty, and the withholding of judgment. *Special grace* is given only to believers. Theologians have typically categorized special grace as prevenient, efficacious, irresistible, and sufficient.[11]

Prevenient grace means that grace comes first, preceding human initiative. "We love because he first loved us" (1 John 4:19). *Efficacious grace* is grace that cannot fail. Grace given to the believer will not be taken away nor will it fail (John 10:27-28). *Sufficient grace* indicates the total adequacy of God's work through Jesus Christ. "Therefore he is able to save completely those who come to God through him" (Heb. 7:25). Finally, *irresistible grace* conveys that God's grace cannot be rejected. It is God who chooses (Eph. 1:4) and provides grace to those "in accordance with his pleasure and will" (Eph. 1:5).

Regeneration, though used only twice in the New Testament (*paliggensia,* Matt. 19:28; Titus 3:5), is an important aspect of salvation. It is the impartation of life from God to the one who believes. It is a new birth from God, or a birth from above, or a second birth: "In reply Jesus declared, 'I tell you the truth, no one can see the Kingdom of God unless he is born again.'" (John 3:3). The regeneration of

[10]Ibid., 330.
[11]See P. E. Hughes, "Grace" in *Evangelical Dictionary of Theology,* Walter A. Elwell, ed. (Grand Rapids, MI: Baker, 1984), 479-482.

the believer results in a new nature (2 Pet. 1:4; Eph. 4:24; 2 Cor. 5:17) and a new life (1 Cor. 2:16; Rom. 5:5).

The Church Growth Dilemma

Church growth grew out of a desire to see men and women accept Christ, to see all of the benefits of salvation described in this chapter given to an unregenerate world. In the historical section of this book, we saw Donald McGavran's burden for the lost people in his mission situation in India. We saw his concern over the small number of converts and his bewilderment that few churches were growing at a rapid pace or had plateaued at best.

As McGavran began to ask why some churches were growing while others declined, he was integrating the two doctrines of soteriology and ecclesiology (i.e. the doctrine of the church which will be examined in the next chapter). McGavran wanted *evidence* that salvation was taking place, that people were coming to Christ. His dilemma could be expressed as follows: How can we *know* that we are reaching people for Christ? How can we determine if an internal decision of the heart has been made?

Jesus said, "By their fruit you will recognize them" (Matt. 7:16). Paul said that the fruit of the Spirit is love, joy, peace, patience, kindness, goodness, faithfulness, gentleness, and self-control (Gal. 5:22-23). Still, McGavran was faced with the situation that it would be impossible to know how many people in India were Christians. No one could know for certain if people were being reached and made disciples (i.e. fruit-bearing believers). It was a non-quantifiable task that defied measurement and thus accountability.

McGavran took a different but fallible approach. Salvation would be "measured" by "responsible church membership." If someone was attending a church and participating actively in the fellowhship, then the probability was high that he or she would be a Christian.

Hence the Church Growth Movement arose when salvation became *quantifiable,* and churches became accountable for their numbers—in terms of membership, attendance, baptisms, and so forth. It must be admitted that this church growth approach is subject to error. However, it creates a level of accountability, and that accountability keeps the church focused on its primary task: reaching people for Christ.

Suggested Reading for Chapter 14

Enns, Paul. *The Moody Handbook of Theology.* Chicago: Moody, 1989.

Erickson, Millard. *Christian Theology.* Grand Rapids, MI: Baker, 1983, 1984, 1985.

Hughes, P. E. "Grace." In *Evangelical Dictionary of Theology,* Walter A. Elwell, ed. Grand Rapids, MI: Baker, 1984.

Klooster, F. H. "Elect, Election." In *Evangelical Dictionary of Theology,* Walter A. Elwell, ed. Grand Rapids, MI: Baker, 1984.

Wagner, C. Peter. *Church Growth and the Whole Gospel: A Biblical Mandate.* San Francisco: Harper & Row, 1981.

White, R.E.O. "Salvation." In *Evangelical Dictionary of Theology,* Walter A. Elwell, ed. Grand Rapids, MI: Baker, 1984.

15

Ecclesiology and Church Growth

Ecclesiology is the study of the church. The English word "church" is a translation of the Greek word *ekklesia,* which literally means "called-out ones." Since the word "church" appears in the name of the Church Growth Movement, it is important that we understand the ecclesiology of church growth. At the heart of the issue is this question: "What is the purpose of the church?" Before we look at this issue, let us examine some figures in Scripture used to describe the church.

Images of the Church

Body of Christ. The body metaphor focuses on authority, unity, and universality. Because it is comprehensive, this is the most frequently used image of the church in the Bible.[1] Authority in the body of Christ resides in Christ Himself who is the Head of the body (Col. 1:18). Believers then are the individual members or parts. The body image also portrays unity, in that there are many members but only one body (1 Cor. 12:12). Finally, the body is also the universal church as well as individual congregations (Eph. 1:22-23). As the body of Christ, the church is the extension of Christ's ministry; the church must do the work of Christ (John 14:12).

Bride of Christ. Paul draws an analogy between the husband and wife relationship in marriage and Christ and His bride, the church (Eph. 5:23). The dominant theme of this image is Christ's love for the church.

The People of God. The picture of the church as the people of God emphasizes God's initiative in choosing the

---

[1]Millard J. Erickson, *Christian Theology* (Grand Rapids, MI: Baker, 1983, 1984, 1985), 1036.

church (2 Cor. 6:16). Like the Abrahamic line that produced Israel, God chose the church to be His people (cf. Ex. 15:13).

Priesthood. Peter refers to Christians as a royal priesthood (1 Pet. 2:9), emphasizing their position as both kings and priests. All believers today have direct access to God and may approach Him boldly (Heb. 4:14-16).

Flock. Jesus is the Shepherd who loves and cares for His flock, the church (John 10:16). This image recognizes Christ's tender care and sacrificial spirit for His church. The sheep (church) belong to Christ and are under His constant watch.

Temple of the Holy Spirit. Believers are the dwelling place for the Holy Spirit. Speaking to believers at Ephesus, Paul wrote, "You too are being built together to become a dwelling in which God lives by his Spirit" (Eph. 2:22). The Holy Spirit gives to the church unity (Eph. 2:21), guidance (John 16:13), and power (Acts 4:31,33).

Government of the Church

Church growth theology rarely mentions the various forms of governments since there is little correlation between church government and the growth of the church. In Millard Erickson's able scriptural analysis of church government, he concluded: "It is probably safe to say that the evidence from the New Testament is inconclusive; nowhere in the New Testament do we find a picture closely resembling any of the fully developed systems of today." Erickson believes that the early churches formed governmental structures that best fit their situation for greatest effectiveness: "It is likely that in those days church government was not very highly developed, indeed, that local congregations were rather loosely knit groups. There may well have been rather wide varieties of governmental arrangements. Each church adopted a pattern which fit its individual situation."[2]

My denomination, the Southern Baptist Convention, adheres to the position that the church is an autonomous and democratic body. Such a theological perspective is called the congregational form of government. Some New

[2]Ibid., 1084.

Testament scholars, however, see the possibility of other types of church governments.

We will briefly examine some of the major positions. The type of government, in the final analysis, depends upon where authority will reside. In the episcopal form of church government, authority is generally in the hands of the bishop (*episkopos*) or bishops. Of course, the most highly developed form of episcopal government is found in the Roman Catholic Church. The bishop of Rome, the pope, is the supreme bishop.

A presbyterian form of government focuses on the key office of elder; but it is usually the elder body rather than the individual office which exercises authority. Paul and Barnabas appointed elders (Acts 14:23), and Paul summoned the elders of Ephesus to be with him in Miletus. "It should be noted . . . that the term elder (*presbuterus*) usually occurs in the plural, suggesting that the authority of the elders is collective rather than individual."[3]

A congregational form of church government places the seat of authority in the local congregation. The church is autonomous and democratic, with every member of the local congregation voting with equal authority. Those who argue for congregational government as normative usually look to the early church example, where the congregation chose Judas's successor (Acts 1:15-26) and the seven men to wait on tables (Acts 6:1-6).

Some Christian groups, such as the Quakers (Friends) and the Plymouth Brethren, have opted to have no governmental structure. All governmental structures, such as committees, officeholders, constitutions and by-laws, and business meetings, are eliminated or kept to a minimum. A dependence on the Holy Spirit to speak directly to the church is the basis for most decision-making.

The Purpose of the Church

The heart of church growth discussion is the purpose of the church. Typically the functions of the church are categorized into four areas.

[3]Ibid., 1075.

Evangelism.   Jesus' last words to His disciples in all of
the New Testament accounts were about evangelism (cf.
Matt. 28:19; Acts 1:8). Obviously Jesus regarded the need for
others to be told of the way of salvation to be of utmost
importance. Furthermore, Jesus commanded His disciples to
reach beyond their own area of Jerusalem to "Judea and
Samaria and to the ends of the earth" (Acts 1:8). The gospel
message was one of urgency to reach as many as possible.

Discipleship.   When Jesus gave His command to
evangelize, He spoke of "making disciples of all nations"
(Matt. 28:19). He obviously had in mind that Christian
conversion was only the beginning; discipleship must follow
with baptism, teaching, and obedience (Matt. 28:19-20).
Believers are to grow in Christ by fellowship or *koinonia,*
holding all things in common (Acts 2:44-45). Further growth
would come from instruction (cf. Acts 18:26), preaching (1
Cor. 14:3-4), and exercise of spiritual gifts (1 Cor. 12).

Worship.   A third purpose of the church is worship, the
praise and exaltation of God. Worship in the early church
involved the gathered church (Heb. 10:25), often meeting at
a set time on a regular basis (1 Cor. 16:2). Elements of
worship included prayer (Acts 12:5), scripture reading (Acts
4:24-26), singing (Eph. 5:19), and observing the Lord's
Supper (1 Cor. 11:23-26). Worship has become a critical issue
in church growth, an issue that we will examine in the final
section on church growth principles.

Social ministry.   Jesus provided a living example of one
who cared about the physical and emotional needs of people.
Such is the essence of His parable about the good Samaritan
(Luke 10:25-37). Indeed Jesus' words in Matthew 25:31-46
suggest that concern for the needs of others would be
evidence of one's true commitment to the Savior. The Book of
James provides intense "sound bites" that state clearly that
faith without works is dead: "Suppose a brother or sister is
without clothes and daily food. If one of you says to him, 'Go,
I wish you well; keep warm and well fed,' but does nothing
about his physical needs, what good is it? In the same way,
faith by itself, if it is not accompanied by action, is dead"
(Jas. 2:15-17). The latter part of the twentieth century saw
evangelicals rediscover their mandate for social concerns

after overreacting to the social gospel earlier in the century. The Church Growth Movement has likewise struggled with its ecclesiology, particularly in its attempt to understand the purpose of the church.

Church Growth: What Is the Purpose of the Church?

To understand the evolution of the Church Growth Movement's ecclesiology, it is necessary to follow C. Peter Wagner in his understanding of mission (i.e. the church's purpose) and evangelism. It is important to understand that, for the most part, Wagner's ecclesiology picked up where Donald McGavran's had ended. In McGavran's books, such as *The Bridges of God* (1955), *How Churches Grow* (1959), and *Understanding Church Growth* (1970), he basically stated that churches have one main job—to multiply themselves. In other words, the purpose of the church is evangelism and everything must be subordinate to it. Today, Wagner's theology, which is representative of church growth ecclesiology, has departed from this narrow concept of the purpose of the church, although evangelism remains the priority purpose.

The Lausanne Covenant, Wagner's primary statement of faith and belief, affirms that in "the church's mission of sacrificial service evangelism is primary," and that "world evangelization requires the whole church to take the whole gospel to the whole world."[4] Wagner's theology holds to the primacy of evangelism, yet the meaning of evangelism in his theology is often misunderstood by some to be synonymous with mission or church growth. Since his church growth theology presupposes the priority of evangelism, it becomes imperative to understand the precise meaning of the word and the context in which it is used. It is necessary first to understand that Wagner's theology sees evangelism as one task, albeit the most urgent task, in the definition of mission. Therefore, to understand evangelism and its priority in church growth theology, his understanding of mission must be examined first.

[4]The Lausanne Covenant, see article 6, "The Church and Evangelism."

The meaning of mission, says Wagner, must be understood in the context of the kingdom of God.[5] John the Baptist preached that the kingdom was open for those who repented of sin and turned in faith to Christ. While preaching in the wilderness of Judea, he said, "Repent for the kingdom of heaven is at hand" (Matt. 3:2); but the kingdom teachings of the New Testament discuss more than just the conversion of people. In instructing His disciples on their mission, Jesus said, "Preach this message, 'The kingdom of heaven is near' Heal the sick, raise the dead, cleanse those who have leprosy, drive out demons" (Matt. 10:7-8). Wagner affirms that the meaning of mission, in the context of the kingdom of God, is a holistic ministry. "Since this is what God sends us to do, this is what mission is all about."[6] Mission thus "aims for the good of the whole person."[7]

Wagner acknowledges that his church growth theology has followed a general evangelical transformation in the understanding of mission. His theological changes have also been the result of criticisms against church growth theology, one of the most obvious being "the narrow conception of mission as evangelism."[8] Rodger Bassham argued that church growth was failing to understand the "whole task of mission." The Church Growth Movement, said Bassham, "appears to have neglected a substantial discussion which has taken place over the past twenty-five years, in which the meaning of mission, evangelism, witness, service, and salvation have been explored and developed."[9]

Until this century mission was most often equated with evangelism. To do mission was to propagate the faith. Harvey Hoekstra labeled this function "classical mission," which he defined as the "complex of activities whose chief purpose is to make Jesus Christ known as Lord and Savior

[5]See C. Peter Wagner, *Strategies for Church Growth* (Ventura, CA: Regal, 1987), 96-99.
[6]Ibid., 99.
[7]Ibid.
[8]Rodger C. Bassham, *Mission Theology: 1948-1975, Years of Worldwide Creative Tension:* Ecumenical, Evangelical and Roman Catholic (Pasadena, CA: William Carey, 1979), 194-195.
[9]Ibid.

and to persuade men to become his disciples and responsible members of his Church."[10]

The classical meaning of mission left little room for activities other than evangelism. Rufus Anderson argued that mission is preaching the gospel and winning converts, after which "social renovation will be sure to follow." He explicitly rejected any purpose of mission that involved the "reorganizing, by various direct means, of the structure of that social system of which the converts form a part."[11]

As the nineteenth century came to a close, the understanding of mission shifted dramatically. The social gospel movement was influencing churches and "missions were metamorphosed from the simple task of winning converts . . . to the complex task of participating actively in social betterment and reconstruction."[12]

Evangelicals began to build defenses against the social gospel. In doing so, evangelicalism was rightly affirming the importance of evangelism but wrongly avoiding any recognition of other ministries as being a part of mission. Wagner was among these evangelicals. Social concerns had little place in his theology of mission. "To allow the cultural mandate to creep into the technical definition of mission," he said, "would have been interpreted as a capitulation to the enemy."[13]

The shift in Wagner's understanding of mission followed the change in evangelicalism in general. Signs of the change were noticeable at the Berlin Congress of 1966, but the shift was explicitly stated in the International Congress on World Evangelization, held in Lausanne, Switzerland, in 1974.

[10]Harvey T. Hoekstra, *The World Council of Churches and the Demise of Evangelism* (Wheaton, IL: Tyndale, 1979), 12. I am following Wagner's development of the meaning of mission, found in *Church Growth and the Whole Gospel*, 87-91. His discussion of Hoekstra and Rufus Anderson is on p. 88.

[11]Cited in Sydney E. Mead, "Denominationalism: The Shape of Protestantism in America," in *Denominationalism*, ed. Russell E. Richey (Nashville: Abingdon, 1977), 85-86 which is cited in C. Peter Wagner, *Church Growth and the Whole Gospel: A Biblical Mandate* (San Francisco: Harper's Row, 1981), 89.

[12]Mead, "Denominationalism," cited in Wagner, *Church Growth and the Whole Gospel*, 89.

[13]Wagner, *Church Growth and the Whole Gospel*, 90.

Wagner was influenced significantly by John R. W. Stott, then the Rector of All Souls Church in London. In Berlin, Stott had held to the classical definition of mission. He presented three plenary session Bible studies on the Great Commission. His understanding of mission then was clear— "The commission of the Church, therefore, is not to reform society, but to preach the Gospel."[14]

Stott, however, led evangelicals in redefining the concept of mission. By the time of the Lausanne meeting, he had become a chief author of the Lausanne Covenant, which stated "that evangelism and sociopolitical involvement are both part of our Christian duty. For both are necessary expressions of our doctrines of God and man, our love for our neighbor and our obedience to Jesus Christ."[15] Shortly after Lausanne, Stott published a book in which he affirmed that the mission of the church "includes evangelism and social responsibility, since both are authentic expressions of the love which longs to serve man in his need."[16]

Wagner's understanding of mission followed a similar pattern. In 1971 he published *Frontiers in Missionary Strategy,* in which he used mission and evangelism interchangeably. He also argued for a definition of mission that was really a definition of presence, proclamation, and persuasion evangelism.[17] Later, Wagner affirmed a change in this aspect of his theology.

> This was before I went to Lausanne and heard such speakers as René Padilla, Samuel Escobar, and Orlando Costas. I was influenced by the Lausanne Covenant, the writings of John Stott, and the ongoing dynamic of the Lausanne Committee, of which I have been a part since its founding. I now believe that the mission of the church embraces both the cultural and evangelistic mandates. *I believe in what is now being called "holistic mission."*[18]

[14]John R. W. Stott, "The Great Commission," in *One Race, One Gospel, One Task,* ed. Carl F. H. Henry and W. Stanley Mooneyham, vol.1, (Minneapolis: World Wide, 1967), 50.

[15]Lausanne Covenant, see article 5, "Christian Social Responsibility."

[16]John R. W. Stott, *Christian Mission in the Modern World* (Downers Grove, IL: InterVarsity, 1975), 35.

[17]C. Peter Wagner, *Frontiers in Missionary Strategy* (Chicago: Moody, 1971), 34.

[18]Wagner, *Church Growth and the Whole Gospel,* 91, emphasis in original.

Holistic mission, then, said Wagner, involves two clear mandates. He used the terminology conceived by Arthur Glasser, the cultural mandate and the evangelistic mandate.[19] The cultural mandate, sometimes called Christian social responsibility, is a responsibility of all Christians. Said Wagner: "Doing good to others, whether our efforts are directed toward individuals or to society as a whole, is a biblical duty, a God-given cultural mandate."[20] Wagner has followed the trend in evangelical circles that now affirms both Christian social ministry and evangelism as essential components of mission.

Wagner announced his transformation to a more holistic ministry in *Church Growth and the Whole Gospel*. In this book Wagner lamented the era of the "Great Reversal," a time in this century when evangelicals reacted adversely to anything that hinted at social ministry. Wagner devoted an entire chapter in his book to the call for Christians to be involved in social ministries.[21]

After *Church Growth and the Whole Gospel* was published in 1981, the Church Growth Movement became recognized as more than a number-counting ministry. "I do not think any of us who live in affluence," he said, "can grasp the full scope of the plight of the world's poor with our minds—it can only be partially felt in our hearts."[22] While the poor had not been neglected in earlier church growth writings, Wagner most clearly depicted their plight and Christians' responsibility in this book.[23] Quoting Howard Snyder, Wagner said: "The teaching is clear, and both consistent and persistent: Of all the peoples and classes, God especially has compassion on the poor, and his acts in history confirm this."[24]

[19]Wagner, *Strategies for Church Growth,* 99.
[20]Ibid., 100.
[21]Wagner, *Church Growth and the Whole Gospel.* The chapter mentioned is chapter 2, "Christian Social Ministry in Perspective."
[22]Ibid., 27.
[23]For example, Donald A. McGavran wrote in *Understanding Church Growth,* rev. ed. (Grand Rapids, MI: Eerdmans, 1980) on 278-279; "God sent his prophets to plead the cause of the poor and to demand justice for the common man."
[24]Wagner, *Church Growth and the Whole Gospel,* 29. The quote mentioned is Howard A Snyder, *The Problem of Wineskins: Church Structure in a Technological Age* (Downers Grove, IL: InterVarsity, 1975), 88.

The cultural mandate presents the church with different avenues of ministry. Wagner categorized the different opportunities into social action and social service. Social action is the group of ministries that attempt to change social structures. It involves socio-political changes. Wagner believed that the church usually is not the best instrument to effect social action.

The church, however, "does not have an option as to whether or not it will be involved in social ministry. The kingdom lifestyle demands it."[25] Social ministry is done in obedience to God, which in turn glorifies God. It may or may not be a means of winning souls. Wagner found an abundance of biblical justification for doing social ministry whether or not people are led to faith in Christ as a result of it.[26]

By the time Wagner wrote *Church Growth and the Whole Gospel,* he had established what he perceived to be the biblical standard for setting priorities for social ministries. The first priority is the family of the Christian, either the nuclear family or the extended family. Wagner cited 1 Timothy 5:8: "But if anyone does not take care of his own relatives, especially the members of his own family, he has denied the faith and is worse than an unbeliever."[27]

Wagner's second priority for Christian social service is fellow believers. Galatians 6:10 is the text he used to support this thesis: "So then, as often as we have the chance, we should do good to everyone, and especially to those who belong to our family in the faith."[28]

The third priority for Christian social service includes anyone who has a need. Wagner warned that the third priority is not an optional group for Christians to serve. "Because it is a third priority it does not mean that this is optional. The poor and hungry and needy and oppressed of the whole world need to be helped by people who live a kingdom lifestyle and who take seriously the cultural mandate. Christians who use these biblical priorities to deny

[25]Ibid., 36.
[26]See Wagner's examples in *Church Growth and the Whole Gospel,* 39.
[27]Ibid., 41.
[28]Ibid.

global responsibility, as some unfortunately have done, are disobedient to God and should repent and mend their ways."[29]

The Priority of Evangelism

Despite Wagner's strong affirmation of the cultural mandate, he still insisted on the priority of the evangelistic mandate in his church growth theology. Many even within the evangelical camp disagreed with him on what they perceived to be a dangerous dichotomy. Although the Lausanne Covenant specifically affirmed the distinction between evangelism and social ministry (article 5), a vocal minority held to a position called "holistic evangelism."[30] That position maintains that evangelism and social ministries should not be separated as two distinct parts of mission.

In *Church Growth and the Whole Gospel*, Wagner noted several individuals who disagreed with him and the Lausanne position. Alfred Krass felt that evangelicals often avoided social issues because they have "learned to read scripture in such a way as to dichotomize between the personal and social, between the private and the historical."[31] Krass cited article 5 of the Lausanne Covenant as a clear example of such a "false dichotomy." Rene Padilla, in the "Response to Lausanne" written by the minority dissenters of the Lausanne Congress, said: "We must repudiate as demonic the attempt to drive a wedge between evangelism and social action."[32]

Wagner was not particularly excited about Padilla's claim that his understanding of the priority of evangelism was "demonic." Orlando Costas, five years later, would call such a position a "diabolic polarization," a "useless debate," and a "senseless and satanic waste of time, energies and

[29]Ibid., 42.

[30]Ibid., 95.

[31]Alfred C. Krass, *Five Lanterns at Sundown: Evangelism in a Chastened Mood* (Grand Rapids, MI: William B. Eerdmans, 1978), 78-79, cited in Wagner, *Church Growth and the Whole Gospel,* 95.

[32]"Theology and Implications of Radical Discipleship" in *Let the Earth Hear His Voice,* ed. J. D. Douglas (Minneapolis: World Wide, 1975), p. 144, cited in Wagner, *Church Growth and the Whole Gospel,* 95.

resources."[33] By this point Wagner was beginning to
question if some of the critics even belonged in the
theological camp of evangelicalism. He believed that one of
the distinguishing features of liberalism is that it is
unwilling to exalt the spiritual over the physical. Speaking
specifically about Costas, Wagner said: "I point this out, not
to show that Costas is a liberal, but to explain why the
position of the Lausanne dissenters on holistic evangelism
has not been embraced to any significant degree by the
contemporary evangelical community. It runs counter to the
way most evangelicals understand their faith."[34]

Wagner refused to accept the position of holistic
evangelism, which states that the cultural mandate and the
evangelistic mandate cannot be separated. His theology now
presupposes that not only are the two separable, but that
evangelism is the priority of the two. Article 6 of the
Lausanne Covenant affirmed this: "In the church's mission
of sacrificial service evangelism is primary." In 1980 the
Consultation on World Evangelization was held in Pattaya,
Thailand. This gathering was even more explicit on the
priority of evangelism: "This is not to deny that evangelism
and social action are integrally related, but rather to
acknowledge that of all the tragic needs of human beings
none is greater than their alienation from their Creator and
the reality of eternal death for those who refuse to repent
and believe."[35]

Wagner stated "that neither *distinction* nor *dichotomization*
nor *granting priority* is equivalent to *polarization*."[36] His
reasons for holding to an evangelistic priority are both
pragmatic and theological. Pragmatically, he states that all
institutions have limited resources of time, money, and
people. Religious institutions are not exempt from the
limitation of resources. Such limitations require assigning
priorities.

---

[33]Orlando E. Costas, *The Integrity of Mission: The Inner Life and Outreach of the Church* (San Francisco: Harper & Row, 1979), 75.

[34]Wagner, *Church Growth and the Whole Gospel*, 96.

[35]Cited in Wagner, *Church Growth and the Whole Gospel*, 96.

[36]Ibid., emphasis in original.

Wagner believes the biblical testimony favors the evangelistic mandate. One of the many passages he cites is Matthew 10:28: "Fear not them which kill the body, but are not able to kill the soul; but rather fear him which is able to destroy both soul and body in hell."[37] Wagner summarized his argument for the priority of evangelism by saying:

> I repeat that fulfilling the cultural mandate is not optional for Christians. It is God's command and a part of Christian mission. But it is true that, when a choice must be made on the basis of availability of resources or of value judgments, the biblical indication is that the evangelistic mandate must take priority. Nothing is or can be as important as saving souls from eternal damnation.[38]

The Practical Consequences of Priorities

As spokesperson for the Church Growth Movement, Wagner unhesitatingly affirmed the priority of evangelism as foundational in church growth theology. The ever-pragmatic leader of the movement, however, was also concerned with the practical consequences of such a priority.

Wagner noted that the historical record for those who hold to the priority of evangelism is very positive. He points to Timothy L. Smith's landmark work, *Revivalism and Social Reform*.[39] Smith found that, though the well-known evangelists and revivalists of the nineteenth century held to a priority of winning people to Christ, they were also instrumental in massive social reforms.

Another of the many examples he cites is Sherwood Wirt's *The Social Conscience of the Evangelical*.[40] Wirt affirmed that the modern evangelical missionary movement was a prototype for holding the priority of evangelism, while also maintaining a strong social conscience.

Wagner concluded that not only is the affirmation of the evangelistic priority conducive to significant social

[37]Ibid., 100.

[38]Ibid., 101, emphasis in original.

[39]Timothy L. Smith, *Revivalism and Social Reform in Mid-Nineteenth-Century America* (New York: Abingdon, 1957).

[40]Sherwood Wirt, *The Social Conscience of the Evangelical* (New York: Harper & Row, 1968).

ministries, but the reversing of the priority could very well lead to a collapse of a Christian movement. He cited the case of the Student Volunteer Movement early in part of this century.[41] The organization was founded upon the slogan: "The evangelization of the world in this generation." Wagner called it "the single strongest force for missions in America in the early part of this century."[42] Yet, in the 1940s, the organization ceased to exist. Its original priority of evangelism had shifted to new emphases such as race relations, international relationships, and economic justice. Wagner also pointed to the rapid decline of many major denominations as further evidence that the failure to grasp the priority of evangelism is a death blow to a Christian movement.

He also believed that the priority of the evangelistic mandate is ultimately the best route for accomplishing social ministries. Wagner's thesis, then, is that the reversal of priorities, such as the cultural mandate over the evangelistic mandate will hurt the cause of evangelism and ultimately of many needed social ministries, as well.

> Although we have insufficient research on this as yet, I am reasonably sure that the evangelical churches which give first priority to the evangelistic mandate are in the long run actually doing more for the poor, the dispossessed, the exploited, and the marginal citizens of America's cities than the more liberal ones. Study a major metropolitan area and see where the physically and mentally handicapped are attending churches in considerable numbers. Locate the churches that have active and growing programs for the deaf. Find the churches of the very poor and see if their theology is of the gospel-preaching, soul-saving variety or if it is oriented to the cultural mandate and concerned with saving the whales and boycotting grapes and outlawing nuclear energy. Most likely such a church will be of an evangelical nature.[43]

[41]See Wagner, *Church Growth and the Whole Gospel,* 117-126.
[42]Ibid., 117.
[43]Ibid., 125.

Suggested Reading for Chapter 15

Erickson, Millard J. *Christian Theology*. Grand Rapids, MI: Baker, 1983, 1984, 1985.

Green, Michael. *Evangelism in the Early Church*. Grand Rapids, MI: Eerdmans, 1970.

Stott, John R. W. *Christian Mission in the Modern World*. Downers Grove, IL: InterVarsity, 1975

Verkuyl, J. *Contemporary Missiology: An Introduction*. Grand Rapids, MI: Eerdmans, 1978.

Wagner, C. Peter. *Church Growth and the Whole Gospel: A Biblical Mandate*. San Francisco: Harper & Row, 1981.

Wagner, C. Peter. *Strategies for Church Growth*. Ventura, CA: Regal, 1987.

16

Eschatology and Church Growth

The Greek word *eschaton* means "last things," so *eschatology* is the study of last things. Theologians have no consensus about the place of eschatology in the total scope of theology. Some regard it as part of another doctrine, such as soteriology or ecclesiology. Other theologians see it as equal to other doctrines; and yet some view eschatology as *the* major doctrine of theology.[1] Certainly eschatology is an important doctrine, but it should not be the topic of all-consuming interest to the Christian. Rather than being a source of divisiveness, eschatology should bring comfort, and inspire purity and hope (1 Thess. 4).

Individual Eschatology

Individual eschatology refers to the future and fate of each individual. This perspective is contrasted with eschatology that studies the future of all creation, sometimes called cosmic eschatology. Typically when we think of the future of every person, we think of the inevitability of death: "Just as man is destined to die once, and after that to face judgment" (Heb. 9:27). For the Christian, individual eschatology means more than death, it means victory over death through Jesus Christ (1 Cor. 15:56-57). Jesus, however, emphasized that physical death does not result in eternal death for the Christian: "Do not be afraid of those who kill the body but cannot kill the soul. Rather, be afraid of the One who can destroy both soul and body in hell" (Matt. 10:28).

[1]For an excellent discussion of the differing views of the importance of eschatology, see Millard J. Erickson, *Christian Theology* (Grand Rapids, MI: Baker, 1983, 1984, 1985), 1149-1153.

Though some question exists about the possibility of intermediate states for believers and unbelievers, the Bible is clear that, for a Christian, to be absent from the body means to be present with the Lord (2 Cor. 5:8). Erickson concluded that the places to which believers and unbelievers go at death is the *same* as their eternal home, but the *intensity* of their immediate state is less than that of their final state. For the unbeliever, then, gehenna is the final and eternal place of punishment (Mark 9:43, 48) after hades gives up the dead to this lake of fire (Rev. 20:13-15). Believers are immediatedly taken to the presence of the Lord to His place of perfect blessedness, while they wait for the final resurrection. Erickson put it this way:

> We conclude that upon death believers go immediately to a place and condition of blessedness, and unbelievers to an experience of misery, torment, and punishment. Although the evidence is not clear, it is likely that these are the very places to which believers and unbelievers will go after the great judgment, since the presence of the Lord (Luke 23:43; 2 Cor. 5:8; Phil. 1:23) would seem nothing other than heaven. Yet while the place of intermediate and final states may be the same, the experiences of paradise and Hades are doubtlessly not as intense as what will ultimately be, since the person is in a somewhat incomplete condition.[2]

Cosmic Eschatology: Points of Agreement

Excessive debate about details surrounding the second coming of Christ often takes our focus away from the key important truths upon which most orthodox theologians agree. In fact the reality of Christ's return is the basis for the believer's hope. The consummation of God's plan for humanity is intricately tied to the second coming of Christ.

Scripture leaves no doubt about the certainty of Christ's return. Three different examples of this promise in the Bible testify to the reality of this event. First, Jesus Himself said He would return: "At that time the sign of the Son of Man will appear in the sky, and all the nations of the earth will mourn. They will see the Son of Man coming on the clouds of

[2]Ibid., 1183-1184.

the sky, with power and great glory" (Matt. 24:30). Second, after Jesus' ascension two angels (literally two men in white) reminded the disciples of Christ's return: "'Men of Galilee,' they said, 'why do you stand here looking into the sky? This same Jesus, who has been taken from you into heaven, will come back in the same way you have seen him go into heaven'" (Acts 1:11). Third, the apostle Paul gave these words of assurance to the Thessalonians: "According to the Lord's own word, we tell you that we who are still alive, who are left till the coming of the Lord, will certainly not precede those who have fallen asleep. For the Lord himself will come down from heaven, with a loud command, with the voice of the archangel and with the trumpet call of God, and the dead in Christ will rise first" (1 Thess. 4:15-16).

Though the event of Christ's return is certain, the precise timing of His coming is not. Jesus emphasized the need for watchfulness rather than revealing the moment of His return: "No one knows about that day or hour, not even the angels in heaven, nor the Son, but only the Father. Be on guard! Be alert! You do not know when that time will come" (Mark 13:32-33).

A further area of agreement in cosmic eschatology is the event usually called the final judgment. Matthew 25:31-46 provides a vivid description of this future event. It shows Jesus Christ (the Son of man) as the judge over all humans (Matt. 25:32). Those receiving judgment will be divided into two groups, and they will go to their respective destinies for eternity: "Then they will go away to eternal punishment, but the righteous to eternal life" (Matt. 25:46).

Cosmic Eschatology: Points of Disagreement

An inordinate amount of energy has been used defining the details of Christ's second coming and related events. Discussion centers on timing and on the millenium or one-thousand-year reign of Christ (Rev. 20:1-6).

Postmillennialism is an optimistic view that the world will get better. As the gospel is preached the world will be converted and evil will be virtually eradicated. After the gospel has made its greatest impact, Christ will return.

Postmillennialists generally do not call for a specific one-thousand-year period but for some extended period. Christ will reign during that time though He will not be physically present. Few advocate this idea today.

Premillennialism holds to an earthly reign of Christ for one thousand years; thus, Christ will return to inaugurate the millennium. This period will be a dramatic contrast to the seven-year tribulation which precedes it. Whereas the tribulation will be a time of devastation, suffering, and chaos, the millennium will be a glorious period of tranquility and righteousness.

Amillennialism views the one-thousand-year period of Revelation 20 as purely symbolic. There will be no literal thousand-year reign of Christ. Like much of the Book of Revelation, amillennialists contend, the millenium of Revelation 20 is symbolic, and the symbolism represents heaven, where there is perfect joy and glory.

Significant agreement exists among evangelicals that premillennialism is the more accurate of the views; but there is still widespread disagreement about the timing of the removal of the church from the world, commonly known as the "rapture." Two views are commonly espoused, as well as other mediating viewpoints.[3]

In theory all premillennialists believe that there will be a period (most believe a literal seven years) of great disturbances before Christ's return.

> The question is whether there will be a separate coming to remove the church from the world prior to the great tribulation or whether the church will go through the tribulation and be united with the Lord only afterward. The view that Christ will take the church to himself prior to the tribulation is called pretribulationism; the view that he will take the church after the tribulation is called posttribulationism. There are also certain mediating positions.[4]

Pretribulationism teaches that the church will not be present during the difficult time of tribulation.

[3]See Erickson's discussion which favors premillennialism, 1215-1217.
[4]Ibid., 1217.

Pretribulationism cites, "For God did not appoint us to suffer wrath but to receive salvation through our Lord Jesus Christ"(1 Thess. 5:9). The church, or believers, will have been taken, or raptured, into the presence of the Lord: "After that, we who are still alive and are left will be caught up together with them in the clouds to meet the Lord in the air. And so we will be with the Lord forever" (1 Thess. 4:17).

The pretribulation view, then, calls for two returns of Christ. At the first return the dead in Christ will be resurrected and believers then living on earth will be raptured. This coming will precede the tribulation. At the second return of Christ those believers who died during the tribulation will be resurrected and Christ will establish His reign for the millennium.

The striking feature of pretribulationism is its emphasis on imminency. Since no prophetic event has to be fulfilled before the rapture, Christ can return at any moment. Many evangelistic sermons proclaim this view, and indeed the Bible itself calls for watchfulness among the believers (Matt. 25:13).

In posttribulationalism the church will be present during the tribulation. This view holds that the wrath (Gk. *orgae*) of God is the punishment and judgment reserved for the wicked. Believers, therefore, will not experience wrath but will experience tribulation. Posttribulationism simplifies end-time events by teaching only *one* return of Christ (at the end of the tribulation, preceding the millennium); and there is a need for only one resurrection of believers. The posttribulationist has difficulty explaining the rapture event described in 1 Thessalonians 4:17. George Ladd suggests that the rapture is a "welcome party" of believers who will greet Christ and then welcome Him back for the millennial reign.[5]

Mediating positions between pretribulationism and posttribulationism abound. Perhaps the most common position of these holds to a rapture at the midpoint of the tribulation. According to this view, the church will not undergo the most severe time of the tribulation in the last three-and-one-half years. A related view is the pre-wrath

---

[5]George E. Ladd, *The Blessed Hope* (Grand Rapids, MI: Eerdmans, 1956), 58-59.

rapture view, which allows for imminence in the sense that the church will be raptured at any time between the middle and the end of the tribulation.[6] Another view holds to a series of raptures, with groups of believers removed from the earth at different times.

Church Growth Eschatology

The Church Growth Movement has not entered the debate over the details of eschatology. With evangelicalism holding various positions on the end times, it is fortunate that the movement has not taken a position that could shift its focus from disciple-making, possibly creating divisiveness. That is not to say that the movement has no eschatology. The Lausanne Covenant reflects and highlights points of agreement

> We believe that Jesus Christ will return personally and visibly in power and glory, to consummate his salvation and his judgment. This promise of his coming is a further spur to our evangelism, for we remember his words that the gospel must first be preached to all nations. We believe that the interim period between Christ's ascension and return is to be filled with the mission of the people of God, who have no liberty to stop before the End . . . .Our Christian confidence is that God will perfect his kingdom, and we look forward with eager anticipation to that day, and to the new heaven and earth in which righteousness will dwell and God will reign forever. Meanwhile, we rededicate ourselves to the service of Christ and of men in joyful submission to his authority over the whole of our lives (Mark 14:62; Heb. 9:28; Mark 13:10; Acts 1:8-11; Matt. 28:20; Mark 13:21-23; John 2:18; 4:1-3; Luke 12:32; Rev. 21:1-5; 2 Pet. 3:13; Matt. 28:18).[7]

What, then, are the implications for eschatology on church growth? The following implications are the consequences of both personal and cosmic eschatology.

1. The Reality of Heaven and Hell. At death or when Christ returns, every human will be assigned to a place of

---

[6]For a book-length discussion on this view, see Marvin Rosenthal, *The Pre-Wrath Rapture of the Church* (Nashville: Thomas Nelson, 1990).

[7]Lausanne Covenant, article 15.

eternal destiny. Each person's destiny will be determined by his or her relationship to Christ during earthly life (Matt. 25:46). The most important task in which a believer can be involved is sharing the good news of Jesus Christ so that persons may have the opportunity to choose Christ and an eternal destiny of heaven.

2. The Urgency of the Evangelistic Task. Our lives on earth are brief, whether ended by death or the return of Christ. We must prioritize our time, money, and effort to evangelize before time as we know it ends. No task is more urgent than evangelism.

3. The Imperative to Make Disciples. Church growth typically measures discipleship by responsible church membership. Though this quantitative approach may have some weaknesses, it focuses our mission on making disciples (Matt. 28:19). The single greatest strength of the Church Growth Movement is that it insists that we move Christians beyond conversion to the point where believers become disciple-makers. Only by involving the whole body of Christ in this urgent task can we hope to reach a lost world.

4. Unleashing the Laity. The "professional clergy," which is really a misnomer, cannot be expected alone to proclaim and urge the world of the need to receive Christ. All the people of God must be equipped to do the work of ministry (Eph. 4:11-13).

5. The Need for Focused Leadership. Although the Church Growth Movement may not have consensus on the details of eschatology, it knows beyond doubt that Christ will return. Because time is brief, churches must focus on the priority of evangelism and disciple-making. Churches must have able and strong leaders who keep that focus before them at all costs.

Suggested Reading for Chapter 16

Acher, Gleason L., Jr., Paul D. Feinberg, Douglas J. Moo, and Richard R. Reiter. *The Rapture: Pre-, Mid-, or Post-Tribulational?* Grand Rapids, MI: Zondervan, 1984.

Clouse, Robert G., ed. *The Meaning of the Millennium: Four Views.* Downers Grove, IL: InterVarsity, 1977.

Cruz, Virgil. "Gehenna." In Walter A. Elwell, ed. *Evangelical Dictionary of Theology.* Grand Rapids, MI: Baker, 1984. 439-440.

Grider, J. Kenneth. "Heaven." In Walter A. Elwell, ed. *Evangelical Dictionary of Theology.* Grand Rapids, MI: Baker, 1984. 499-500.

Lightner, Robert "Hell." In Walter A. Elwell, ed. *Evangelical Dictionary of Theology.* Grand Rapids, MI: Baker, 1984. 506.

Motyer, J. A. "Hades." In Walter A. Elwell, ed. *Evangelical Dictionary of Theology.* Grand Rapids, MI: Baker, 1984. 492.

Rosenthal, Marvin. *The Pre-Wrath Rapture of the Church.* Nashville: Thomas Nelson, 1990.

Van Gemeren, William A. "Sheol." In Walter A. Elwell, ed. *Evangelical Dictionary of Theology.* Grand Rapids, MI: Baker, 1984. 1011-1012.

Part III

Principles
of
Church Growth

17

Principles of Church Growth

Sometime ago, I attempted to consolidate the church growth principles I had learned over several years. I stopped when the list approached one hundred. Although some of the principles were overlapping or related, the project made me realize just how expansive and detailed the Church Growth Movement had become.

In this section we will examine some of the major church growth principles that have emerged in the past four decades. In an attempt to include as many principles as possible, each of the following chapters will include church growth precepts grouped into major themes. Even so, some principles may be overlooked. With the Church Growth Movement ever seeking new ways to make disciples for Christ, the number of principles will grow as others fade away.

Church Growth Principles
Versus Biblical Principles

Most church growth principles in the following chapters come from the Bible. For example, we will examine the role of prayer in church growth. Prayer is the very heart of early church growth in the Book of Acts. In this case the church growth principle is also a biblical principle.

Some of the principles, however, do not come from the Bible, yet they are not *unbiblical*. Church growth identifies factors that contribute to the expansion of churches. If these factors are not contrary to Scripture, then they are considered valid for church growth work. An example of such a principle is the explosion of contemporary worship experiences in churches across the nation. The Bible does not prescribe a type of worship, a style of music, or a method of welcoming guests. The only requisite for worship is that it bring glory to God by ascribing worth to His name. If many Christians are growing spiritually and lost people are drawn closer to Christ through contemporary worship, then it is a principle worth discerning. Wagner says, "As a starting point, church growth often looks to the 'is' previous to the 'ought'. . . . What Christians experience about God's work in the world and in their lives is not always preceded by careful theological rationalizations. Many times the sequence is just the opposite: theology is shaped by Christian experience."[1]

Evaluating Church Growth Principles

At the conclusion of each chapter, an evaluation of the church growth principle will be given. The principle will be evaluated in light of either its theological integrity, or its correlation to growth in church, or both.

The previous section dealing with the theology of church growth will provide the foundation upon which some of the principles will be evaluated. The key question is not only whether the principle is found in the Bible, but if the principle is contrary to Scripture.

It may seem unusual that some principles will be evaluated in light of their correlation to church growth. After all, did not the principle come forth as a result of its contribution to the growth of churches? At this point I am deeply indebted to C. Kirk Hadaway for his analysis of church growth principles in *Church Growth Principles: Separating Fact from Fiction.*[2]

Hadaway's thesis is that the observation of rapidly-growing churches can not alone give us true church growth principles: "Unfortunately, most of these principles, keys, vital signs, and steps to church growth are simply hunches.

---

[1]C. Peter Wagner, "The Church Growth Movement after Thirty Years," in *Church Growth: State of the Art,* ed. C. Peter Wagner with Win Arn and Elmer Towns (Wheaton, IL: Tyndale, 1986), 33.

[2]C. Kirk Hadaway, *Church Growth Principles: Separating Fact from Fiction* (Nashville: Broadman, 1991).

They are often based on careful observation and are usually plausible, but they have not been tested or verified."[3] Hadaway took the case study approach and supplemented it with intensive research procedures. "The problem with studying an unusual group, like the fastest-growing churches in America, is that the researcher has no way of knowing whether or not the characteristics they share are any different from the characteristics of churches which are not growing." Hadaway then emphasizes: "Further, such research provides no way of knowing which church growth-producing factor is more important than any other."[4]

Many church growth principles, notes Hadaway, are derived from the extreme cases of the largest and fastest-growing churches. Can these principles make a difference in the average American church with an attendance of less than one hundred persons? "Most churches have the opportunity for growth, but few have the potential to become another Crystal Cathedral. It may well be that the strategies used by the fastest-growing churches in America are not the most feasible strategies for achieving renewed growth in most small congregations."[5] The next chapters will use the extensive research of Hadaway and others in evaluating church growth principles both theologically and practically.

Church Growth Principles and Spiritual Growth Principles: A Conflict?

If church growth principles become the emphasis, will churches neglect other areas of importance? In past centuries, churches that stressed evangelism and growth were often at the forefront in social ministries and Christian nurture. The historical record for those who hold to the priority of evangelism is very positive. In the chapter on ecclesiology and church growth, it was noted that the evangelistic churches of the nineteenth century were among the leaders in great social reform. Can the same be said for

[3]Ibid., 9.
[4]Ibid., 10.
[5]Ibid.

church growth churches today? Have aggressive,
evangelistic churches given up some other key aspect of the
task of the church in order to pursue a growth strategy?

Perhaps the most rewarding aspect of Hadaway's research
is his conclusion that today's fast-growing churches tend to
be leaders in other ministries as well. "Recent research into
the correlates of 'growth in mature faith' and 'effective
Christian education' has shown that adults in growing
churches tend to indicate more growth in faith on the
average than do adults in churches which are not growing."
Hadaway further discovered that virtually all phases of the
growing churches' ministries were enhanced. "Growing
churches also were found to exhibit greater overall levels of
strength and effectiveness in other areas of church life, such
as worship, congregational warmth, quality of the Christian
education program, spiritual development, congregational
loyalty, and social-service orientation."[6]

The good news for church growth enthusiasts is that our
churches do not suffer when we emphasize positive
numerical growth. To the contrary, a growing church creates
an atmosphere conducive to enhancing all other areas and
ministries of the church. With that in mind, it becomes
imperative for us to discover those church growth principles
that really make a difference. Applying many of these
principles will result in a larger church that has reached
more people for God and whose members have discovered a
deeper commitment to our Lord.

Suggested Reading for Chapter 17

Hadaway, C. Kirk. *Church Growth Principles: Separating
Fact from Fiction.* Nashville: Broadman, 1991.

Schaller, Lyle E. *Growing Plans.* Nashville: Abingdon, 1983.

Wagner, C. Peter. *Church Growth and the Whole Gospel: A
Biblical Mandate.* San Francisco: Harper & Row, 1981.

Wagner, C. Peter, ed., with Win Arn and Elmer Towns.
Church Growth: State of the Art. Wheaton, IL: Tyndale,
1986.

[6]Ibid., 11-12.

18

Prayer: The Power
Behind the Principles

Upon approaching the conclusion of writing my doctoral dissertation several years ago, I was left with the task of evaluating the theology of the Church Growth Movement. At that time the one glaring deficiency that I had mentioned was the failure of the movement to develop an appreciation for the relationship between prayer and church growth. Prayer was the very source of power for the explosive growth of the early church. Before Pentecost, the small band of believers "joined together constantly in prayers" (Acts 1:14). A key factor in the continued waves of growth in the early church was the devotion of the believers to prayer (Acts 2:42).

On many occasions in the early church, the threat of opposition endangered the growth of Christianity. When the Sanhedrin threatened the followers with punitive action if they continued to speak about the "name" (Acts 4:18), the church met for unified prayer and attained new levels of evangelistic boldness (Acts 4:31). Again, when Herod attempted to destroy the evangelistic impetus through persecution, the church united in prayer and growth continued (Acts 12:5): "Here then were two communities, the world and the church, arrayed against one another, each wielding an appropriate weapon. On the one side was the authority of Herod, the power of the sword and the security of the prison. On the other side, the church turned to prayer, which is the only power which the powerless possess."[1]

The prayers of the "powerless" defeated all the weapons of the world. Peter was rescued from prison by an angel, and

---

[1] John R. W. Stott, *The Spirit, the Church, and the World* (Downers Grove, IL: InterVarsity, 1990), 208-209. Stott's commentary on Acts is an excellent work, especially for church growth theorists desiring to see growth principles of the early church.

the gospel continued to spread (Acts 11:11). Herod was struck down by the Lord and died a gruesome death (Acts 11:23). The oppressing action against the church continued only briefly. The gospel, because of the power of prayer, spread unhindered.[2]

Since the Book of Acts is often used as an apologia for church growth principles, I wondered why the movement had said so little about the impact of prayer on church growth. The literature that emanated from the early years of the Church Growth Movement was very method oriented. The reader was sometimes left with the impression that any church could grow if it only applied in correct proportion the right methods. Critics asked if God was involved in the movement at all.

Of course, no church growth leader truly discounted the power of prayer and dependence upon God in the growth of the church, but literature did not reflect such an emphasis. As the movement began to mature, the literature began more and more to reflect this most vital principle of church growth.

A Shift in the 1980s

C. Peter Wagner, having experienced a paradigm shift in the area of signs and wonders, began researching the spiritual dimensions of churches. He spent several years studying the influence of supernatural signs and wonders on the growth of churches. He stated his findings in *How to Have a Healing Ministry without Making Your Church Sick* in 1988.[3] We will examine implications of the signs-and-wonders movement in chapter 30. Wagner's research led him to a deeper understanding of the role of prayer in church growth. By 1992, Wagner had published the first of three books dealing with prayer in the growth of the church. The

---

[2]See my article for a concise summary of prayer and church growth in the Book of Acts: Thom S. Rainer, "Church Growth and Evangelism in Acts," *Criswell Theological Review*, 5 (1990) 57-68.

[3]C. Peter Wagner, *How to Have a Healing Ministry without Making Your Church Sick* (Ventura, CA: Regal, 1988).

third book specifically addresses the relationship of prayer to the growth of the local church.[4] Other literature on church growth and prayer followed Wagner's lead.

George Barna wrote one of the better summaries on the topic in his book *User Friendly Churches*.[5] In this study of some rapidly growing churches in America, he found that prayer was the foundational ministry of the church. The church emphasized prayer in at least four major areas.

First, church members were exposed to biblical teachings about prayer in the Christian life. The pulpit and the various programs and ministries of the church encouraged and taught prayer. There was little doubt in the minds of the average church member that prayer was a priority.

Second, the church leaders, beginning with the pastor, modeled dynamic prayer lives. Large segments of time were devoted to prayer despite busy schedules. Some pastors spent more time praying about their sermons than preparing their messages.

Third, the rapidly growing churches learned that praises for answered prayers were an integral part of prayer itself. The people learned that prayer really is effective as they heard about the many answered prayers.

Fourth, growing churches engendered accountability for prayer. The prayer life of members, the prayer ministries of the church, and the prayer life of church leaders were regularly held before the church.

Church growth is discovering more than new methods: it is discovering the power behind the principles and methods. In the next chapter we will examine the key growth principle of leadership and vision. Before ever discussing the topic, however, we need to realize that vision comes from God and must result from a leader's prayer life.

---

[4]The triology is known as "The Prayer Warrior Series." The first two books are *Warfare Prayer* (1992) and *Prayer Shield* (1992). As of this writing, I do not have the name of the third book dealing with prayer and church growth in the local church, which will probably be published in 1993. All books are published by Regal (Ventura, CA).

[5]George Barna, *User Friendly Churches* (Ventura, CA: Regal, 1991). See chapter 10, "You Do Not Have Because You Do Not Ask."

Prayer and Vision

If visionary leadership is one of the key components to church growth, we then must determine how a leader develops a vision. Though it is the topic of the next chapter, vision is so tied to prayer that it deserves mention here.

Prayer is indispensable to understanding God's vision for churches. Paul wrote that we should seek wisdom and vision from God, not the world: "Do not deceive yourselves. If any one of you thinks he is wise by the standards of this age, he should become a 'fool' so that he may become wise. For the wisdom of this world is foolishness in God's sight" (1 Cor. 3:18-19). Not only must we look beyond the world's ideas for vision, we must look beyond the visions of other churches. Though we can certainly learn from other growing churches, the vision God gives to one church is not the same as He gives to another church. The vision of leadership for a church must come directly and specifically from God.

As we pray to God for a vision for our churches, He will miraculously open our eyes to possibilities. After several weeks of supplication for God to give me a vision for the church I pastor, Green Valley Baptist Church in Birmingham, an exciting development transpired. I was in a car with our four associate pastors, Charles Dorris, Marion Eubank, Chuck Carter, and Tim Miller. We drove through a newly populated area of the county that had no significant church work in sight. We discussed the possibility of starting a new church in the area, but were concerned that it was only about four miles away, so close that it would be difficult for a new church to establish a separate identity from the mother church.

Then I realized that we did not have to establish a church with a totally separate identity. We could start a new campus while sharing our gym, large fellowship hall, and other facilities. We could use some of the same staff and ministries and realize economies of scale. We could work together to provide resources of people, money, and time to start more new churches. Soon the vision became clear: a group of churches working together under the same umbrella of ministry dedicated to the task of starting new churches.

I later realized that the vision God gave me was similar, but not identical, to that of some other churches around the world. This type of church planting is called the *satellite* method, and I am convinced that the vision would never have been given without prayer. I am also convinced that the vision would never have become a reality had not prayer been the foundation of the spiritual warfare that would follow.

Prayer and Spiritual Warfare

Satan will oppose any church growth principle that God blesses. The conclusive piece of clothing in fitting ourselves with "the full armor of God" (Eph. 6:11-18) is to "pray in the Spirit on all occasions with all kinds of prayers and requests" (Eph. 6:18). Any church leader who has seen God bless the growth of his or her church has also seen the opposition of "the rulers . . . the authorities . . . the powers . . . and . . . the spiritual forces of evil in the heavenly realms" (Eph. 6:12).

Prayer must be the means by which we see God's vision for our churches, and it must also be one of the principal weapons in the warfare against those powers that would impede the growth of the church. Wagner's empirical research affirmed this: "The more deeply I dig beneath the surface of church growth principles, the more thoroughly convinced I become that the real battle is a spiritual battle and that our principal weapon is prayer."[6]

At some point in any church growth leader's ministry, Satan will unleash his forces to thwart the growth of God's church. The battle may come from unexpected sources, for example church members whose comfort zone or power niche has been disrupted by the church's growth. The battle may come from outside the church, such as governmental agencies. Lyle Schaller has said that one of the great battles American churches will face in the twenty-first century is land acquisition. Many local and state governmental agencies are becoming increasingly hostile to Christian churches in zoning and acquisition requests.

[6]C. Peter Wagner, *Church Planting for a Greater Harvest* (Ventura, CA: Regal, 1990), 46.

Regardless of the area, opposition *will* come to the church growth leader. He or she can battle the opposition effectively only with spiritual warfare saturated with the power of prayer. Remember the words of James: "Submit yourselves, then, to God. Resist the devil, and he will flee from you. Come near to God and he will come near to you. Wash your hands, you sinners, and purify your hearts, you double-minded" (Jas. 4:7-8).

Implementation of a Church Prayer Ministry

I am often asked: "What is the first step you would take toward growing a church?" My answer is consistent: Start a prayer ministry.

A prayer ministry will be effective only when the pastor and other church leaders themselves are prayer warriors. The first step toward a dynamic prayer ministry is evaluating our own prayer life. Recent studies have shown that the average American pastor spends from fifteen to twenty-two minutes daily in prayer. One of four pastors spend less than ten minutes daily in prayer! Church leaders must set the pace by spending significant qualitative and quantitative time with God.

The second step in an effective prayer ministry is teaching the people about the biblical priority of prayer. Each church leader must decide the most effective means by which prayer can be taught. The pastor, of course, has the effective vehicle for teaching via the pulpit ministry. With the small groups exploding across the land, this ministry is fast becoming a resource for discovering the power of prayer.

At some point the church leader will want to establish a churchwide prayer ministry, involving as many people as possible. This ministry must not be just another church program. The prayer ministry must become the very lifesource of the church. Many good resources are available for understanding the principles and methods of establishing a prayer ministry. Leaders may consult denominational agencies or other churches with dynamic prayer ministries. Remember, however, that we must be sensitive to God for a comprehensive ministry that will best fit our specific situation. I will use as an example the ministry components of my own church, Green Valley Baptist Church. This ministry is led in a wonderful fashion by Aulene Maxwell in our church. We have found in her what I believe are the essential ingredients of a person to lead a prayer ministry: sweet, loving, an optimistic spirit, good organizational skills, and, of course, a burden for prayer. Aulene has organized our church into several facets of prayer ministry.

1. Intercessory prayer room. This room is totally devoted to prayer. Different church members give one hour weekly to praying over the literally hundreds of prayer requests listed in the room. This room is also used during worship services as intercessors pray for the services.

2. Prayer cards and prayergrams. Each person in our worship services including members and guests completes a registration card, which is put in the offering plate. On the back of the card is a place for prayer requests. Hundreds of requests come in this way! We also send prayergrams affirming our prayer support to those in need. (See insert.)

3. Prayer chains. Many telephone chains for prayer have developed within the church.

Sample Prayergram
(Green Valley Baptist Church, Birmingham, Alabama)

PRAYERGRAM

"...Pray one for another ..."
James 5:16

Intercessory Prayer Ministry
1815 Patton Chapel Road
Birmingham, AL 35226

(205) 822-2173

" ... Pray without ceasing ..."
I Thessalonians 5:17

A ministry of
Green Valley Baptist Church
Dr. Thom Rainer, Pastor

"And all things, whatsoever ye shall ask in prayer, believing, ye shall receive."
Matthew 21:22

" ... My house is the house prayer ..."
Luke 19:46

God Answers Prayer

Sample Registration Card

(Front and back, with prayer request space on back)

Welcome to
Green Valley Baptist Church   Date _____

Dr./Rev./Ms.
Mr./Mrs./Miss _____   Phone (___) _____
Address _____   Apt. ____   Wk. Phone (___) _____
City_____   State____   Zip _____

Is This Your . . .
☐ First Time? I came as a guest of _____
☐ Second Time?   ☐ Third Time?   ☐ Attender   ☐ Member

Present Church Membership _____

Your School Grade	**Or Age Group**	**Please Circle:**
K 1 2 3 4 5 6 7 8	18-29 30-35 36-40 41-45	Single
9 10 11 12 College	46-49 50-55 56-64 65-66+	Married

Names of your children living at home   Birthday

_____
_____
_____

(Please see other side)

- -

I'd like information on:
☐ How to become a Christian
☐ Next Membership Class
☐ Spiritual Growth
☐ Teacher Training
☐ Missions
☐ Adult Bible Study
☐ Music Activities
☐ Singles Activities
☐ College Activities
☐ Youth Activities
☐ Preschool Children Activities
Prayer Needs: _____
_____
_____

Would you like a Prayergram sent to the
person prayed for? ☐ Yes ☐ No. If Yes,
provide address.
_____
_____

I would like to:
☐ Commit my life to Christ
☐ Renew my commitment to Christ
☐ Be baptized
☐ Be enrolled in next membership class
☐ Help where needed
☐ Enroll in Sunday School
☐ Join the Church
☐ Reservations for Wed. Night Dinner
_____
_____
_____
_____
_____
_____
_____
_____
_____
_____
_____

(Please see other side)

4. Prayer groups. Many other prayer groups have developed within small groups in the church.

5. PIPPs—Pastor's Intercessory Prayer Partners. Fifty devoted people who have been called to pray for me and my ministry daily.

6. Prayer emphases. Many times we have given special emphasis to prayer, such as a twenty-four-hour period devoted to prayer and fasting.

Finally, the church should be called regularly to a time of corporate prayer. For many churches the long-standing Wednesday night prayer time has fallen victim to frantic schedules of today's family. Nevertheless, the church should find regular times to bring all the people together for corporate prayer.

Evaluation

A prayer ministry in the church needs little theological justification. If nothing else, the power of prayer in the explosive growth of the church in Acts should motivate church leaders to make prayer a priority.

Prayer should be primary in the church because God's Word mandates it. Even if we could find no positive correlation between prayer and church growth, the mandate of prayer would require our obedience. It is fascinating, however, to learn how God *is* working through prayer to lead churches to unprecedented levels of growth. We noted earlier George Barna's comments on the priority of prayer in growing churches. C. Kirk Hadaway studied "breakout" churches (former plateaued or declining churches now experiencing growth) and plateaued churches. He found that "*71 percent* of breakout churches reported an increased emphasis on prayer over the past several years as compared to only 40 percent of churches which continue on the plateau."[7]

Prayer *is* the power behind the principles. There simply is no more important principle in church growth than prayer.

---

[7]C. Kirk Hadaway, *Church Growth Principles: Separating Fact from Fiction* (Nashville: Broadman, 1991), 164, emphasis added.

The prayers of the early church unleashed the power of God to add thousands to the church. It happened then. It is happening in some churches today. And it can happen in your church.

Suggested Reading for Chapter 18

Barna, George. *User Friendly Churches*. Ventura, CA: Regal, 1991.

Barna, George. *Without a Vision, the People Perish*. Glendale, CA: Barna Research, 1991.

Hadaway, C. Kirk. *Church Growth Principles: Separating Fact from Fiction*. Nashville: Broadman, 1991.

Rainer, Thom S. "Church Growth and Evangelism in Acts." *Criswell Theological Review*, 5 (1990). 57-68.

Rainer, Thom S. *Evangelism in the Twenty-First Century*. Wheaton, IL: Shaw, 1989. See especially Ed Lyrene's chapter on "Evangelism and Prayer."

Stott, John R. W. *The Spirit, the Church, and the World*. Downers Grove, IL: InterVarsity, 1990.

Wagner, C. Peter. *Church Planting for a Greater Harvest*. Ventura, CA: Regal, 1990.

Wagner, C. Peter. *How To Have a Healing Ministry without Making Your Church Sick*. Ventura, CA: Regal, 1988.

Wagner, C. Peter. *Warfare Prayer*. Ventura, CA: Regal, 1992.

Wagner, C. Peter, ed., with Win Arn and Elmer Towns. *Church Growth: State of the Art*. Wheaton: Tyndale, 1986.

19

Leadership and Church Growth

Nearly twenty years ago, C. Peter Wagner boldly proclaimed a central church growth principle: "In America, the primary catalytic factor for growth in a local church is the pastor. In every growing, dynamic church I have studied, I have found a key person whom God is using to make it happen."[1] Wagner further stated that strong pastoral leadership is the first of many church growth signs of health: "Vital Sign Number One of a healthy church is a pastor who is a possibility thinker and whose dynamic leadership has been used to catalyze the entire church into action for growth."[2] Wagner later devoted an entire volume to the subject of pastoral leadership, *Leading Your Church to Growth.*[3]

There is little doubt that leadership in general and pastoral leadership in particular is a major factor in the church growth process. In this chapter we examine many leadership principles affecting the growth of the church. We should examine these principles not only in light of their church growth successes but also in view of biblical teachings about true leadership.

In some regard, implementing growth principles mentioned in this book or elsewhere will result from leadership focused on obedience to the Great Commission (Matt. 28:19). This single-minded devotion to reaching people must be nurtured in the heart of the leader and passed on to followers.

---

[1]C. Peter Wagner, *Your Church Can Grow,* rev. ed. (Ventura, CA: Regal, 1984), 60.
[2]Ibid., 63.
[3]C. Peter Wagner, *Leading Your Church to Growth* (Ventura, CA: Regal, 1984).

The Pastor as Leader

We most often think of the pastor as the key church growth leader. Indeed the responsibility for growth in a church ultimately falls on the senior pastor of a congregation. Though such non-leadership factors as demographics, the history of the church, and the age of the church will affect growth potential, pastoral leadership may prove decisive in moving a church from non-growth to growth. Hadaway notes how new leadership can dramatically change the face of a church: "The majority of breakout churches in the survey (59 percent) called a new pastor in the same year or in the year before they began to grow off the plateau."[4] Hadaway found that one of the key components of the pastoral leadership for breakout growth was vision: "They inherited churches with problems and were unable to force any issues because they had not earned the right to do so. Instead, they played the role of the catalyst—sharing their vision with the church, linking it to latent purposes which members still shared, creating a sense of excitement, and providing encouragement to those in the church who could see the vision and who were willing to work for it."[5]

As one surveys the wealth of church growth literature on pastoral leadership, several characteristics of growth pastors emerge. Perhaps the one now most frequently mentioned is the one which Hadaway just described—vision.

Vision.   When George Barna wrote *Without a Vision, the People Perish*,[6] he addressed the most critical issue of pastoral leadership today. Society and the church are changing today more rapidly than anytime in history. While theological truths must remain constant, the church must ask if it is being left behind by the technological and societal revolution. If the world does not understand the church, if the church is not relevant to the world, then the unchangeable message of the gospel is never communicated to the lost.

[4]C. Kirk Hadaway, *Church Growth Principles: Separating Fact from Fiction* (Nashville: Broadman, 1991), 91.

[5]Ibid.

[6]George Barna, *Without a Vision, the People Perish* (Glendale, CA: Barna, 1992).

A church growth leader, particularly a pastor, must follow God's plan for the church in order to lead the people in this time of greatest need. How does a pastor capture God's vision for the church? The pastor must know himself—his gifts, passions, talents, values, attitudes, experiences, and assumptions. God led the pastor to the church for a particular time for a particular reason. Like Esther in Persia the pastor is in the church "for such a time as this" (Esth. 4:14). Undoubtedly God will use the personality, the attributes, and the gifts of the pastor in shaping the vision. To know himself is often the pastor's first step in capturing God's vision.

The pastor must also know the church he serves. Many leaders believe that they know their people and, to some extent, the pastor-people relationship produces knowledge about each other. I was surprised, however, at how little I knew about the people of my church when we conducted two anonymous churchwide surveys in a period of about eighteen months. The surveys were extensive and were completed by over one-half of the resident adult membership. For me the results were an unusual blend of surprise, encouragement, pain, confusion, and direction. I discovered that we had at least three churches within a church, with two broad groups displaying common characteristics with their age peers. I discovered a group who thought the church was moving too slowly, another who perceived that change was too rapid, and yet another who felt we had achieved a good, steady pace and direction. These surveys prepared me for differing reactions each time our church faced a decision of some consequence. A survey is an indispensable tool for vision.

Pastors may further know their churches through spiritual gift inventories. These inventories are available from several different sources. Though they are not infallible tools, the inventories provide good indicators of the spiritual gift mix of Christians. We will examine this tool further in the next chapter.

Another piece of the vision puzzle is learning the community and ministry environment. Demographic information helps us to understand the statistical composition of our community, but our research should not end there. Each ministry area has a personality, although these personalities may not be monolothic. Some communities may be receptive to new ministries while others are not. Some leaders in my home state of Alabama have attempted to transplant the ministries of churches from the West Coast in total. The results are often disastrous for both pastor and church.

The most important element of vision is prayer. A pastor who has a consistent prayer life seeking God's wisdom will discover the exciting direction that God has planned for the church.

Initiating.   Some leadership books speak of good leaders as being "proactive" or "future active." A church growth leader must initiate action toward the God-given vision. The leader does not wait for something new to happen; he is making it happen! Being a church growth pastor is hard work. It takes time, commitment, vision, and an ability to stick with the vision for the long haul.

Sharing the ministry.   One of the hindrances to growth in many churches is a pastor's unwillingness to let go of ministry. I consulted a few years ago with a church whose average attendance had remained around 140 for fifteen years. I learned that this plateau coincided with the tenure of the present pastor. It did not take long to discover this pastor's ministerial routine. He alone visited the sick in the hospital; ministered to the homebound; counseled the troubled; and even called all members on their birthdays! In doing so, the pastor deprived the people of their God-given call to do the work of ministry (Eph. 4:12) and failed in his task to be the equipper for ministry (Eph. 4:11-12).

Pastors must overcome the insecurity that says: "Nobody can do the ministry but I!" This attitude reflects a condescending view of laity or a fear that the pastor will be perceived as failing to do his job. Some pastors even fear that they will lose recognition and admiration if others do the work of ministry.

"Ranchers."   Lyle Schaller first mentioned the pastor as a rancher over fifteen years ago.[7] Wagner commented: "It fits the bill perfectly. Notice that in a church led by a rancher the sheep are still shepherded, but the rancher does

---

[7]Lyle E. Schaller, *Survival Tactics in the Parish* (Nashville: Abingdon, 1977), 53.

not do it. The rancher sees that it is done by others."[8] How can a pastor find and equip others to shepherd the congregation? While there are several possible answers to this question, the interested reader may skip to chapter 29 and the discussion of small groups. I know of no better shepherding model in the world than that of small groups.

Good stewards.   Good leaders are also good stewards. Stewardship usually refers to responsibility to God with money and material gain. Good leaders must also develop good stewardship of their time, their prayer lives, their work and leisure habits, their Bible study, and their family.

Confident, decisive, and optimistic.   Because a visionary church growth pastor will have developed a vision from God, he can respond to situations with confidence and decisiveness. In fact decision-making will become increasingly easier as the vision or plan for the church unfolds. A visionary pastor is optimistic about the future because God has given him a clear picture of that future. There is a goal to be reached and a prize to be received (Phil. 4:14). Barna found that visionary pastors had "an entrepreneurial spirit that enabled them to envision possibilities, conceive ways of making those possibilities come to fruition, and marshal and direct the resources to make good things happen . . . . They tended to be proactive more than reactive."[9]

Common Mistakes of Church Growth Leaders

I have the wonderful opportunity of interacting with hundreds of church growth leaders, especially pastors and other church staff leaders. The Church Growth Movement has made an indelible impression on their lives. They are excited, visionary, and optimistic. Yet even the best leaders sometimes stumble, and a few fail. Although the common mistakes discussed here are not exhaustive, they are characteristics inherent in many church growth leaders' lives today.

Struggles in personal and spiritual life.   A church growth leader has difficulty slowing down. Often prayer time and time in God's Word seem like interruptions to a busy

[8]Wagner, *Leading Your Church to Growth*, 59.
[9]George Barna, *User Friendly Churches* (Ventura, CA: Regal, 1991), 146.

schedule. Pastors' families and other leaders' families are often neglected. The words of Paul to Timothy are conveniently forgotten: "If anyone does not know how to manage his own family, how can he take care of God's church?" (1 Tim. 3:5).

While there are many good resources for enhancing one's walk with Christ, the key for most church growth pastors is accountability. I have made myself fully accountable to a small group of men in our church. All of these men are older than I, and share with me in such key areas as my relationship to God, my wife, my children, and other church members. In a church with which I recently consulted, all of the ministers on staff have small accountability groups; but these groups developed after one of the former staff members was discovered to be commiting adultery with a church member. His tragic words to his pastor were : "If only I had been accountable . . ."

Moving too rapidly. It is extremely difficult to know when to move or to wait. If church growth leaders waited on everyone in the church to buy the vision, the vision would never become a reality. Nevertheless, pastors can get too far ahead of their people. Carolyn Weese said it well: "Visionaries can envision more ministry and programs than there are people to fill those ministries and programs. Visionaries tend to get so far out in front of their people that the people often mistake them for the enemy. Visionaries are willing to take risks. When they do take risks, they leave themselves vulnerable to be misunderstood, criticized, or undercut by members of their staff, leadership, or congregation."[10]

A church growth leader must constantly urge his people forward. He faces the danger of going to battle without any soldiers. Sometimes patience can be the greatest but most difficult virtue for a church growth pastor.

Failure to communicate. A visionary leader often sets out to accomplish the task without adequately communicating to the people in the church. Not desiring to get bogged down in details, a pastor may proceed to

[10]Carolyn Weese, *Eagles in Tall Steeples* (Nashville: Oliver Nelson, 1991), 23.

accomplish some facet of the vision while few people understand his purpose. He must repeatedly communicate the vision and how it will be accomplished.

Lack of follow through. Because the visionary pastor is typically not interested in details, many grandiose ideas never get much further than the dreams of the pastor. While the church growth leader does not have to be involved in all of the details himself, he must have equipped staff or lay leaders to make the dream a reality.

"Emulation fever." Case studies, visits to growing churches, seminars and conferences led by megachurch pastors, and books idealizing the ministries of other churches tempt many pastors to copy those models in their churches. Who has not heard of "the Saddleback model" or "the Willow Creek model" becoming the basis for ministry for a church? The leaders of the model churches would be the first to tell the pastors to learn from their churches, but to be careful in reproducing any facet of the model in their own local church context.

Difficulty letting go. A church growth pastor must be willing to relinquish control and hands-on involvement in every ministry of the church. He must equip and empower others to do the work of ministry, even if he perceives that no one can get the job done as well as he can. The more ministry is shared throughout the church, the greater the opportunities for growth.

Difficulty keeping the vision alive. Visionary leadership is harder work than leadership without vision. Visionary leadership requires constant and consistent communication and the persistence to measure everything in the church by the vision. Visionary leadership moves people out of their comfort zones and often, as a result, creates some opposition within the church. Most visionary leaders have felt the temptation to return to the unbiblical comfort of the status quo rather than keeping the vision alive.

Discouragement. Once a pastor understands God's vision for his church, that vision becomes a consuming passion that never leaves his thoughts. When critics attack the vision, the pastor feels that the attack is personal.

Discouragement is inevitable at times. Furthermore, the energy that must be expended just to keep the vision alive is tremendous. Burnout is more common than most pastors admit. Without a dynamic relationship with God through daily renewal in prayer and time in God's Word, the pastor will find his own energy quickly expended. The leader must remember that he can only do everything through Christ who gives him strength (Phil. 4:13). Kingdom building is spiritual warfare. The enemy will do everything he can to discourage and distract the pastor. The leader's response must be the daily putting on of the full armor of God (Eph. 6:10-18).

Evaluation

Most church growth literature ranks leadership as one of the most important growth factors in the local church. Indeed Wagner and other church growth leaders identify leadership as the primary catalytic factor. Hadaway's statistical evidence cited earlier in the chapter seems to indicate a direct correlation between strong pastoral leadership and church growth.

It is difficult to find a relationship between church growth and pastoral leadership in the New Testament. The difficulty lies in the absence of evidence rather than in any conflicting evidence. One could argue with biblical certainty, however, that God has used strong leadership empowered by Him to accomplish His purpose. Certainly the Old Testament examples of Moses, Joshua, David, and Nehemiah support the postulate that leadership has been an important factor in the accomplishment of God's plan.

Another important issue is pastoral tenure. Does a long-term pastorate engender church growth? Most church growth writers believe long tenure helps a church to grow. This is not to say, however, that long pastorates produce growth. Many plateaued and declining churches were represented by long-term pastorates as well.

Two studies indicate the most productive years of pastors. Lyle Schaller found that the greatest growth of churches occurred in the years five through eight of a pastor's tenure.[11] Hadaway's research of Southern Baptist pastors

[11]Lyle E. Schaller, *Growing Plans* (Nashville: Abingdon, 1975), 96.

concluded that the most productive years were three through six.[12] Unfortunately the average tenure of Southern Baptist pastors is less than three years.

At the very least we conclude that a visionary pastor is a major contributor to the growth of a church. That pastor must be able to maintain God's vision well beyond his first three years of tenure, often the most difficult years, in order to see the vision bear fruit.

Suggested Reading for Chapter 19

Barna, George. *User Friendly Churches*. Ventura, CA: Regal, 1991.

Barna, George. *Without a Vision, the People Perish*. Glendale, CA: Barna, 1991.

George, Carl F. and Robert E. Logan. *Leading and Managing Your Church*. Old Tappan, NJ: Revell, 1987.

Hadaway, C. Kirk. *Church Growth Principles: Separating Fact from Fiction*. Nashville: Broadman, 1991.

Hocking, David. *The Seven Laws of Christian Leadership*. Ventura, CA: Regal, 1991.

Schaller, Lyle E. *The Pastor and the People*. Rev. ed. Nashville: Abingdon, 1986.

Schaller, Lyle E. *Survival Tactics in the Parish*. Nashville: Abingdon, 1977.

Wagner, C. Peter. *Leading Your Church to Growth*. Ventura, CA: Regal, 1984.

Wagner, C. Peter. *Your Church Can Grow*. Rev. ed. Ventura, CA: Regal, 1984.

Weese, Carolyn. *Eagles in Tall Steeples*. Nashville: Oliver Nelson, 1991.

[12]Hadaway, 77.

20

Laity, Ministry, and Church Growth

A few years ago I purchased a book by Greg Ogden with a provocative title, *The New Reformation: Returning the Ministry to the People of God.*[1] That title described well what I believe to be one of the most exciting developments in the church today: a return to the biblical mandate for all Christians to do the work of ministry. The Church Growth Movement focused on this vital issue early in its history. C. Peter Wagner said nearly twenty years ago: "As far as church growth is concerned, lay liberation has opened up fantastic new possibilities. If laypeople become excited about what they can do for God and for their church, the sky is the limit."[2]

Why is the return of the laity to ministry called "the new Reformation"? Nearly five hundred years ago Martin Luther and others began a revolution to liberate the church from the hierarchial structure that had attempted to prohibit the average Christian from having direct access to God through Jesus Christ. Of course, no structure could really block that direct relationship, but most Christians then were not aware of their true freedom in Christ. The Reformation released believers from going to God through a human mediator. Jesus Christ is the one and only high priest through whom we come into God's presence.

Greg Ogden argues that the Reformation never fully delivered on its promise to release all the people of God to do the work of ministry. A clergy/laity dichotomy still exists in the mentality of many churchgoers. For them, the clergy are the doers of ministry—contrary to the clear biblical

[1]Greg Ogden, *The New Reformation: Returning the Ministry to the People of God* (Grand Rapids, MI: Zondervan, 1990).

[2]C. Peter Wagner, *Your Church Can Grow*, rev. ed. (Ventura, CA: Regal, 1984), 80.

teachings that God's people *laos* are to do the ministry and works of service (Eph. 4:12). For most Christians today, church is a place they attend and where the pastor works.

The contribution of the Church Growth Movement to the unleashing of the laity is its constant, pragmatic questioning of "how?". It is not enough to affirm the biblical principle of lay ministry; there must be means by which such equipping and ministry can take place. Ogden identifies six major paradigm shifts since 1960 which have helped the people of God to do the ministry of God.[3]

First, there is a renewed understanding of the role of the Holy Spirit. The third Person of the Trinity is more than a propositional truth; He is the living God who encounters the people of God. "The work of the Spirit includes mediating the direct presence of God to the life of the believer."[4]

Second, Christianity is now more than an institutional faith for many believers. To be a Christian means to have Christ in us, a moment-by-moment awareness that Christ resides in our lives, empowers us, directs us, and loves through us.

Third, the church is becoming people-focused rather than pastor-focused. The church is being understood as a living organism, in which all the people (pastors and laity alike) contribute to the body of Christ. The renewal of small groups is a visible sign of this new mindset. In this setting, Christians are no longer the audience; they are contributing participants in ministry.

Fourth, a new awareness that all God's people are ministers has caused increased emphasis on discovery and using spiritual gifts.

> As the reality of the church as an organism has been rediscovered, we are finding that in God's design all the people in the church are gifted for ministry. Ministry is not to be equated with what professional leaders do; ministry has been given to all God's people. So the pastor's role is not to guard ministry jealously for himself, but instead to turn the spotlight on this multigifted body. In the process,

3Ogden, 13-25.
4Ibid., 15.

God's people are discovering that in fact they are gifted to
act.[5]

Fifth, a new ecumenical movement has emerged, a
movement transcending denominational loyalties. This
movement focuses on reaching the lost and releasing
Christians to answer their God-given call to the ministry.
This evangelical, ecumenical spirit can most likely find its
initial impetus under the leadership of Billy Graham, who
provided the direction and resources for the International
Congress on World Evangelization at Lausanne, Switzerland
in 1974.

Sixth, the direction of worship has undergone such change
that the worship event is, in the minds of some, a new
Reformation itself. Worship is shifting from a setting of
performance with only the "actors" participating, to a setting
of participation, where all of God's people direct their hearts
to God. We will examine the worship paradigm shift in
chapter 23.

This new Reformation is not a foregone conclusion in
many churches. The idea of paying for ministry as opposed
to doing ministry is still the paradigm of many churchgoers.
In order for the new Reformation to become reality, new
roles for both the pastor and the people must be accepted.

The Pastor in the
New Reformation

In the previous chapter we looked at the role of a church
growth pastor. Now let us see briefly the implications of this
role in releasing the laity to answer their call to ministry.
Ogden is on target when he assumes that the key to
realizing the new Reformation is a

> transformation of the pastor's posture. A congregation
> tends to assimilate the personality, stance, and approach
> of its pastor and reflect that identity as a mirror image.
> There is a reactive dynamic or interplay between the
> pastor and congregation. For example, if the pastor's basic
> approach to God's people is as scholar-teacher, the people

[5]Ibid., 21.

will tend to become students-learners. If the pastor views the church and his role as a social activist, the church will become a center from which to trumpet causes of justice. If the pastor projects the image of a father-mother, the people will view themselves as dependent children. But if the church is to be a ministering community, the pastor must be an equipper who empowers God's people to fullness of service.[6]

A pastor must be willing to make three major changes in order to fulfill his role as an equipper. These changes are often painful; for most pastors and laity alike, they are fundamentally different from "the way we've always done it."

Proactive.   The pastor must first realize that he is the beginning of the necessary change. The church will not participate in the new Reformation without his leadership. All of the preaching, teaching, and writing opportunities available to the pastor must proclaim the new Reformation. Ultimately the pastor must make some major changes in the way he does his ministry so that the people can see that his commitment is more than just words.

Abandoning the dependency models.   Ogden calls the traditional model of pastoral ministry today "the dependency model." He sees that this model is fostered in the minds and actions of both the pastor and the congregation.[7]

The pastor feels pressure to be omnicompetent. He is the scholar who studies; the counselor who listens and advises; the shepherd who visits; the orator who speaks; the teacher who teaches; the businessman who administers; the fund-raiser who pleads; the encourager who comforts; and the evangelist who witnesses. He knows that different members of his congregation have different expectations of him. Somehow, while meeting the church members' multifaceted needs, he must care for his own family as well.

Some pastors fear the abandonment of this model of dependency. Afterall, they are "the professionals." Can mere lay people without their education and training do what the pastor does? The pastor is well aware that many in the

[6]Ibid., 85.
[7]Ibid., see especially 86-95.

congregation firmly believe that they pay the pastor to do the ministry.

Then there is the little-spoken issue of the pastor's ego. Many in our profession live for the daily "strokes" we receive. Can we possibly tolerate the scenario in which the lay people receive the accolades as they enter the front lines of ministry? Are we willing to be a behind-the-scenes equipper who receives little recognition?

Yet other pastors foster the dependency model out of guilt. If the pastor is not doing something that is activity-oriented, is he really doing something worthwhile? Can pastors turn ministry over to others and focus their attention on equipping (Eph. 4:12), prayer, and the Word (Acts 6:3-4)?

These realities make it hard for most pastors to abandon the dependency model. A leader who is willing to make the change to the biblical model must be prepared to withstand the waves of criticism and resistance that will often follow.

Embracing the equipper model. We will examine shortly an equipping model to unleash the laity for ministry. Accepting and implementing this new model is not accomplished in a few weeks. Patience, strength, and persistence are three requisites for the pastor as he attempts to lead the people to a new paradigm that will ultimately result in a church where most of God's people are in ministry, and where church growth becomes as natural as the growth of the early church (Acts 6:7).

The New Reformation Realized: The People of God in Ministry

The ultimate implementation of equipping and releasing requires long-term pastoral commitment, especially in churches firmly entrenched in tradition. Whereas a new church may adapt to the new Reformation in a matter of months, a one-hundred-year-old downtown church may need several years to make a paradigm shift.

Education. The beginning of the process is education. The pastor has various means by which he may communicate the message of equipping and unleashing the church. He must expose the people to the biblical model on a consistent and persistent basis. Unlearning the traditional model of dependency will take time and patience. The pastor must be cautious. Many of the people need time to assimilate an entirely new way of thinking.

Restructuring. Most churches are not structured for the laity to do ministry. Persons involved in the church often spend their time on committees or boards rather than in front-line ministry. Wagner comments that "as the church grows it gets more and more unwieldy . . . and tend[s] to multiply boards and committees ad infinitum." Instead of providing opportunities for ministry, this leaderless structure, says Wagner, "drags down the church."[8]

Most pastors can empathize with my story of Brent. Shortly after Brent was baptized in our church, he called me with a straightforward question: "What do I do next?" Brent knew that there was more to being a Christian, and he wanted to be a part of the action. My plight was that there were no openings for positions in our church. Even if there had been openings, I doubt that I would have suggested that Brent fill a slot. The structure had failed both of us.

I am now convinced that the small-group structure is the biblical and best way to mobilize the laity. As Jethro counseled Moses to structure the nation of Israel (Ex. 18:13-27) into groups, so pastors should structure the church. Real ministry takes place in small groups. Small groups encourage face-to-face ministry; this will not take place in traditional church structures. Such a re-organization will require time, patience, and toughness. Yet the short-term pain is well worth the long-term gain. We will look at the small group structure in more detail in chapter 26.

Spiritual gift discovery. When I was pastor of Azalea Baptist Church in St. Petersburg, Florida, my associate pastor Chuck Carter and I led the church in discovering their spiritual gifts. The process was threefold. First, I preached a series of sermons on the gifts. Next, we held an all-day seminar that concluded with each participant's taking a gifts inventory. The final step was an interview by

---

[8]C. Peter Wagner, *Leading Your Church to Growth* (Ventura, CA: Regal, 1984), 11.

the pastors with each of those who participated in the seminar.

I remember well the reaction of the first person I interviewed. Her most prominent gift was helps. On the inventory she was not even on the scale for the gift of teaching. When she saw the results, a great wave of relief came over her. "So that's why I hate to teach Sunday School!" she exclaimed. She eventually found a place of volunteer service in the church office and became a radiant worker for Christ.

In my Southern Baptist Convention we have a deacon family ministry plan where each active deacon is assigned shepherding responsibility for a certain number of families. Yet I have seen godly deacons become frustrated because they are not doing their job as prescribed by the program. Why? Many of the deacons do not have the gift mix that lends itself to a shepherding ministry. In other words, they are trying to do a ministry without the necessary spiritual resources.

When spiritual gifts discovery takes place in a church, liberation and joy results. Exciting, joyful ministry will eventually transpire because people are doing ministry according to their gifts.

Rethinking ministries. Traditionally ministries in churches were synonymous with programs. If we thought we needed a more evangelistic thrust, we instituted an evangelism program. If we perceived the need for greater discipleship, we started a discipleship program. A few leaders in the church therefore organized the programs for the year and waited for people to fill the slots. It is no surprise that these programs rarely survived more than a year of two in a local church.

In his classic book, *Unleashing the Church,* Frank Tillapaugh describes the plight of many good church members who wonder if the local church has any effectiveness at all. He described one couple who had lost their zeal for the church:

> As they reflected on their past church experiences there was little joy or satisfaction. Looking back over a period

stretching across three decades, it had been a desperate grind. They had served on endless committees that never seemed to accomplish much. They had watched pastors come and go. They had seen the churches level out in attendance, hold their own and then go into decline. For some time they had been discouraged and disillusioned about the potential of the local church.[9]

Tillapaugh recalls the faithfulness of this couple who wondered why their church work now seemed meaningless: "But the element of the dynamic aliveness that comes from involvement in meaningful ministry was, for the most part, lacking. So much of the church-related work seemed trivial. Hours had been poured into decisions concerning buildings and parking lots. They had spent so much time discussing church business, and yet had invested little in people."[10]

This couple expressed the sentiments of untold numbers of churchgoers who find themselves in similar circumstances. The only ministry they are allowed to do in the church is that which already exists in the church program.

Rethinking ministry means allowing the people to begin or engage in ministries according to their God-given gifts and burdens. If a churchgoer has a burden for ministry that does not fit in an existing church program, he or she should be free to begin that ministry. Such an approach carries risk, but it is compatible with the growth of the early church. While the apostle Paul provided doctrinal teaching, guidelines, and leaders, he ultimately left the churches he founded under the divine care of the Holy Spirit. Seeking God's direction, "with prayer and fasting, [he] committed them to the Lord in whom they had put their trust."[11]

One of the most dynamic ministries with which I have been associated is the Food Bank Ministry of the Green Valley Baptist Church. It is now one of the largest food ministries in metropolitan Birmingham, but it began as a

[9]Frank R. Tillapaugh, *Unleashing the Church* (Ventura, CA: Regal, 1982), 11.
[10]Ibid.
[11]See Thom S. Rainer, "Church Growth and Evangelism in the Book of Acts," *Criswell Theological Review*, 5 (Fall, 1990), 64-65, where I discuss the principle of indigenization of the early churches.

burden in the hearts of some of our laypersons. It is led by a layperson. Its staff includes about seventy lay volunteers. I praise God that these people are a part of the new Reformation and that our church structure took advantage of their God-given call to ministry.

Evaluation

One of the most exciting principles of church growth is unleashing laity to do the work of ministry. Implementing this principle means returning to New Testament basics where the dichotomy between clergy and laity does not exist. This requires affirming the priesthood of the believers for which the Reformers passionately fought.

Hadaway discovered a direct correlation between numerical growth of the church and significant ministry to the community. His comments are noteworthy:

> It is clear that breakout churches (and growing churches generally) tend to have a greater presence in their community. They are less inward looking and see the role of the church as helping people, whether they are members of their congregation or not. As a result, persons in the community are aware that the church exists and that it is available in time of need. The goals of providing ministry to the community were not designed to produce growth in these churches, but it would appear that growth can be an unintended consequence. The ministering church is seen as an open, accepting congregation, rather than a restricted social club. Further, those who have received help or support and those on the outside who have worked on joint ministry projects with the church may establish relationships with the pastor or members, come to know Christ (if they do not already), and eventually join the fellowship.[12]

---

[12]C. Kirk Hadaway, *Church Growth Principles: Separating Fact from Fiction* (Nashville: Broadman, 1991), 169.

Suggested Reading for Chapter 20

Barna, George. *User Friendly Churches*. Ventura, CA: Regal, 1991.

Hadaway, C. Kirk. *Church Growth Principles: Separating Fact from Fiction*. Nashville: Broadman, 1991.

Ogden, Greg. *The New Reformation*. Grand Rapids, MI: Zondervan, 1990.

Rainer, Thom S. "Church Growth and Evangelism in the Book of Acts." *Criswell Theological Review*, 5 (Fall, 1990), 57-68.

Slocum, Robert E. *Maximize Your Ministry*. Colorado Springs, CO: NavPress, 1990.

Tillapaugh, Frank R. *Unleashing the Church*. Ventura, CA: Regal, 1982.

Wagner, C. Peter. *Leading Your Church to Growth*. Ventura, CA: Regal, 1984.

Wagner, C. Peter. *Your Church Can Grow*. Rev. ed. Ventura, CA: Regal, 1984.

Wagner, C. Peter. *Your Spiritual Gifts Can Help Your Church Grow*. Ventura, CA: Regal, 1979.

21

Church Planting and Church Growth

C. Peter Wagner calls church planting "the single most effective evangelistic methodology under heaven."[1] Those Christian denominations experiencing the most rapid growth have been those that stress church planting. Wagner lauds the Church of the Nazarene, Assemblies of God, and the Southern Baptist Convention for their church planting emphasis. Says Wagner:

> It is not by accident that the Southern Baptists have become the largest Protestant denomination in America. One of their secrets is that they constantly invest substantial resources of personnel and finances in church planting on all levels from local congregations to associations to state conventions to their Home Mission Board in Atlanta. Although they will be the first to admit they don't do it enough, every year they strive to start more churches or church-type missions than the previous year. Much of what I have learned about church planting I have learned from Southern Baptists.[2]

Church Planting: The Impact on Church Growth

Does church planting positively affect the growth of the church? The answer is an unqualified "yes." Total church growth, which is closely related to kingdom growth, is enhanced. New churches have both a higher growth rate

---

[1]C. Peter Wagner, *Church Planting for a Greater Harvest* (Ventura, CA: Regal, 1990), 11. This is one of the best books written on church planting in print. Wagner cogently covers the vital issues in this volume. Much of this chapter is a synopsis of Wagner's main points.
[2]Ibid., 15.

and a higher conversion growth rate. A study was conducted of churches of all denominations in the Santa Clarita Valley of California. The surprising statistical conclusion was that older churches were baptizing four persons for every one hundred members, while newer churches were baptizing sixteen persons per one hundred members!

Why does this conversion growth discrepancy exist between newly started churches and older churches? One reason is that a new church offers another option to the unchurched. Regardless of the location, a new church will attract a segment of the unchurched that existing churches cannot reach. Wagner puts it this way:

> Some church planners have an aversion to starting churches of the same denomination in geographical proximity to each other. This may be wise in rural or small town settings, but it makes little sense in most of today's urban areas. In the same neighborhood one often finds a considerable variety of ethnic groups, social classes, and other social networks, each of which require a different kind of church. Church leaders who think geographical location is more important than social networks to the average unchurched American are living far from reality.[3]

We must abandon the competitive turf mentality that plagues many churches today! I observed a situation where a Baptist church moved from a transition neighborhood in the inner city to the suburbs of the same city. I thought a riot would erupt! The rioters were some of the members and leaders of other churches in the suburban area who were screaming that the church had trespassed on their turf. Such mentality is not of Christ and not of concern for kingdom building. The pastor of that church has led the newly located church to exciting growth, and their former inner-city building is now occupied by a thriving predominantly black megachurch. We must forever abandon the narrow-minded mentality of religious protectionism.

Church planting is not only beneficial for overall kingdom growth, it is also good for the local church that is visionary

[3]Ibid., 34.

enough to start a new church. A sponsoring church may send members and money to a new church and the sponsoring church inevitably sees God honor that commitment. This is a basic understanding of stewardship: God blesses what we give. Excitement is evident when new churches are started, and that excitement attracts new members to the sponsoring church.

Yet some methods of church planting do not require a local church to give up people or money. This is true of the satellite and multicampus models, which we will examine in more detail shortly. Both of these church planting models create extensions of a local church. Additional growth at any of the one church's locations results in new growth for the total church system.

Obstacles to Overcome

Undoubtedly the visionary church and its leaders will meet some opposition as they attempt to plant new churches. Most opposition results from problems of attitude.

Giving up members. There is pain in seeing members of a church family move to a new church. The members who decide to plant the new church are typically the most devout and best stewards. The sponsoring church is really giving its best. Much of the resistance to starting new churches results from the pain of anticipated separation. Church members must catch the vision of a mission mindset. The focus must be on kingdom growth rather than short-term losses the church may experience.

Loss of Funds. When a sponsoring church has enough vision to send some of its people to start a new church, it is aware that it is giving away tithers and above-tithers. This lowers the sponsoring church's budget and cash flow. God, however, honors the commitment of the parent church. Wagner noted a study showing that a sponsoring church usually replaced its people sent to the new church within six months. The same holds true for finances. He also discovered that the pattern depends significantly on the attitude of the parent church, particulary the pastor. "If the pastor has a negative attitude toward the church planting process it might negatively affect the parent church's subsequent growth."[4]

Start-up cost. Some denominations spend as much as $500,000 to start a church.[5] If such expenditures were the norm, the argument that high start-up costs make church planting prohibitive might have validity. At Green Valley Baptist Church, however, we were able to start our first satellite campus for approximately $9,000. Since we had received a gift for new church work for about that same amount, the church did not have to take any money out of the budget! Wagner discovered that an Assemblies of God district in North Carolina had planted 85 churches in the 1970s at a cost of about $2,500 each! Lyle Schaller has long maintained that financial subsidies hinder new churches. The money needed to pay for staff, land, buildings, and general operating expenses should come from the growth of the church rather than an up-front allocation.

Hurting other churches. Many fear that established churches will be hurt if a new church is started in an area of existing churches. Since we are to love other brothers and sisters in Christ, perhaps church planting in an area of existing churches should not take place. Such an approach presents a problem since almost every place in the metropolitan areas of the United States have several churches. Most studies, however, have identified improvements in the entire Christian community when new churches are planted.[6]

Wagner is right when he says that, regardless of other churches' approval, the task of church planting must not be hindered. I am well aware, from my church's experience in planting a new church, that the whims of all churches in the area will never be satisfied. How then should we respond? Wagner says to love them and plant churches anyway:

> I believe it is important and beneficial to enjoy the
> approval of existing churches when a new church is

[4]Ibid., 38.

[5]Ibid,. 39.

[6]See specifically Wagner's citing of a study of churches on the Oahu island of Hawaii in *Church Planting for a Greater Harvest,* 40. All churches on the island experienced a growth in attendance after a Southern Baptist church was planted there.

planted. But while such an approval is a plus, it should not be regarded as a prerequisite. As the parable of the shepherd indicates, the needs of the lost are a higher consideration than the needs of those who are safe and sound in the churches. As we learn from the modern shopping mall theory of merchandising, two churches even in close proximity to each other will reach many more unchurched than either one could hope to do alone.[7]

Harder work. An unspoken but very real concern of some people in existing churches is that growth (or even maintenance) of their church will be more difficult with a new church in the area. I believe that a new church can raise the outreach consciousness for an area. Greater effort may need to be expanded, but such is Great Commission obedience (Matt. 28:19).

Options for Planting Churches

Church planting will indeed be a method for church growth that will take many believers from their comfort zone; but Christianity was never meant to be a business-as-usual faith. The early church was always on the cutting edge of reaching people for Christ. Even when persecution broke out against the church, Christians scattered throughout Judea and Samaria. They shared their faith and started churches as they fled (Acts 8:1-4).

How then do we start churches? As a Southern Baptist, I was not familiar with the many options available to plant a church. My background had exposed me to only the traditional method of church planting. Now, in my denomination and others, many new options for church planting abound. In fact Russell Chandler, award winning journalist and religion writer for the Los Angeles Times, wrote that Southern Baptists and others are now on the cutting edge of new forms of church planting: "Southern Baptists talk about 'satellite' churches. Elmer Towns, head of the Church Growth Institute in Lynchburg, Virginia, calls the concept 'the geographical expanded parish church.'

[7]Ibid., 40-41.

Others refer to it as the 'perimeter' church. Whatever we call the idea, churches practicing it are the pacesetting ministries on the leading edge of the coming millennium."[8] Let us examine some of these options open to starting new churches as we approach the twenty-first century.

Traditional. In the traditional model of church planting, a sponsoring church sends a nucleus of members to start a new church in a geographical area. The new church is usually located within driving distance of the sponsoring church. The goal is for the new church to become totally autonomous as soon as possible. The success rate of these new churches is very high. Members of the nucleus are typically dedicated givers and workers. Because of the good base, the chances of survival are excellent. The disadvantage, especially in congregationally-governed churches, is that this system does not have any mechanism of accountability for the new church to become a parent church. For example, my church, Green Valley Baptist, was started by Philadelphia Baptist Church in Birmingham. Twenty-seven years elapsed before Green Valley started a church! Why? One of the primary reasons is that Green Valley as a church was accountable to no one or no group. An autonomous church has its advantages, but lack of accountability is a definite disadvantage.

Colonization. Colonization is identical to the traditional model with one major exception. The nucleus of members sent by the parent church move to a different geographical area. Those members must sell their homes, find new jobs, and send their children to new schools. A radical level of commitment to the Great Commission is a requisite.

Adoption. A Southern Baptist church in Texas heard of three churches in the area that had made a decision to close their doors. The pastor of the thriving church made a commitment to provide the people, the funds, and the leadership to keep the churches open. Though new churches were not planted, three churches were kept alive and the

[8]Russell Chandler, *Racing Toward 2001: The Forces Changing America's Religious Future.* (Grand Rapids, MI: Zondervan and Harper, 1992), 240. Chandler's book is an excellent study of trends in religion as we approach the twenty-first century.

impact was similar. While it is easier to have babies than to raise the dead, God needs mission-minded leaders to turn around dying churches.

Church splits. When churches split, the result is usually pain and dissension on both sides of the split. God definitely does not approve of divisiveness in the body of Christ. Yet God can use a bad situation for good. Wagner addresses the predicament positively:

> What can we say to this phenomenon? I'm sure that God does not approve of church splits or the causes of them listed by McGavran and Hunter. Nor would I go on record as advocating church splitting as a church planting methodology. It is much better to pray and plan and minister in harmony. Nevertheless, when the dust settles, I have to believe that God loves both of the resulting churches and accepts them as the bride of Christ . . . . He can be glorified through the offspring of accidental parenthood.[9]

Satellite. For many the satellite model is the most exciting development in church planting. John Vaughan describes this method in *The Large Church*: "Large churches with satellite groups combine the best of two growth strategies . . . . Although many of these churches are committed to building a large central church, most are just as committed to penetrating and reaching the city through the use of small groups coordinated fully, in most instances, by the parent congregation."[10] The satellite model is similar to the secular model of branch banking. Each new location has a high degree of autonomy, but it is still part of the same church. In other words, there is one church with many locations. This method may be the way of the future in American churches. The new church location can reach a new geographic area but still have all the combined resources of the parent and other satellite churches. This model also engenders accountability. Each of the locations look to one another to start new churches. This mutual

---

[9]Wagner, 65
[10]John N. Vaughan, *The Large Church* (Grand Rapids, MI: Baker, 1985), 23.

accountability to the vision of church planting is probably the single greatest strength of the satellite model.

Multicongregational.   The multicongregational model of church planting allows planting a new church in the facility of an existing church. This method works best in a multiethnic area. An English-speaking church, for example, shares its facilities with Korean and Chinese churches. Each church uses the building at different hours. The different groups may choose to be autonomous, or they may decide to be subgroups of a larger, single church.

Multicampus.   This model is slightly different from the satellite approach. Multicampus refers to one church in more than one location. Unlike the satellite model, the multicampus church has one membership roll, one budget, and one staff. The two more well-known examples of this model are Mt. Paran Church of God in Atlanta, Paul Walker, pastor; and The Church on the Way in Van Nuys, California, Jack Hayford, pastor.

Sodality models.   In the church-planting models previously described, the institution planting new churches was the local church. In the sodality model of church planting some agency other than a local church starts the new church. That agency can be a denominational agency, a parachurch organization, or it could refer to the starting of churches by individuals.

Evaluation

At the beginning of this chapter C. Peter Wagner was quoted as describing church planting as the single most effective evangelistic method under heaven. For pastors and other leaders truly committed to the church growth imperative of the Great Commission, church planting is not an option.

Examine the rapid growth of the early church in the Book of Acts; the role of church planting for evangelistic success is critical. The work began with key leaders such as Paul and Barnabas who followed the leading of the Holy Spirit to start new churches in multiple locations (cf. Acts 13:2-3). Christ's church today needs more leaders and followers who are willing to leave the comfort of their local churches to do something great for God. God is calling established churches to be good stewards of what He has given them. Remember the essence of the Great Commission is not "come to my church." It is "therefore go." May we obediently go.

Suggested Reading for Chapter 21

Chandler, Russell. *Racing Toward 2001: The Forces Shaping America's Religious Future.* Grand Rapids, MI: Zondervan and Harper, 1992.

Chaney, Charles L. *Church Planting at the End of the Twentieth Century.* Wheaton, IL: Tyndale, 1982.

Hoge, Dean R. and David A. Roozen, eds. *Understanding Church Growth and Decline 1950-1978.* New York: Pilgrim, 1979.

Redford, Jack. *Planting New Churches.* Nashville: Broadman, 1978.

Vaughan, John N. *The Large Church.* Grand Rapids, MI: Baker, 1985.

Wagner, C. Peter. *Church Planting for a Greater Harvest.* Ventura, CA: Regal, 1990.

22

Evangelism and Church Growth

A few years ago a word from the philosophy of science entered the vocabulary of the Church Growth Movement. *Paradigm,* the way we view things, or our model for the world, became a word in church growth lingo. Wagner first used the word when he said that he had experienced a paradigm shift, or change in world view, in the way he saw modern-day miracles. His former world view, one of a dispensational leaning, did not allow for "sign gifts" in this post-apostolic era. His new world view affirms the manifestation of all of the gifts of the Spirit.[1]

Another paradigm shift is taking place in the area of evangelism. Because of the close relationship between evangelism and church growth, this paradigm shift has touched all areas of the Church Growth Movement. From a personal perspective, the shift has been painful. As one who practiced and preached "cold call" confrontational evangelism, I have struggled with the decreasing effectiveness of this method. What then is the paradigm shift in evangelism? Perhaps a personal illustration will tell the story best. Over ten years ago I accompanied an Evangelism Explosion team going door-to-door, seeking an opportunity to share the gospel with a stranger. After several unsuccessful visits, Jim allowed us to enter his apartment. We went through the carefully scripted plan of salvation, and Jim asked Christ into his life. Within two

[1]The signs-and-wonders issue will be discussed in detail in chapter 30. Wagner has written extensively about his pilgrimage in this area. For a full treatment of both his journey and the entire issue as it relates to the Church Growth Movement, see C. Peter Wagner, *How To Have a Healing Ministry without Making Your Church Sick* (Ventura, CA: Regal, 1988).

weeks Jim had made his faith public in the church, and he was baptized soon after. A few weeks later Jim had made some friends in his Sunday School class and became increasingly active in the church. He is now a leader in that church.

The good news is the excitement of the change in Jim's life: from unchurched, lost, without relationships with Christians to an active, fruit-bearing disciple of Christ in a local church. The not-so-good news is that I have not witnessed a similar story since. Evangelism Explosion teams (or other confrontational programs such as Continuing Witness Training in the Southern Baptist Convention) are experiencing difficulty finding prospects who will allow them to share their faith. Even those who make decisions to accept Christ rarely become active in the local church. Since the heart of church growth is disciple-making, evangelism that produces no disciples is certainly not the type of evangelism that Christ had in mind when He gave the Great Commission. In fact, the success stories of Evangelism Explosion in the churches I have served are those encounters with lost people who already had relationships with people in the church.

In his book *User Friendly Churches,* which examined disciple-making churches, George Barna found that cold-call evangelism was not a factor in these churches that reached many people for Christ:

> Falling into the familiar patterns and routines that have worked in the past is a trademark of stagnant churches. Cold-call evangelism is one such pattern that appeals to many such churches.
>
> During the first three-quarters of this century, it was not uncommon for churches to develop evangelistic teams that would get together one or two nights a week and go knocking on people's doors, attempting to share the gospel on people's front door steps, or in their living rooms.
>
> Times have changed, however, and successful churches grow because they have generally understood the change. They may have an evangelism team, but the efforts of that team are directed either to "response evangelism"— visiting those people who request such a visit, or "event evangelism"— providing public interest events that

include some type of evangelistic thrust. They know that the chances of meeting a responsive individual who gets a cold call at their front door are minimal. They know that their good-hearted attempt at service may close the person's mind to the gospel. Given the range of other, proven means of affecting change in the person's heart, they simply do not believe that the methodology warrant's the high risk of failure.[2]

The Reasons Behind the
New Paradigm

Though the paradigm shift in evangelism has not happened overnight, it has taken place at such a rapid pace that many Christians and churches simply are unaware of the change. Five basic changes in society have contributed to the shift. Churches must understand and respond to these changes if we are to have any hope for reaching significant numbers of people for Christ in the twenty-first century.

The new pagans.   Until the late 1960s Christians could speak the "language of Zion" with a level of assurance that most of America understood them. Most of America based their values upon the Judeo-Christian value system. Yet in the span of about one generation, our culture has changed dramatically. Situational ethics and personal freedom have become the new basis for decision making. Right and wrong is no longer black and white. One person's "right" is another person's "wrong."

If Christians believe that most of the nation adheres to biblical beliefs, they are working under a false assumption. The sad truth is that Americans are generally ignorant of the Bible. Even if they decide that the Bible is their accepted authority, they know too little about it to make much difference.

One poll showed that, while 93 percent of Americans have a Bible in their home, only 12 percent of all adults read it daily. Less than one third knew that the expression "God helps those who help themselves" is not in the Bible. Less

[2]George Barna, *User Friendly Churches* (Ventura, CA: Regal, 1991), 180. Used by permission.

than one-half knew that Jonah is a book in the Bible.[3] Is it
any wonder that non-Christians have difficulty
understanding us?

This phenomenon explains one of the reasons why our
gospel presentations make little sense to unbelievers. We
tell them that they are sinners in need of forgiveness, but
their new morality does not understand sin and, if it did, it
would redefine the concept. The Church Growth Movement
grasped this reality several years ago when it incorporated
the Engel scale in its literature.[4]

When James Engel of Wheaton College developed a linear
scale to measure progress in the evangelistic process, church
growth writers quickly used the instrument in their works.
The Engel scale depicts eight progressive steps an
unbeliever makes before becoming a believer in Jesus
Christ. The scale then shows three further steps after
salvation.

-8 Awareness of a supreme being, but no effective
   knowledge of the gospel

-7 Initial awareness of the gospel

-6 Awareness of the fundamentals of the gospel

-5 Grasp of the implications of the gospel

-4 Positive attitude toward the gospel

-3 Personal problem recognition

-2 Decision to act

-1 Repentance and faith in Christ

The person is regenerated and becomes a new creature.

+1 Post-decision evaluation

+2 Incorporation into the body

+3 A lifetime of conceptual and behaviorial growth in
   Christ

[3]George Barna, *The Frog in the Kettle* (Ventura, CA: Regal, 1990), 118.
[4]The Engel scale can be found in many church growth books. The best
explanation of the tool is found in C. Peter Wagner, *Strategies for Church Growth*
(Ventura, CA: Regal, 1987), 124.

Most churches that have an evangelistic thrust approach lost persons as if they are "-4" or "-3" on the Engel scale. This would have been a fair assumption three decades ago. Today most of the "new pagans" would be a "-8" or a "-7" on the scale. If we are to be effective evangelists, we must recognize that most people are a lot further from the cross than they were a few decades earlier.

Vanishing time. Barna calls time the new "money" in that time is now Americans' most valuable commodity.[5] Innovators in marketing have understood this need and have given us microwaves, fax machines, automated teller machines, fast foods, home delivery, and convenience stores. Anything that can save us time becomes a marketable product.

Part of the explanation behind the loss of time is the number of women in the work force. More than half of all women now work outside the home.[6] With both husband and wife employed, time becomes more and more scarce. Time becomes a fiercely guarded, jealously protected commodity.

Into this scenario walks an evangelistic team without notice. Even if the team is allowed into the home, resistance has already developed. Many consider this an invasion of privacy or a theft of time.

Unmet needs. Every minute of advertising that bombards our society speaks of how a product or service can meet a need. In fact, some marketing today *creates* needs in the minds of the consumer, while showing how products can satisfy those needs.

Evangelism which does not recognize the hungering for fulfillment will not communicate the gospel effectively. Of course, the need for a Savior is the greatest need for humanity. Yet, most of the time other more temporal needs must be met to gain a hearing.

Break-up of relationships. Trial relationships, better known as living together before marriage, came into vogue in the 1960s. Many argued that this would provide time for consenting adults to see if they were really meant for each

[5]Barna, *The Frog in the Kettle,* 39.
[6]Ibid., 98.

other. In other words, trial relationships would ultimately result in stronger marriages. Statistics from the census bureau, however, ended that argument. People who live together before marriage, say the statistics, are even more likely to divorce.[7]

Speaking of divorce, one researcher recently predicted that two out of three currently married couples would get a divorce.[8] We already know statistically that 60 percent of all second marriages end in divorce.[9]

Children are hit the hardest by the break-up of relationships. Presently, one out of four homes has a single parent with one or more children. The trend indicates that at least 60 percent of all children born in 1990 will live in a single-parent home before reaching eighteen.[10] All children are growing up too fast. The average age of sexual intercourse for the first time is declining. One-third of teenagers who have reached driving age own a car. Yet children who live at home spend less than thirty minutes weekly in meaningful conversation with their mothers, and less than half that time with their fathers.

Americans today are intensely lonely. Yet our life-styles discourage lasting, life-changing relationships. Evangelism that produces real church growth must understand this deep longing for relationships. The religion that can bridge the relationship chasm among men, women, and children today will win the multitudes.

Lack of relevancy. Most churches today simply are irrelevent to most of society. The language, methodology, music, organizations, buildings, and sermons typically do not reflect the world in which most people live. A walk into a church (if we really could get them into the front door) would be a trip into a nostalgic past at best, and boring irrelevancy at worst.

Can the church of the twenty-first century speak to the new pagans? Is there a way for our evangelism to reach

---

[7]Ibid., 67.
[8]Russell Chandler, *Racing Toward 2001: The Forces Shaping America's Religious Future* (Grand Rapids, MI: Zondervan and Harper, 1992), 98.
[9]Barna, *The Frog in the Kettle,* 67.
[10]Ibid., 67-68.

them without compromising our theology? All indications are that we can more effectively reach the lost; but there is a price to be paid. The price is the pain of change. Are Christians in America ready to make such changes, to "do church" differently than most have ever known? Let us look at possible areas that can make our evangelism relevant while keeping our theology sound.

Evangelism Which Results In Real Church Growth

A church that is willing to take the following five steps should be forewarned. Significant change brings significant pain. Too many people simply do not understand why church cannot be "the way we've always done it." I recently spoke to the pastor of a megachurch that lost *five hundred members* after this process of change began. He knew something had to be done because, although they were baptizing over one hundred people yearly, they were not touching the surface of the numbers of new pagans. Their losses have now bottomed out, and they are beginning to reach a new subset of the population. For three years of change, however, the pain was intense and personal. Are leaders today willing to make such sacrifices? Are Christians willing to follow this leadership? The answers to these questions are eternal in significance.

Small groups. I will not discuss small groups extensively here since it is the subject of chapter 29. The emphasis to be made at this point is that there may be no greater evangelistic tool for developing relationships than small groups. Those churches that are proceeding deliberately and enthusiastically in this area will undoubtedly see the greatest evangelistic harvests in the years ahead. Our relationship-hungry society is willing to go into homes and other "neutral" sites as their first steps toward associating with Christians. Openness is increasing in small groups that is not found in most other areas of the church.

Your schedule or mine? One of the most innovative moves of the American church in the past was scheduling worship services at 11:00 a.m. to meet the needs of a then predominantly agricultural society. The farmers had time to milk the cows, do the chores, and still get to church on time. Unfortunately most churches today believe that the 11:00 worship hour was mandated by Christ and practiced by the apostle Paul. Needless to say, ours is no longer an agricultural nation. Are we willing to make dramatic changes in the times and days of worship and other activities in order to give the unchurched a choice that can best fit their schedule?

Relevant. Once the unchurched enter the front door, will they feel intimidated by what they see, hear, and feel? In the next chapter we will look at the issue of worship, the new front door.

Ministry that is meaningful. Baby boomers and baby busters will not stand for ministry as usual in our churches. The unchurched must see that, if they are to be a part of the believing community, they will be involved in life-changing ministries (review chapter 20). They will no longer accept monotonous committee meetings, business conferences with a quorum of 5 percent, and positions that simply fill a slot. The people of our society want to know that they can touch lives and make a difference if they are to be involved in our churches.

A new look at evangelism training. Despite the dire comments made earlier about cold-call evangelism, programs such as Continuing Witness Training and Evangelism Explosion will have a place in our churches. They cannot, however, be viewed as the sum of our evangelism ministry. Christians do need training to share Christ cogently and confidently. However, the trainees should be taught that their training will be most effective among persons with whom they have developed a relationship. In other words, evangelism training is "in" but cold-call evangelism is "out."

Evaluation

Few churches are reaching the new pagans of our nation. Most churches are, at best, reaching the children and close relatives of church members. Sadly, too many churches are reaching few or none for Christ.

Rethinking our evangelistic methodology does not mean compromising our theology. In fact we must be careful that we do not confuse our methodology for theology.

On the other hand, we must be careful lest we dilute the gospel in our eagerness to be relevant to the world. Sin is still sin. Discipleship still means cross-bearing. The new pagans still need a Savior. For them and us, Jesus is still our only hope.

Suggested Reading for Chapter 22

Barna, George. *The Frog in the Kettle.* Ventura, CA: Regal, 1990.

Barna, George. *User Friendly Churches.* Ventura, CA: Regal, 1991.

Chandler, Russell. *Racing Toward 2001: The Forces Shaping America's Religious Future.* Grand Rapids, MI: Zondervan and Harper, 1992.

Rainer, Thom S., ed. *Evangelism in the Twenty-First Century.* Wheaton, IL: Shaw, 1989. See especially chapter 3 by C. Peter Wagner, "Evangelism and the Church Growth Movement"; and chapter 5 by Paige Patterson, "Lifestyle Evangelism."

Wagner, C. Peter. *Strategies for Church Growth.* Ventura, CA: Regal, 1987.

23

Worship and Church Growth

In James Emery White's outstanding book on worship, *Opening the Front Door: Worship and Church Growth,* an unlikely marriage takes place. White recognizes that linking worship and church growth may seem inappropriate:

> A colleague shared with me that someone told him that speaking of worship in relation to non-churched persons was "heresy," for worship had nothing to do with anyone but Christians. Though I am sure this person was well-intentioned, such a view is not in accord with the biblical materials, or even with current practice. Virtually every Protestant church in the United States concludes its worship experience with an invitation or "altar call" for salvation. This is a clear indication that we already *functionally* join worship and church growth.[1]

While worship *is* the response of believers who give glory and worth to God, the biblical testimony indicates that non-believers are often in worship services as well. In his First Letter to the Corinthians, Paul instructed the believers to conduct their worship services in such a manner that the non-believers would be affected positively. Paul obviously believed that the worship service had a dual purpose for believers and the non-Christians (1 Cor. 14:23-25).

Yet worship has been linked with church growth primarily because worship services are increasingly becoming the entry point for the unchurched into churches. White comments: "If a nonchurched person does decide to investigate involvement in a local church, what is the 'front door' by which he or she

[1]James Emery White, *Opening the Front Door: Worship and Church Growth* (Nashville: Convention, 1992), 15, emphasis in original.

will enter? An examination of the statistics of the Southern Baptist Convention, the largest Protestant denomination in the United States, suggests that the front door of the church is no longer a small group network such as the Sunday School but has changed to the worship service."[2]

Why has the change taken place in American churches? A primary reason is that most people interested in a church would like to "try it out" with anonymity. It is easier to get lost in a large crowd than in a small group. Second, in a large crowd the seeker is not put on the spot to participate. The small group environment may be too threatening to the guest who envisions having to read the Bible, comment on biblical passages, introduce himself or herself, or—dread above all dreads—pray in public. Finally, no commitment is required in a larger group. The seeker perceives that if he or she visits a church in a small-group setting, other members of the group will be attempting to "sign them up." By visiting the worship service first, guests can evaluate the church without being pressured.

Prepare for Conflict

Before we look at changes taking place in worship services in America, we must recognize potential conflict. For example, enormous conflict is inevitable when changes of music are made. White says, "Growing churches which have transitioned their church to non-traditional forms of music have often, as a result, received enormous criticism."[3] Elmer Towns says the greatest revolution in the modern church is taking place in worship; but, he cautions, it is also the source of the greatest controversy.[4] Russell Chandler agrees that the debate will continue, but the trend is set: "Nowhere is the dissonance greater than in discussions about what's 'proper' in 'Christian' music. Expect the syncopated tempo to pick up as we head for 2001."[5]

[2]Ibid., 16.
[3]Ibid., 82.
[4]Elmer Towns, *Ten of Today's Most Innovative Churches* (Ventura, CA: Regal, 1990), 15.
[5]Russell Chandler, *Racing Toward 2001: The Forces Shaping America's Religious Future* (Grand Rapids, MI: Zondervan and Harper, 1992), 299.

The controversy and conflict, however, will extend beyond music. I chuckle at the cartoon that shows a disgruntled church member leading his pastor to the hanging gallows, much to the delight of the rabid congregation. The caption reads, as one member speaks to another, "I tried to tell him not to change the order of service."

Why are worship changes so controversial? For many the music and elements of worship bring back warm memories of receiving Christ, sitting next to Mom and Dad, or making a major decision toward greater discipleship. When those traditional elements are changed, many feel loss or even grief.

Still others may confuse a method of worship with correct theology. When that method or style is changed, they exclaim that the church has been unfaithful to its biblical moorings. The church, they say, has compromised truth for the enticements of the charismatics, liberals, or secularists.

Perhaps the basic explanation behind the worship debate is that change is painful. For many church is supposed to be the stable force in a world of rapid change. If the church, especially the worship service, offers no stability, then they feel that nothing in the world can offer them a sense of belonging.

Worship in the Twenty-First Century

What are some of the changes we can expect as we enter a new century? Before we answer that question, we must recognize that the anticipated changes will take place in most churches, but not all churches. Worship styles have never been monolithic in America; and there is no reason to expect that to change. What we forsee, however, is a trend in many churches in the following directions.

Why are these trends taking place? The influence of the Church Growth Movement has inspired churches seeking to reach people to ask the unchurched why they do not attend church. Their answers were as follows:

1. Churches are always asking for money.
2. Church services are boring and lifeless.

3. Church services are predictable and repetitive.
4. Sermons are irrelevant to daily life as it's lived in the real world.
5. The pastor makes me feel guilty and ignorant, and I leave church feeling worse than when I entered the doors.[6]

In other words, the unchurched said that *worship services* were the biggest *barrier* to their attending church. As a consequence, many churches began to change, so that their "front door" might really be open to the unbelievers and unchurched.

Quality. The average American has become accustomed to quality: slick productions in television and movies; shiny, clean malls; and businesses seeking to improve their products and services. While devout Christians may tolerate worship services that are less-than-good, we cannot expect the unchurched to be so tolerant. Unkempt facilities, abrasive sound systems, inundating organ music, uncomfortable pews, and irrelevant sermons are but a few of the distractions that will send the unchurched away, maybe forever. "One of the first marks of growing churches that is instantly perceived is a *commitment to excellence,* an attitude that strives for quality and rejects mediocrity."[7]

Atmosphere. White has identified five elements of atmosphere in growing churches: celebrative, friendly, relaxed, positive, and expectant.[8] Growing churches have enthusiastic and celebrative worship services. They have learned that the true meaning of enthusiasm is *en theos,* or "in God." Yet C. Peter Wagner remarked several years ago that most church services are "more like a funeral than a festival."[9]

Friendliness in a church often begins with the worship leader and pastor. They set the tone for the rest of the congregation. Most churches think of themselves as friendly; in reality, however, church members are friendly to each other but unfriendly to outsiders. We have two ways at

[6]White, 19-20.
[7]Ibid., 55, emphasis in original.
[8]Ibid., 62.
[9]C. Peter Wagner, *Your Church Can Grow* (Ventura, CA: Regal, 1984), 113.

our church, Green Valley Baptist, by which we measure our friendliness. The first is our seating habits. Are we sitting with the same people in the same seats on Sundays and Wednesdays? Or are we reaching out to guests and new members by introducing ourselves and sitting with them? Second, as pastor I send a letter to all guests in our worship services. Included in the letter is a hand-stamped response card. We ask the guest to complete the card anonymously and mail it to us after completing these three lines:

1. My first impression of the church was _____.
2. The worship service was _____.
3. If I could make one suggestion it would be _____.

Approximately 25 percent of our guests respond in this manner. These cards help us measure our friendliness to outsiders.

What is meant by "a relaxed atmosphere"? It is important to answer this question because two-thirds of the unchurched persons want an informal style of worship.[10] White visited many growing churches to determine what those churches were doing to create a relaxed atmosphere:

> Though this work does not recommend a particular style, it is certainly clear that research shows that "formality and liturgy are often barriers" to church growth. It was not uncommon as I visited growing churches to be the only one in attendance wearing a coat and tie (particularly for Saturday evening and early Sunday morning services). A coffee pot with donuts is common in the vestibule and other gathering areas both before and after services or Sunday School, encouraging individuals to perceive that they are in a relaxed, warm atmosphere. Taped music is often playing in the background, adding to the "relaxed" atmosphere of conversation and fellowship.

A positive spirit and sense of expectancy enhance the atmosphere of growing churches. These churches are joyful; smiles are obvious on the faces of the congregation and choir. The focus is on the possibilities through Christ (Phil. 4:13). The positive is accentuated because the people believe that

[10]White, 68.

God can transform lives. They enter every service with a feeling that God is doing something in their midst.

Welcoming guests. Several years ago I was presented to a church in view of a call as pastor. During the time of welcome, each guest was asked to raise his or her hand. The few who were willing to comply were presented a "visitor card" and given a "visitor badge" to wear. Then, at the conclusion of the service, the names of these visitors were read before the congregation, and the embarrassed souls were asked to stand so that the members could identify them. I later asked the search committee how many people returned after their first visit. Their response was anticipated: "Very few—and we just don't understand why."

If we have attended a church for some length of time, we often forget the discomfort of walking into a new place. Then, if we are "spotlighted" as different from everyone else, we have little desire to return. Yet many members just cannot understand why guests do not return to their friendly church.

Some principles are now being followed in growing churches in the treatment of guests. The first is the principle of anonymity. Growing churches let the guests themselves determine if they want to be identified. For example, this chapter includes the same registration card used for prayer requests at Green Valley Baptist (chapter 18). Everyone, guests and members alike, is asked to complete the card. The guests are not isolated and treated differently. Only the block they check (first-time guest, second-time guest, etc.) on the card identifies them as non-members, and they are never singled-out during the service. Because everyone places a card in the offering plate, the guests do not feel conspicuous.

Speaking of the offering, many growing churches are giving a disclaimer before the offering is taken. Guests are told specifically that the offering is for the members and regular attenders who give to support the ministries of the church. Such a statement eliminates a major fear in the minds of the unchurched: "All they are interested in is my money!"

Every facet of the service in many growing churches is planned with guests in mind. Those who come are called "guests" ("you have been invited") rather than "visitors" ("you dropped in on us").

Registration Card
Green Valley Baptist Church
Birmingham, Alabama

Welcome to
Green Valley Baptist Church   Date _____

Dr./Rev./Ms.
Mr./Mrs./Miss _____   Phone (___) _____
Address _____   Apt. ____   Wk. Phone (___) _____
City_____   State____   Zip _____

Is This Your . . .
☐ First Time? I came as a guest of _____
☐ Second Time?   ☐ Third Time?   ☐ Attender   ☐ Member

Present Church Membership _____

Your School Grade	Or Age Group	Please Circle:
K 1 2 3 4 5 6 7 8	18-29 30-35 36-40 41-45	Single
9 10 11 12 College	46-49 50-55 56-64 65-66+	Married

Names of your children living at home   Birthday

_____

_____

_____

(Please see other side)

- -

I'd like information on:
☐ How to become a Christian
☐ Next Membership Class
☐ Spiritual Growth
☐ Teacher Training
☐ Missions
☐ Adult Bible Study
☐ Music Activities
☐ Singles Activities
☐ College Activities
☐ Youth Activities
☐ Preschool Children Activities
Prayer Needs: _____

_____

_____

Would you like a Prayergram sent to the
person prayed for? ☐ Yes ☐ No. If Yes,
provide address.

_____

_____

I would like to:
☐ Commit my life to Christ
☐ Renew my commitment to Christ
☐ Be baptized
☐ Be enrolled in next membership class
☐ Help where needed
☐ Enroll in Sunday School
☐ Join the Church
☐ Reservations for Wed. Night Dinner

_____

_____

_____

_____

_____

_____

_____

_____

_____

_____

(Please see other side)

The best parking is reserved for guests. In-house announcements and terminology are avoided. Language we church members have heard all of our lives makes no sense to the unchurched: "The BYW of the WMU will meet immediately preceding the Discipleship Training hour. And all VBS workers are to meet after the Wednesday fellowship dinner." Speak their language and be sensitive to their situation and they just might return.

Music. The trends in music are perhaps the sources of greatest controversy. "People guard their taste in music, especially in the life of the church, more dearly than doctrine."[11] White notes four major trends in music in worship services: "It is contemporary and upbeat, it is of the highest quality, there is lots of it; and it is led and presented in innovative ways."[12] Although exceptions are noted, contemporary Christian rock music is the fastest growing style of music in growing churches. One must remember that, for the majority of the baby boomers, rock is the traditional form of music.

While some may feel that the invasion of Christian rock music into worship services is heresy, White observes that this situation is not new. The hymns of Martin Luther were anything but traditional to his generation: "What Luther did was take the tunes from the 'Top 40' of the Wittenburg bar circuit and equip them with Christian words. Many of the great hymns born of the Protestant Reformation, such as 'A Mighty Fortress Is Our God,' were tunes that Luther took, changed the lyrics, and put into the life of the church in order that the common people could both identify and participate."[13] Other well-known song writers of the past have taken music from "questionable sources" and reworded them for the church: Bach and Ira Sankey are two examples. "Historically, the church has always seized contemporary music and adapted it to Christian lyrics. This was one of the dynamics behind the Second Great

[11]Ibid., 82.
[12]Ibid., 83.
[13]Ibid., 86. See also Roland Bainton, *Here I Stand: A Life of Martin Luther* (Nashville, Abingdon, 1950), 340-347.

Awakening, especially in New England. Simply put, the use of contemporary music in worship is far from innovative."[14]

Variety and scheduling. Growing churches are offering worship services at different times and days so that the unchurched may have a choice that best fits their schedules. Multiple Sunday morning worship services and weeknight and Saturday evening services are increasingly common.

Within the services themselves, growing churches are offering a variety of media and speakers. Drama, video, hymns and choruses on overhead screens, and a number of innovations in worship will likely be the norm in the twenty-first century.

Sermons. White identifies seven characteristics of the preaching style in growing churches.[15] The first of these characteristics is that the preachers are specifically targeting a group in their sermons. A sermon for a lost person will be different than one for a mature Christian. Sermons to children, baby boomers, and senior adults will each have characteristics of their own. The reality of the context of worship is that representatives of most target groups may be present to hear all sermons so the preacher must decide his key target for each message.

Second, all sermons must be biblical. The authority and centrality of the Bible cannot be compromised. As third and fourth characteristics, those biblical sermons must be practical and relevant. The content must speak to the needs of the hearers in such a way that it makes a difference in their lives.

Fifth, sermons today must be interesting and even entertaining. While such descriptions may seem out of place in the context of a worship service, sermons that do not catch the attention of the listeners will be useless, despite their rich content. Ours is a generation of television, movies, and entertainment. Dull and lifeless sermons will send all the guests and many members in different directions.

Another characteristic of sermons in growing churches reflects the widespread biblical illiteracy among not only the

---

[14]White, unpublished material provided to author.
[15]White, *Opening the Front Door,* see chapter 9, "Sermon," 107-123.

unchurched but many regular churchgoers as well. Sermons must be simple, especially those that are designed to reach the largest number. More in-depth preaching and teaching must take place in settings other than the worship service which is designed to reach the unchurched.

Finally, sermons in growing churches are positive and encouraging. The world has enough bad news. Even if the message is a hard-hitting sermon on the consequences of sin, it can be communicated in light of the good news of the Sin Forgiver.

The decline of revivals. Revivals have become progressively shorter throughout the twentieth century. From month-long camp meetings to two-week revivals, to eight-day revivals, to four-day revivals, we are now seeing the increasing use of one-day revivals. The decline of revivals can first be attributed to the church's failure to get lost people to attend. The town revival was, in years past, a social as well as a religious event. Everyone could be expected to attend. An unredeemed person in revival services today is the exception rather than the rule.

The loaded and busy schedules of our people have contributed to the demise of revivals. Not many people, even regular churchgoers, are able or willing to set aside four to eight consecutive evenings to attend a revival. Worship services of the twenty-first century will use special one-day events as successors to revivals. Financial-planning seminars, marriage-enrichment conferences, and divorce-recovery workshops are some of the examples of the one-day events built around worship services.

Making the Transition

An aging church member shared with me the pain of the change he was witnessing in his church. "I know we must be relevant and speak to the lost people today," he said. "But it hurts to watch the music I love and the worship I'm accustomed to disappear from the scene. Doesn't anyone care how I feel?"

Many others share his pain, especially those born before 1946, the start of the baby boom. We who are church leaders and church-growth minded must seek every opportunity to reach the lost for Jesus Christ—even changing our worship services if necessary. However, we must also remember that those who resist or dislike the changes are God's children as well. Perhaps the following suggestions can ease the pain of transition for those churches who decide to make a change.

Proceed deliberately.   Too much change made too rapidly can be disastrous for the pastor and the congregation. The churches that are making worship changes at a pace with which the people can cope will experience the greatest long-term benefit. The median age of the church should be a factor in determining the pace of change. Remember that you can not please everyone. Ultimately the evangelistic motive of the church must be considered the highest priority.

Love those who disagree.   If worship changes cause great dissension in the church, any innovations will be rendered ineffective. For the leader who moves the church even gradually, the criticisms will come. Every effort should be made to keep the mandate of Christ-like love before the people. "This is the message you heard from the beginning: We should love one another" (1 John 3:11).

Multiple services.   Additional services to meet the worship preferences of different groups can also provide an interim solution that may last for years. I know of one church that specifies in all of its printed material: 9:30 a.m.— contemporary worship; 11:00 a.m.—traditional worship.

Multiple campuses.   When additional campuses, such as the satellite concept discussed in chapter 21, are established for outreach, the new campus can have from the onset an alternative worship style. Green Valley Baptist Church determined that its first satellite campus would begin with a more contemporary worship. The decision was largely based on demographic studies that showed the median age of the community was under thirty.

Evaluation

Perhaps the greatest potential danger in moving toward "seeker-friendly" services is that worship services could cease to be authentic Christian worship. If virtually everything is geared toward unbelievers, the believers will have no opportunity to worship the living God. In reality few churches have made such a radical transition. If the desire is to have a worship service geared completely for unbelievers, another service must be offered for Christians.

Another unresolved theological question concerns worship on days other than Sunday. Some would assert that, although first-day worship is not commanded in Scripture, its practice in the New Testament testimony is sufficient evidence for its continuation. Others regard the practice of Sunday worship as a tradition of the apostolic church that can be changed by Christians of later generations. White concludes from the biblical testimony:

> The seventh day (Saturday) was no longer regarded as a day to be especially observed by worship and rest from labor (see Rom. 14:5; Gal. 4:8; Col. 2:16; Acts 15:28). The resurrection, the heart of the gospel, occurred on a Sunday. When the New Testament writers designated the various days on which the resurrected Christ appeared and spoke to His disciples, it was uniformly on a Sunday (see Matt. 28:9; Luke 24:13; John 20:19). And the coming of the Holy Spirit in Acts 2 occurred on Pentecost (a Sunday). Therefore while worship on the Lord's Day (Sunday) is descriptive of the practice of the early church and thus important to take note of for our practice, *nowhere is it directly commanded.*[16]

Perhaps the clearest warning church growth enthusiasts should heed is the warning of potential compromise. Because worship services that are relevant to culture are growth-enhancing, the danger is that such cultural adaptation or contextualization can lead to theological compromise. The message can never change for it is about the unchangeable Christ (Heb. 13:8).

[16]Ibid., 149, emphasis in original.

Suggested Reading for Chapter 23

Hadaway, C. Kirk. *Church Growth Principles: Separating Fact from Fiction.* Nashville: Broadman, 1991.

Hayford, Jack W. *Worship His Majesty.* Dallas: Word, 1987.

Hayford, Jack W., John Killinger, and Howard Stevenson. *Mastering Worship.* Portland, OR: Christianity Today and Multnomah, 1990.

Murren, Doug. *The Baby Boomerang.* Ventura, CA: Regal, 1990.

Towns, Elmer. *Ten of Today's Most Innovative Churches.* Ventura, CA: Regal, 1990.

Wagner, C. Peter. *Your Church Can Grow.* Rev. ed. Ventura, CA: Regal, 1984.

White, James Emery. *Opening the Front Door: Worship and Church Growth.* Nashville: Convention, 1992.

White, James F. *Introduction to Christian Worship.* Rev. ed. Nashville: Abingdon, 1990.

24

Finding the People

In the previous chapter we saw the relatively new phenomen of worship providing a point of entry for outreach. We also examined the ways in which we can make our services "seeker-sensitive," so that first time guests might return gladly.

Even a church with an excellent worship service, however, must not wait for the people to come. The emphasis of the Great Commission (Matt. 28:19) is to go. What might we do to reach people who would not otherwise come to our churches?

In this chapter we will look at seven good ways to discover prospects. These seven methods fall into two broad categories: church promotion and relationship building. Developing a community presence, special events, marketing, seeking new residents, and surveying by needs are all good methods to find prospects. These methods focus on what the church can do for the prospect. The next two, however, focus on building a relationship. Training members in life-style evangelism and developing small groups are keys to reaching the unchurched as we enter the twenty-first century.

A list of seven ways to find prospects is certainly not an exhaustive approach. These methods, however, are prominent in growing churches. The approaches will undoubtedly change in coming years. The Church Growth Movement continues to discover and assess the most successful types of outreach.

Community Presence

One of the outstanding churches in America today is First Baptist Church of Leesburg, Florida, led by Pastor Charles

Roesel. This church is one of the consistent leaders in baptisms in the Southern Baptist Convention. First Baptist has various community ministries such as homes for battered women and unwed mothers. These ministries touch the physical, financial, and emotional needs of people in the community. Most important, the church often reaches the greatest spiritual need as many of those who benefit from the ministries also accept Jesus Christ as their Lord and Savior.

Perhaps the church most frequently mentioned as the model for community presence is Bear Valley Baptist Church in Denver. The church has unleashed hundreds of members to do ministry. The people in the church are constantly reminded that they are the ministers and that they have the freedom and the permission to begin ministries under broad and reasonable guidelines.[1]

Churches with a community presence find prospects in two ways. First, those who are served by the community ministries are often prospects for salvation and for the church. The church that views these people as prospects may discover that the prospects are "down and outers." The attitude of Jesus is necessary as the church does outreach in New Testament style, ministering to "the least of these" (Matt. 25:40). Are churches today ready to give up their comfort zones by letting different kinds of people come into their buildings?

Second, the church discovers prospects as people in the community get involved in these ministries. There is a deep hunger in the hearts of many people to touch lives and to make a difference. Unfortunately, most churches do not offer opportunities for "outsiders" or members to be involved in front-line ministry. If you lead a church toward involvement in the community that makes a difference, the church will become a magnet for many prospects.

Special Events

Can special events such as high attendance days, friend days, Christmas and Easter spectaculars, seminars,

[1]See Frank Tillapaugh, "Giving an Ingrown Church an Outward Focus," in Calvin Ratz, Frank Tillapaugh, and Myron Augsburger, *Mastering Outreach & Evangelism* (Portland, OR: Christianity Today and Multnomah, 1990), 58. The book-length treatment is Tillapaugh's *The Church Unleashed* (Ventura, CA: Regal, 1982).

conferences, and dramas result in growth and discover prospects? C. Kirk Hadaway says: "The answer is *'yes,'* if *used properly.*"[2] What is necessary, according to Hadaway, is follow-up if special events are to be effective. The attenders cease to be prospects in many churches because they "are not visited quickly, and persons who join during the event may not return."[3] The church must understand the purpose of special events if they are to reach the unchurched. "If the primary reason is 'tradition,' 'our members enjoy them,' or 'to revive our church,' then they are unlikely to produce growth. In fact, they may actually work against growth by siphoning off the energy of members from activities which do produce growth."[4]

The churches that are discovering prospects through special events typically produce an event that is sensitive to the unchurched. Shades Mountain Independent Church in Birmingham, Alabama, creates a major Christmas production for the community each year. Music minister Kim Cannon now divides these productions equally between music and drama; in the past they were predominantly music. The reason? Drama, especially good drama, is seeker sensitive. Television and movies have developed a society that is highly affected by the visual media.

Marketing

When George Barna's book *Marketing the Church*[5] was published in 1988, some Christian leaders expressed concern that the church was "selling out" to an unbiblical, secular model for reaching the unchurched. The very use of the word "marketing" seemed to many inappropriate in the context of the church. Barna explained that we must first "think of marketing as the activities that address the needs of a target audience, thereby allowing the business to satisfy its goals."[6] If we understand that the "business" of the

[2]C. Kirk Hadaway, *Church Growth Principles: Separating Fact from Fiction* (Nashville: Broadman, 1991), 27, emphasis in original.
[3]Ibid.
[4]Ibid., 28, emphasis in original.
[5]George Barna, *Marketing the Church* (Colorado Springs, CO: NavPress, 1988).
[6]Ibid., 30.

church is, among other things, reaching people for Christ, then we will discern the best ways to reach these people. Whether by word of mouth, newspaper advertisement, direct mail, or many other methods to reach the unchurched, the church has involved itself in marketing. The problem for most is terminology. Much of what Barna advocates under the name of marketing is the same activity that many churches call "outreach."

Traditional marketing approaches of churches have been home visitation, passive media (e.g. a sign in front of the church), and paid passive media, such as newspaper advertisement. Barna's research has shown that these tactics are of little value in getting people to our churches.

The approaches that do appear to have some success are personal invitation, small groups, and programs that meet needs. It is my conviction that these three are so important that most churches today should be channeling much more of their resources in these directions. The small group is so important that its effectiveness will be discussed again later in this chapter.

Barna also sees effectiveness in telemarketing and direct mail, but the level of success depends on the quality of the effort: "Direct mail can work well for the church. However, with the average household now receiving in excess of 1,500 unsolicited pieces of mail per year, it takes a polished, professional piece to cut through the clutter and make such a significant impression that it will alter an established behavior pattern. If your mailing is done amateurishly, you will undoubtedly lose your shirt in the process. If it is handled professionally you might emerge a winner."[7]

New Residents

A number of churches discover prospects through new residents who move into the community. Several companies provide lists of newcomers at a modest cost. Newcomers are often receptive to churches or the Christian faith at their time of dislocation. A move to another area is a "crisis

[7]Ibid., 115.

event," a time when the newcomer is open to other changes, such as changes to a new church or to receiving Christ. A church that pursues a strategy to reach new residents must be persistent. Contacting one thousand families yearly may result in ten new families added to the church. This method of outreach, if used with other approaches, could provide a steady flow of prospects.

Surveys

Surveys can be effective if their purpose is to meet the needs of the unchurched, and if they do not violate the privacy of the unchurched. On the next page is a copy of the survey Green Valley Baptist uses in the community. The steps we follow are the following:

1. We knock on a door and ask the person to complete a survey after we leave.

2. We state that the purpose of our survey is to meet community needs.

3. After they complete the survey, we ask them to leave it on the doorknob (the survey has a perforated top that enables it to be hung in this fashion).

4. We return to pick up the survey within an hour, without further disturbing the resident.

5. If the resident requested any activities or information, we follow up at an appropriate time. For example, we were very surprised at the number of women requesting aerobic classes. We began offering two classes that filled up immediately. We, of course, sent letters to those who requested the class. This class provided an entry point into the church for many who would not otherwise come.

6. We send a thank-you note to everyone who responded.

We have had good success with this method of outreach. The key is the ability to fulfill the promise to meet a need. If the prospect comes to our church and feels that we are not all we said we were, the chasm is bigger and the alienation is greater.

Sample Survey Form

Thank You . . .

. . . for taking the time to complete this simple information card. When you have completed the information, please place this card on your door, and we will return within the hour and pick it up.

Green Valley Baptist Church
1815 Patton Chapel Road — Hoover
Dr. Thom Rainer, Pastor

Family Name:_____
Address:_____
Phone: _____Zip_____
Person completing this form: _____

Family Members
Name   -   Age
Head of
House:_____
Spouse:_____
Children: _____
          _____
          _____

What do you think is the greatest need in our area?
_____
_____
_____

Why do you think most people do not attend church?
_____
_____
_____

(over)

If you were looking for a church, what kinds of things would you look for?
_____
_____

Please check any activities you would like to see offered to meet the needs of our area:
___Home Bible Studies
___Aerobics/Fitness Classes
___Saturday Evening Worship Services
___Sporting Activities
___Topical Studies
___Summer Christian Education for Children
___Mothers Day Out
___Marriage Enrichment Seminars
___Single Parents Ministry
___Parents Night Out
___Youth Activities
___Financial Planning
___Big Brother/Big Sister
Others: _____
_____
_____

I'd like information on:
___How to become a Christian
___Adult Bible Studies
___Children's Bible Studies
___Singles Activities
___Youth Activities
___Spiritual Growth
___Green Valley Baptist Church
___Please Place Me On Your Mail-Out

We at Green Valley care about you and our community. Would you let us know how we can help you?

Comments, Requests or Prayer Needs:
_____
_____
_____

(over)

Life-style Evangelism

These next two methods of finding prospects depend on building relationships. They are not quick solutions. The pastor or other leader must view this process as long-term. If these methods are successfully implemented, the benefits not only include more prospects, but eventually more fully assimilated and productive church members.

When we speak of life-style evangelism, we refer to a life that is growing and maturing in Christ, while letting the words and deeds of that life draw others to Christ. What can the church do to engender life-style evangelism, where the members naturally bring and attract the unchurched to the church? This question is of critical importance since almost three-fourths of church members began attending at the invitation of a member or a friend.[8]

Hadaway notes four critical factors in infusing the church with an atmosphere that produces evangelistic life-styles.[9] The first is emphasizing the eternal importance of evangelism: an open, evangelistic spirit. The members must see that sharing their faith is a natural overflow of the Christian life.

Second, evangelistic training must be an ongoing ministry of the church. As was noted in chapter 22, the role of Evangelism Explosion or Continuing Witness Training is changing, but that does not preclude the necessity for training our members in how to share their faith. The training must be used in the everyday lives of the members.

Third, our churches must have something worthwhile for the guests who do finally come to our churches. If our members capture the spirit of life-style evangelism while our worship services are dull and dry, the invitations to come will quickly cease, and church members will become discouraged.

Finally, we must encourage new Christians to share their new-found faith. Hadaway explains:

> New Christians are generally more enthusiastic about their relationship with Christ than anyone else, and they have more contacts with persons who are not in church.

[8]Hadaway, 30.
[9]Ibid., 30-31.

Further, the sudden change in the lives of new Christians gives non-Christian friends dramatic evidence of the power of God . . . . The process usually occurs naturally, out of the new Christian's excitement about his or her relationship with Christ. All that is generally needed is the "permission" of the church to witness—even though the new believer may know little about the Bible or about "proper witnessing techniques." The expectation that all Christians should be witnesses out of the overflow of their thankfulness to God may be all that is needed to free new Christians to share their faith.[10]

Small Groups

In chapter 29, when we look at the full scope of small groups and their potential, we will see the multiple benefits of this ministry. As a tool for securing prospects, small groups may prove to be the outreach method of the future. In the small groups meeting from our church, each group keeps a vacant chair in the presence of all group members. This vacancy reminds the participants that each of them has a responsibility to bring others in the group. Since entry into the group will most likely result from relationships at work, in school, in a club, or in the neighborhood, these prospects will have a high probability of one day being fully assimilated into the church.

The Two Controversial Principles: Homogeneous Units and Receptivity

The Church Growth Movement has received an enormous amount of criticism for attempting to find prospects through receptivity and homogeneity. Because these principles are so controversial, we will take the entire next chapter to discuss and evaluate their roles.

Evaluation

Churches that obey the Great Commission are "going" churches, they seek to find prospects rather than waiting for

[10]Ibid., 31.

prospects to come to them. Though each method discussed in this chapter has strengths, the most successful approaches begin with developing relationships. Because our society is becoming a society of isolationists, the need for relationship evangelism increases daily.

Relationship building emanates from our Lord's command to "love one another" (1 John 3:11). If an unloved world can sense true love in our lives, they will be drawn to us. Like the Philippian jailer who could not fathom the sacrificial joy and love of Paul and Silas, they too may ask us: "What must I do to be saved?" (Acts 16:30).

Suggested Reading for Chapter 24

Barna, George. *Marketing the Church.* Colorado Springs, CO: NavPress, 1988.

McIntosh, Gary and Glen. *Finding Them, Keeping Them: Effective Strategies for Evangelism and Assimilation in the Local Church.* Nashville: Broadman, 1992.

Rainer, Thom S., ed. *Evangelism in the Twenty-First Century.* Wheaton, IL: Shaw, 1989. See especially chapter 5, "Lifestyle Evangelism," by Paige Patterson.

Ratz, Calvin, Frank Tillapaugh, and Myron Augsburger. *Mastering Outreach and Evangelism.* Portland, OR: Christianity Today and Multnomah, 1990.

Tillapaugh, Frank. *The Church Unleashed.* Ventura, CA: Regal, 1982.

25

Receptivity and Church Growth

The two previous chapters have dealt with getting people into the church, what is commonly known as "opening the front door." This chapter is somewhat of an appendage to that theme. We are specifically looking at two principles of "opening the front door" that have evoked much discussion and debate. It must be understood that these principles, especially the homogeneous unit principle, are not necessarily primary principles of church growth. I have heard some critics of the Church Growth Movement equate the homogeneous unit principle with the totality of church growth. To the contrary, I see very little written in church growth literature today on homogeneity.

A book on church growth, however, would be incomplete without some discussion of these principles. The reader may notice the more technical approach of this chapter compared with the other chapters on principles. This approach is necessary because critics must be heard, answered, and properly footnoted.

The Principle of Receptivity

Focusing on receptive people has been viewed as a great contributor to church growth. George G. Hunter, III called church growth's awareness and evangelization of receptive peoples "Church Growth Movement's greatest contribution to this generation's world evangelization."[1] C. Peter Wagner believes "that at a given point in time certain people groups, families, and individuals will be more receptive to the

[1]George G. Hunter, III, *The Contagious Congregation: Frontiers in Evangelism and Church Growth* (Nashville: Abingdon, 1979), 104.

message of the Gospel than others."[2] This perspective is
called the "resistance-receptivity theory."

Wagner's pragmatism becomes clearly evident here. The
theory postulates that resources of time, personnel, and
money should be focused where there is greatest receptivity
to the gospel. "Although God can and does intervene and
indicate otherwise, it only makes good sense to direct the
bulk of the available resources to the areas where the
greatest numbers are likely to become disciples of Jesus
Christ."[3] Wagner does not advocate neglecting resistant
areas, but these areas should receive lesser resources than
receptive areas.

Wagner finds biblical justification for the principle of
receptivity in what he labels "the harvest principle" of the
Bible: the fundamental principle of farming is that of the
harvest. It is the vision of the fruit. The farmer's goal is to
gather in a crop of whatever he planted. Jesus assumed this
when He spoke to His disciples about the harvest: "Lift up
your eyes and look at the fields, for they are already white
for the harvest!" (John 4:35). He mentioned that in some
cases one person sows the seed while another gathers the
fruit, but they rejoice together because their combined labors
have resulted in a harvest (John 4:36-37).[4]

Wagner cites Jesus' parable of the sower whose seeds fell
into four places (see Matt. 13:1-23). Only one of the four
places was a fruitful location for the seed. The seed (the
Word of God) that fell on good ground produced fruit in
great quantities (Luke 8:11). The "soil," according to this
interpretation, is "people who have been so prepared that
they hear the word and understand it."[5]

Wagner concluded that effective strategies of evangelism
attempt to identify the most receptive people. "Soil testing"
should also be used to evaluate present allocation of
resources and methodologies. If results are good, (for
example, if numerical increases are evident) significant

[2]C. Peter Wagner, *Church Growth and the Whole Gospel: A Biblical Mandate*
(San Francisco: Harper & Row, 1981), 77.
[3]Ibid., 77-78.
[4]C. Peter Wagner, *Strategies for Church Growth* (Ventura, CA: Regal, 1987), 59.
[5]Ibid., 62.

allocation of resources should continue. "If they are not, emotional ties should not prevent us from scrapping any methodology which is not working."[6]

Wagner cites Jesus' own ministry. Jesus said, "The harvest truly is plentiful but the workers are few. Ask the Lord of the harvest, therefore, to send out workers into his harvest field" (Matt. 9:37-38). Wagner views this pronouncement as a clear indication that Jesus mandated the need for large numbers when the harvest is ripe.[7] Jesus Himself established a strategy of evangelism for His disciples. In Matthew 10:11-14, He instructed the disciples to test the receptivity of a city or town. If the disciples were not received by the people, they were to depart from the place and shake the dust from their feet. "Shaking off dust was a culturally-recognized sign of protest, in this case protesting resistance to the gospel."[8]

Wagner cannot be a theologian without also being an activist. His pragmatic approach to church growth precludes the luxury of theologizing alone. He must act on his theology. How does one then implement an evangelistic strategy based on the principle of receptivity?

Wagner credits Edward R. Dayton for producing the most widely used "resistance-receptivity axis." This axis is used now by the Strategy Working Group of the Lausanne Committee for World Evangelization.

Resistance/Receptivity Scale[9]

Highly Resistant to the Gospel									Highly Receptive the Gospel
-5	-4	-3	-2	-1	0	+1	+2	+3	+4	+5
Strongly Opposed		Somewhat Opposed		Indifferent			Somewhat Favorable		Strongly Favorable

---

[6]Ibid., 64.

[7]Ibid., 67.

[8]Ibid.

[9]This scale comes from Wagner, *Strategies for Church Growth*, 78. See also 78-86 for Wagner's detailed discussion of the three receptive areas. Wagner cites his source as Edward R. Dayton, *That Everyone May Hear*, 2nd ed. (Monrovia: MARC, 1980), 47.

One church growth strategy is to discover where receptive people are located, especially those on the furthest right of the scale. The research of Wagner and others produced three areas where the most gospel-receptive people are probably located.

Receptivity should first be expected where churches are already growing. Although such an area may already have a number of churches, it is likely that a large number of people there are still unchurched yet gospel-receptive.

A second likely area of receptivity is where people are encountering significant change: social change, political change, economic change, or psychological change. More than other groups, these people are responsive to becoming disciples of Christ during periods of change and transition.

The third major group of receptive people is the masses, the common working people and the poor. Wagner said that "religion usually enters society among the masses and works its way up."[10] Specific exceptions to this rule, however, have been recognized. In the United States receptivity to the gospel crosses class lines, but in England the working class is the most resistant.

Church growth strategy then attempts to allocate resources to the most receptive areas. Wagner is adamant that even the resistant fields be allocated resources of people, time, and money, albeit a smaller resource allocation than the receptive fields.

> No church growth advocate I know has ever suggested that we bypass the resistant. The Great Commission says that we are to preach the gospel to all creatures. Donald McGavran from the beginning has taught that we should "occupy fields of low receptivity lightly." In many cases Christian workers can do nothing more than establish a friendly presence and quietly sow the seed. God continues to call many of his servants to do just that, and I am one who supports and encourages them.[11]

[10]Ibid., 84.
[11]Ibid., 88-89. Wagner cites Donald A. McGavran, *Understanding Church Growth*, rev. ed. (Grand Rapids, MI: Eerdmans, 1980), 176-178.

An Evaluation of the Principle
of Receptivity

The pragmatism of the Church Growth Movement is evident in the principle of receptivity. Ralph H. Elliot is a representative critic of this philosophy. He essentially finds two broad problems with the principle. First, because church growth strategists use sociological and anthropological tools to determine receptivity, Elliot finds little emphasis on the sovereignty of God and the role of the Holy Spirit. Second, he believes that the application of the principle would lead to the neglect of the most needy, simply because they are not receptive. He is particularly concerned about the neglect of the city and the church growth preference of the suburbs.[12]

Such critics misunderstand church growth when they fail to see the movement's dependence on the power of God in church growth strategy. Sociology and anthropology should not be set in opposition to the work and power of the Holy Spirit. Human effort does not exclude the work of God. Certainly there is a danger in determining receptive areas if the work is done at a purely human level. Wagner himself recognizes that it "is quite possible for God's servants to become haughty and self-reliant and insensitive to the leading of the Holy Spirit."[13] While such dangers exist, says Wagner, they "should not cause us to overreact and blind ourselves to spiritually-oriented reasons why intelligent strategy planning for church growth should include some predicting."[14]

Elliot's concern about the neglect of the most needy areas assumed that the areas of "the dispossessed and the powerless" will always be the least receptive areas to the gospel. The principle of receptivity does not mean abandoning the lower socioeconomic classes with less political clout. To the contrary, if the people in a poor area are receptive to the gospel, the principle would call for

[12]See Ralph Elliot, *Church Growth That Counts* (Valley Forge, PA: Judson, 1982), 73-77.
[13]Wagner, *Strategies for Church Growth*, 75.
[14]Ibid.

greater focus of resources to that area. Church growth strategists such as Wagner, attempting to fulfill the evangelistic mandate, "direct the bulk of the available resources to the areas where the greatest numbers are likely to become disciples of Jesus Christ."[15]

The Homogeneous Unit Principle

No single tenet of church growth theology has received so much criticism as the homogeneous unit principle.[16] Wagner has advocated the homogeneous unit principle in America. He has thus drawn the brunt of criticism in earlier years as the Church Growth Movement gained momentum in America. He is not, however, the originator of the term, nor is he the first proponent of the principle within the Church Growth Movement. Credit on both accounts goes to Donald McGavran, the father of the movement.

McGavran's Influence

"Men like to become Christians without crossing racial, linguistic, or class barriers."[17] When Donald McGavran began to advocate that principle as a tenet of church growth, an avalanche of criticism and debate ensued. Cries of "racism," "narrow-mindedness," "exclusiveness," and "psychological manipulation" were voiced as a reaction to the much-debated principle. Although McGavran addressed the issue in 1955 in *The Bridges of God,* the tenet was most clearly expressed in *Understanding Church Growth in 1970.* McGavran discussed a sociological observation: differences in human beings and their culture result in difficult

[15]Wagner, *Church Growth and the Whole Gospel,* 77-78.

[16]Church growth rarely uses the terminology "homogeneous unit principle" today because of the highly-emotive responses it evokes. The phrase "people approach to world evangelization" is nearly synonymous with "homogeneous unit principle," and represents his choice of wording. I will continue to use "homogeneous unit" because it is a more familiar phrase to those knowledgeable of church growth, and because it is the wording used in Wagner's landmark book, *Our Kind of People: The Ethical Dimensions of Church Growth in America* (Atlanta: John Knox, 1979).

[17]Donald A. McGavran, *Understanding Church Growth,* rev. ed. (Grand Rapids, MI: Eerdmans, 1980), 223.

barriers: "This principle states an undeniable fact. Human beings do build barriers around their own societies. More exactly we may say that the ways in which each society lives and speaks, dresses and works, of necessity set it off from other societies. Mankind is a mosaic and each piece has a separate life of its own which seems strange and often unlovely to men and women of other pieces."[18]

While such a sociological observation may be readily accepted, the application of the principle to the sharing of the gospel and the growth of the church poses new questions. Is the crossing of societal and cultural barriers a prerequisite for one to become a Christian? Is a propagator of the gospel faithful to the message when he or she limits his or her witness to like-cultural groups? Is an overt attempt to expand homogeneous Christian groups obedience to Christ or discrimination?

It must be recognized that McGavran always taught the unity of all people in Christ. "The biblical teaching is plain that in Christ two peoples become one. Christian Jews and Gentiles became one new people of God, parts of the One Body of Christ."[19] However, McGavran emphasized that "the One Body is complex." Speaking of the first-century church, he says, "Since both people continue to speak separate languages, does not the oneness cover a vast and continuing diversity?"[20] McGavran thus urged that the gospel cross all barriers; but such is not the same as insisting that cultural differences be ignored in the formation of Christian groups: "The principle is also readily discerned when it comes to pronounced class and racial barriers. It takes no great acumen to see that when marked differences of color, stature, income, cleanliness, and education are present, men understand the Gospel better when expounded by their own kind of people. They prefer to join churches whose members look, talk, and act like themselves."[21]

[18]Ibid.
[19]Ibid., 224.
[20]Ibid.
[21]Ibid., 227.

A key to understanding McGavran's devotion to the homogeneous unit principle is found in the latter portion of his statement above: "They prefer to join churches whose members look, talk, and act like themselves." For both McGavran and Wagner, the guiding principle in theology and hermeneutic is the growth of the church and the priority of evangelism. Even McGavran recognized potential abuse of an evangelism that reaches out only to "our kind of people":

> The creation of narrow Churches, selfishly centered on the salvation of their own kith and kin only, is never the goal. Becoming Christian should never enhance animosities or the arrogance which is so common to all human associations. As men of one class, tribe, or society come to Christ, the church will seek to moderate their ethnocentrism in many ways. She will teach them that persons from other segments of society are also God's children. God so loved the world, she will say, that He gave His only Son that *whosoever* believes in Him might have eternal life.[22]

McGavran thus urged the implementation of the homogeneous unit principle for pragmatic reasons: people are more likely to become Christians if they are not required to leave their own group. Yet, he cautions that such a principle "is certainly not the heart of church growth,"[23] nor should it be used to promote or maintain an underlying policy of segregation or class superiority.

Wagner and *Our Kind of People*

Although Donald McGavran is the author of the homogeneous unit principle as a tenet of church growth, C. Peter Wagner was once its most vociferous proponent. Wagner gained this reputation with the publication of *Our Kind of People* in 1979. Even McGavran recognized that his student had become most closely identified with the homogeneous unit principle:

[22]Ibid., 242-243, emphasis in original.
[23]Ibid., 243.

As the debate in America raged concerning the rightness of the Homogeneous Unit, C. Peter Wagner determined to write his doctoral dissertation at the University of Southern California, maintaining that properly understood the concept is thoroughly Christian and very helpful in that discipling of *panta ta ethne* commanded in the New Testament. His dissertation was published in 1979 by John Knox Press—a landmark book entitled *Our Kind of People*. Anyone who wants to probe the depths of the radical turnaround in theory of evangelism and mission which the concept has caused must read this book.[24]

As soon as *Our Kind of People: The Ethical Dimensions of Church Growth* was published, Wagner's theology and hermeneutic were attacked relentlessly. While the furor focused on the contents of the book, the words on the jacket of the book undoubtedly set many people ill at ease before they read the first page: *"Our Kind of People* attacks the Christian guilt complex arising from the civil rights movement and puts it to rest with a skillful mixture of scriptural precedent and human psychology. In doing so, Wagner transforms the statement that '11 a.m. on Sunday is the most segregated hour in America' from a millstone around Christian necks into a dynamic tool for assuring Christian growth."[25] Wagner is introduced on the jacket as "a follower of Donald McGavran, the movement's founder [who] . . . is well researched in his study of the implications of segregated congregations."[26]

To the prospective reader who takes a cursory glance at the jacket, the implications of the book may have seemed shocking. On the surface the reader may have concluded that Wagner was opposed to the civil rights movement, was an ardent supporter of segregation, and proved his points "with a skillful mixture of scriptural precedent and human psychology." Perhaps such language at least partially explained some of the emotional reviews of Wagner's book, such as the review that proclaimed Wagner's theology to be "Evangelism without the Gospel."[27]

[24]Ibid., 239-240.
[25]Wagner, *Our Kind of People,* book jacket.
[26]Ibid.
[27]Tom Nees, "Evangelism Without the Gospel: Church Growth in *Our Kind of People," Sojourners* 9 (February, 1980), 27.

In his book, Wagner challenged the prevailing consensus of many theologians that the integration of churches would be the panacea for church race relations. Liston Pope articulated the point in *The Kingdom beyond Caste,* published in 1957. In it he called the American church "the most segregated major institution in American society."[28] Sunday morning worship, he lamented, "is the most segregated hour in the week."[29] Pope argued that congregational integration must take place to reflect the true nature and purpose of the church. His pessimism about the future of black churches implied that neither black nor white churches should exist. Wagner responded that "Pope does not seem to be concerned with, or even aware of, the possibility that he is advocating ethnocide for black culture in America."[30]

Another influential book was written during the civil rights era of the 1960s. Gibson Winter, in *The Suburban Captivity of the Churches,* viewed segregated, homogeneous churches as "unholy alliance[s] of religious and racial segregation, an alliance whose real purpose is to preserve insulated, residential communities."[31]

As the 1960s drew to a close, some ethicists began to write in ways that resembled Wagner's homogeneous unit principle. In his book *Black Power and White Protestants,* Joseph Hough advocated models of pluralism rather than desegregation and assimilation.[32] Hough argued that the models of integration were little more than token integration of predominantly white churches. The "new Negro pluralism,"[33] however, maintained the dignity and self-determination of black churches. "Thus," concluded Wagner, "the civil rights movement began to affect theologians and ethicists, opening up possibilities for an understanding and application of the homogeneous unit principle in America."[34]

[28]Liston Pope, *The Kingdom beyond Caste* (New York: Friendship, 1957), 105.
[29]Ibid.
[30]Wagner, *Our Kind of People,* 25.
[31]Gibson Winter, *The Suburban Captivity of the Churches: An Analysis of Protestant Responsibility in the Expanding Metropolis,* paperback ed. (New York: Macmillan, 1962), 30.
[32]Joseph C. Hough, Jr., *Black Power and White Protestants: A Christian Response to the New Negro Pluralism* (New York: Oxford, 1968).
[33]Ibid., 212.
[34]Wagner, *Our Kind of People,* 27.

Church Growth and the Whole Gospel, it has been said earlier, was a decisive book and definitive defense of the Church Growth Movement. Wagner's apologia addressed many points, among them the homogeneous unit principle.[35] Two years lapsed between publication of that book and *Our Kind of People.* Wagner therefore had enough time to absorb and address the criticisms. After the publication of *Church Growth and the Whole Gospel,* he reflected on the uproar, defended some of the points, and articulated what he considered to be the most salient issues of the homogeneous unit principle. Since then, however, Wagner has been conspicuously reticent to speak about the principle. The phrase "homogeneous unit" is rare in recent books by Wagner.[36] He believes that too much time has been wasted on a principle that is certainly not the major tenet of the Church Growth Movement.[37]

In *Church Growth and the Whole Gospel,* Wagner made several comments about the homogeneous unit principle and its potential risks. One was the risk of "implicitly placing a seal of approval on segregation, discrimination, racism, the caste system, and apartheid."[38] He noted that Ralph D. Winter made a presentation at the Lausanne Congress on World Evangelization in 1974 on the homogeneous unit principle. A few weeks later Winter heard that his recorded statements were being used in South Africa to demonstrate that Lausanne approved apartheid. Wagner remembered the situation well:

> Winter was shocked. Approving apartheid was so far from Winter's mind that the whole affair seemed ludicrous. But just as a knife can be used as an instrument of mercy in a surgical operation or as an instrument of horror in a murder, the homogeneous unit principle can be used for good or for bad. Properly applied, it can be an effective force to reduce racism; wrongly applied, it can suppport

[35]See Wagner, *Church Growth and the Whole Gospel,* especially 166-183.

[36]In *Strategies for Church Growth,* published in 1987, the words "homogeneous unit principle" do not appear. Its less-revealing synonym, "people approach to world evangelization," appears twice. A year earlier Wagner edited *Church Growth: State of the Art,* in which both phrases appear a total of only five times.

[37]C. Peter Wagner, personal interview, 25 July 1987.

[38]Wagner, *Church Growth and the Whole Gospel,* 169.

racism. It must be admitted that the principle carries with
it an element of risk.[39]

Wagner also recognizes that "homogeneity aids the
evangelistic mandate, heterogeneity aids the cultural
mandate."[40] He believes that evangelism is the first priority.
"If strenuous evangelism means to multiply homogeneous
churches, multiply them . . . . The evangelistic mandate is
more important than the cultural mandate."[41] Wagner also
stresses that believers should be taught "that God's people
are all one in Christ."[42] That is the message in the kingdom
of God:

> In the kingdom of God, a kingdom of *shalom,* there is no
> war, no hatred, no oppression, no exploitation, no racism,
> no xenophobia, no greed, no militarism, no segregation, no
> discrimination, no redlining, no unfair housing practices.
> Kingdom people respect the integrity of cultures other
> than their own and relate to people in other cultures in
> love, mutual concern, and interdependence. They know
> how to share without either subservience or paternalism.
> They enjoy each other's differences while affirming a basic
> human unity. They promote human rights. They work
> diligently toward an open society where people are free to
> make their own choices without coercion.[43]

Those who know Wagner, even if they disagree with his
concept of the homogeneous unit principle, staunchly deny
any hint of racism or cultural superiority in his theology or
his life.[44] However Wagner has not helped himself or the
homogeneous unit principle with statements that may seem
to imply that segregation should be the norm for Christians.
Perhaps had he made two broad statements about
homogeneity the furor would not have been so intense.
First, rapid evangelization takes place best when people of a

[39]Ibid.
[40]Ibid.,170.
[41]Ibid.
[42]Ibid., 170-171.
[43]Ibid., 174-175.
[44]One such example is John M. Perkins, a black leader who disagrees with the
homogeneous unit principle but who affirms Wagner personally. In a conversation
I had with Perkins in 1987, Perkins called Wagner "a gentle Christian man who
knows no racism."

culture share their faith in Jesus Christ with others within their own culture. Second, Christians must not insist that a person abandon his or her culture in order to become a Christian. Such is the essence of the homogeneous unit principle.

An Evaluation of the
Homogeneous Unit Principle

Many critics have reacted emotionally to the homogeneous unit principle. Neither Wagner nor church growth proponents are racists or segregationists, and the critics who make such charges do not understand them or their message. The homogeneous unit principle *is* a controversial concept. It is therefore important to cull through the emotional rhetoric to understand fully its implications.

One of the most cogent arguments against the homogeneous unit principle comes from Rene Padilla in his study of Wagner's hermeneutic. Padilla takes issue with Wagner's assertion that the "spread of Christianity was accomplished among numerous homogeneous units."[45] On the one hand, Wagner argues that the gospel indeed did "transcend racial, cultural, and linguistic barriers, but its spread continued along homogeneous unit lines."[46] His most frequently mentioned example is the Gentiles, who were not required to become Jews in order to become Christians. While Padilla recognized this aspect of the spread of the gospel, he nevertheless emphasized that the "breaking down of the barriers that separate people in the world was regarded as an essential aspect of the gospel, not merely as a result of it."[47] He furthermore believes that Wagner's theology of the homogeneous unit is "a missiology tailor-made for churches and institutions whose main function in society is to reinforce the status quo."[48]

---

[45]C. Peter Wagner, *Our Kind of People,* 113.
[46]Ibid., 124.
[47]C. Rene Padilla, "The Unity of the Church and the Homogeneous Unit Principle," in *Exploring Church Growth,* ed. Wilbert R. Shenk (Grand Rapids, MI: Eerdmans, 1980), 300.
[48]Ibid., 301.

The later Wagner seems in some sense to agree with Padilla, in that he is less vocal about the homogeneous unit today than he was when *Our Kind of People* was published in 1979. He regrets that "the homogeneous unit principle has assumed such proportions that it is considered the sum and substance of the Church Growth Movement."[49] It is also apparent that he has mellowed considerably in his position on the issue. The tone of *Our Kind of People* was that homogeneity was a principle that should be pursued aggressively to assure church growth. Wagner now says homogeneity is "descriptive, not normative . . . phenomenological, not theological."[50] The very fact that Wagner does not claim theological support for a growth strategy of homogeneity is significantly different than his position in *Our Kind of People,* where a biblical apologia is set forth. Wagner stated in *Church Growth and the Whole Gospel* that "the homogeneous unit principle [is] a penultimate dynamic, not an ultimate ideal."[51] Such a statement is strikingly similar to Padilla's perspective of the homogeneous unit principle: "We must admit that at times the witness of separate congregations in the same geographical area on the basis of language and culture may have to be accepted as a necessary, but provisional, measure for the sake of the fulfillment of Christ's mission."[52]

The two positions of the homogeneous unit principle that were seemingly polarized have each moved closer to the middle. Wagner's concept of the principle as "penultimate dynamic" is very close to Padilla's admission that it is "necessary, but provisional." The homogeneous unit is a possible starting point for evangelizing: no one should be required to leave his or her culture to become a Christian. Yet homogeneity is not an ideal state. Once evangelized, said Wagner, "teach believers that God's people are all one in Christ."[53]

---

[49]Wagner, *Church Growth and the Whole Gospel,* 166.
[50]Ibid., 167.
[51]Ibid., 168.
[52]C. Rene Padilla, "The Unity of the Church and the Homogeneous Unit Principle," 301. Padilla quotes Leslie Neubirgin, "What Is 'A Local Church Truly United'?" *The Ecumenical Review,* 29 (April, 1977), 124.
[53]Wagner, *Church Growth and the Whole Gospel,* 170-171.

Suggested Reading for Chapter 25

Elliot, Ralph. *Church Growth That Counts.* Valley Forge, PA: Judson, 1982. This is one of the most-often quoted books critical of the the Church Growth Movement.

Hunter, George G, III. *The Contagious Congregation: Frontiers in Evangelism and Church Growth.* Nashville: Abingdon, 1979.

McGavran, Donald A. *Understanding Church Growth.* 2nd Rev. ed. by C. Peter Wagner. Grand Rapids, MI: Eerdmans, 1990.

Shenk, Wilbert R. *Exploring Church Growth.* Grand Rapids, MI: William B. Eerdmans, 1982. Another largely critical book of the Church Growth Movement, this book includes C. Rene Padilla's chapter attacking the homogeneous unit principle, "The Unity of the Church and the Homogeneous Unit Principle."

Wagner, C. Peter. *Church Growth and the Whole Gospel: A Biblical Mandate.* San Francisco: Harper & Row, 1981.

Wagner, C. Peter. *Our Kind of People: The Ethical Dimensions of Church Growth in America.* Atlanta: John Knox, 1979.

Wagner, C. Peter. *Strategies For Church Growth.* Ventura, CA: Regal, 1987.

26

Planning, Goal Setting, and Church Growth

Does planning and goal setting preclude the sovereignty of God and the leadership of the Holy Spirit? Are churches depending on human strength rather than God's power when they plan? These questions are critical since statistical evidence supports church growth's thesis that planning and goal setting contribute to the growth of the church. C. Kirk Hadaway notes that churches that plan for growth usually experience growth. Of the churches he studied, 69 percent of the growing churches were planning churches, compared to only 32 percent of plateaued churches.[1] Some church growth writers repeat the cliche: "To fail to plan is to plan to fail." Let us look at some of the reasons leaders are urging churches to plan for growth.

Planning for Growth

C. Peter Wagner cites at least six advantages to planning:[2]

1. It increases efficiency. God's resource of time, energy, and money are best used for good stewardship.

2. It permits midcourse corrections.

3. It unites the team with a singular plan and vision. Each member of the team understands his or her role in the vision.

4. It helps measure effectiveness. Progress is measured according to the plans.

[1]C. Kirk Hadaway, *Church Growth Principles: Separating Fact from Fiction* (Nashville: Broadman, 1991), 114.
[2]C. Peter Wagner, *Strategies for Church Growth* (Ventura, CA: Regal, 1987), 32-34.

5.   It makes accountability natural.

6.   It can become a model to help others.

Does having a plan alone naturally engender growth? The answer is a qualified "yes." It is possible that planning can be counterproductive because so much of the energy and enthusiasm can be used in the planning process itself. That is why, urges Bill Sullivan, action needs to follow quickly after the plan has been established.[3]

Planning has several elements. The key element is *vision.* In chapter 19 we examined the critical factor of leadership and how leadership must articulate a vision. From that vision emerges *goals,* the by-products of vision. We will look at goals in detail following this section. Next come *strategies,* which are the specific means by which these goals will be met. Once a specific strategy has been articulated, this plan must be *communicated and owned* by the church. It must become "our plan" instead of the pastor's or the group's. Finally, the plan must be *evaluated and readjusted* on a regular basis, at least annually.

Does such a planning process really contribute to growth? Apparently the answer is "yes." Hadaway's research again affirms the pragmatic value of this approach: "Survey results show that 85 percent of churches which have grown off the plateau have reevaluated their programs and priorities during the past five years, as compared to 59 percent of churches which have remained on the plateau. Similarly, 40 percent of 'breakout churches' have developed a long-range plan, as compared to only 18 percent of continued plateau churches."[4]

While there is a strong positive correlation between planning and growth, the correlation is even higher with goal setting. Goal setting motivates the church to put the plan into action.

Goal Setting

Related to church growth's method of strategy planning is its emphasis on goal setting. Wagner calls it "the awesome

[3]Bill M. Sullivan, *Ten Steps to Breaking the 200 Barrier* (Kansas City, MO: Beacon Hill, 1988), 45.
[4]Hadaway, 120.

power of setting goals."[5] He equates goal setting with faith: "The overwhelming consensus of individuals whom God has blessed with large, growing churches is that it could never be done without the faith required to set goals. I agree with Arthur Adams who says, 'Faith is the most important qualification of a leader. A commitment to something so strong that it shapes the leader's life is contagious.'"[6]

Wagner realizes that goals, to be conducive to church growth, must not be arbitrary. His idea of "good goals" includes five characteristics.[7]

First, goals must be *relevant.* They must be related to the needs of both the church and the community. A goal-setting church has an awareness of its strengths, weaknesses, and ministries.

Second, goals must be *measurable.* A vague goal that cannot be measured over a specified time frame is worthless. Furthermore, Wagner believes that a system of accountability must be built into the goal-setting process.

Third, the goal should be *significant.* "Shy away from meager goals and learn to trust God for the big things."[8] Many churches simply lack the faith necessary for significant growth.

Fourth, the goal must also be *manageable.* "Coming up with pipe dreams and setting ridiculous goals is counterproductive and produces so much frustration that some people who do it no longer want to practice goal setting."[9] Yet Wagner believes it is better to set an ambitious goal and fail, than attempt nothing and succeed.

Finally, goals must be related to both the *pastor and the people* in a local church. The people must demonstrate commitment to goals by giving time, money, and energy.

Why is goal-setting an important tool for church growth? How does goal-setting lead churches to growth? Perhaps more than any other factor, it gives specific direction to the

[5]C. Peter Wagner, *Leading Your Church to Growth* (Ventura, CA: Regal, 1984), 186.

[6]Ibid.

[7]Ibid., 187-190.

[8]Ibid., 188.

[9]Ibid., 189.

vision of the church. Few churches have plans, but even fewer churches set goals to fulfill their plans.

Goal-setting, if it is both challenging and realistic, can produce motivation and excitement. Leaders need to realize that most of our church members are hungering to be a part of a church that makes a difference. If those members can see real evidence that the church and its leadership are committed to new and challenging directions, enthusiasm will be natural and spontaneous.

Goal-setting can make a church future-oriented rather than tradition-bound. Tradition is healthy. It keeps us aware of our heritage and past. It gives us a sense of gratitude for those who have gone before us and for their accomplishments. Traditionalism, however, is unhealthy. It makes the past a point of focus and source of worship. It takes our eyes off what God can do, because we choose to make the way things have been done in the past the way God must work in the future. Traditionalism kills vision because it will not budge from "we've never done it that way before." Goal setting is a way to refocus and to dream again.

Evaluation

The solid evidence suggests that a positive correlation exists between church growth, planning, and goal setting. This evaluation must ask the question: Is such methodology biblically sound? In chapter 9, "Theology Proper and Church Growth," we concluded that human efforts to grow a church do not run counter to a theology that affirms the total sovereignty of God. Still we must ask: Is this a biblical model or a model from another source, such as the business world?

Few critics have argued with church growth's biblical defense of human intervention in spreading the gospel. The point to be considered, however, is the emphasis on strategy planning. Is it a biblical mandate that "is not . . . optional in human life and activity"?[10] Or is the emphasis the result of a pragmatic hermeneutic that leads to strategy planning, because such planning results in numerical growth?

---

[10]Wagner, *Strategies for Church Growth,* 24.

Wagner provides some biblical examples of strategic planning, but his concern is more pragmatic than theological. He contends that Christians must first have a proper relationship with God. If such a relationship exists "we are free to plan strategy using the methods and technology that will best accomplish the work of God in the world."[11] In other words, planning and strategy will result in numerical church growth. The biblical examples of planning strategy that Wagner offers come largely from Proverbs, in which practical advice for regular planning is given.[12] He also perceives Paul to be a pragmatic planner in his strategy to reach the Gentiles.[13]

Rather than accept Wagner's premise that there is a "biblical pattern of consecrated pragmatism [and] . . . strategy planning,"[14] it is probably best to consider strategy planning as more pragmatic than biblical, while affirming its value in church growth endeavors. When Wagner speaks of the advantages of having a strategy for church growth, his points are much like those one would hear in business. His points are not unbiblical, and they are concerned with the goal of winning the most people to Christ. Their sources, however, are more from pragmatic concern than solid biblical evidence.

Church growth advocates also believe that goal setting is a natural activity for people. "It may well be something that God intended for human beings in creation."[15] Wagner likes the pragmatism of goal setting. His empirical studies have concluded that "faith projections" have a positive effect on accelerated church growth. He frequently cites the example of the Yoido Full Gospel Church in Seoul, the world's largest church. Its pastor, Paul Yonggi Cho, firmly believes in goal setting. Wagner remembers his first meeting with Cho in

[11]Ibid., 24.

[12]Wagner cites Proverbs 13:16; 13:19; 16:9; and 18:15 in *Strategies for Church Growth*, 30-31.

[13]Wagner views 1 Corinthians 9 as an example of Paul's pragmatic planning. In *Strategies for Chruch Growth*, 31, he says: "And although he (Paul) himself might have been somewhat uncomfortable, especially with his stratcgy for reaching the Gentiles, he affirms, 'This I do for the gospel's sake' (1 Corinthians 9:23)."

[14]Wagner, *Strategies for Church Growth*, 32.

[15]Ibid., 158.

1976 when the church had "only" 50,000 members. In their initial meeting, Cho told Wagner that his church had a goal of 500,000 members by 1984, the one-hundredth anniversary of Protestantism in Korea. Inadequate facilities were a factor in the failure to reach the goal in 1984, but the church exceeded the 500,000-member mark by 1985.[16]

Planning and goal-setting can be healthy for the church and its growth. In our enthusiastic efforts to plan for the growth of the church, however, we must never attempt to initiate any stage of planning without intense prayer as we seek guidance from the Holy Spirit. The tools of planning and goal-setting can be of tremendous benefit. They can be steps of faith; but they must be guided carefully by the hand of God. If such guidance takes place, planning will be a "foundation using gold, silver, and costly stones." If not, the work will be "wood, hay or straw . . . revealed with fire . . . and burned up." (1 Cor. 3:12-15).

Suggested Reading for Chapter 26

Hadaway, C. Kirk. *Church Growth Principles: Separating Fact from Fiction.* Nashville: Broadman, 1991.

Schaller, Lyle E. *Growing Plans.* Nashville: Abingdon, 1983.

Sullivan, Bill M. *Ten Steps to Breaking the 200 Barrier.* Kansas City, MO: Beacon Hill, 1988.

Wagner, C. Peter. *Leading Your Church to Growth.* Ventura, CA: Regal, 1984.

Wagner, C. Peter. *Strategies for Church Growth.* Ventura, CA: Regal, 1987.

---

[16]Ibid., 158-159. Wagner also lauds the goal-setting efforts of Filipino Christians. "Of all nationalities, Filipinos seem to be as enthusiastic about goal setting as any other." He cited the successful goal-setting work of the Philippine Christian and Missionary Alliance; the Conservative Baptists in the Philippines; the Association of Bible Churches; the Baptist Conference of the Philippines; and the Church of the Nazarene.

27

Physical Facilities
and Church Growth

Some of the most-often asked questions about church growth concern physical facilities. How large should our sanctuary be? When should we have multiple worship services? Do we need to build extra education space? Is our church attractive? Is it non-threatening to guests? Do we have enough parking? What do we do with our huge sanctuary?

It is understandable that church leaders ask such questions. The physical facilities usually represent the largest dollar investment of the church. A mistake in this area could lead to financial disaster.

Some leaders perceive adjustments in church facilities to be the panacea for church growth. I know of a church in Florida that had suffered a seven-year attendance plateau. They made the decision to add new education space and remodel existing education space in hopes of attracting people. After investing several hundred thousand dollars, attendance plateaued and even declined in subsequent months. Now the church's new debt burden left the people discouraged and defeated.

Physical facilities alone cannot set the future course of a church. They can, however, combine with other elements to be a contributing or detracting factor. In this chapter we will look at the facilities from two perspectives: how much is needed for growth and how appearance affects growth.

Room for Growth

An often-heard principle of church growth is that when eighty percent of any facility is in use, it is time to make provisions for more room.[1] This rule-of-thumb is applied typically to five areas: parking, sanctuary, land, nursery (preschool), and education space. When large malls were built, owners made sure that their facilities never completely filled, except perhaps during two or three holiday periods. The owners wanted passersby to know that additional parking was always available and convenient. Such a mentality is common among churchgoers today. A packed sanctuary or parking lot sends the message that there is no more room.

Perhaps the most critical space factor is parking. Once parking is nearly depleted, prospective guests will literally drive away! Before we added a new parking lot at Green Valley Baptist, I actually saw guests drive to our church and then drive away. I wanted to chase after each of them! William Easum adds: "Most relationships are formed outside the neighborhood, such as at work or the health club; America's love affair with the automobile makes it easy for people to drive ten to twenty miles to a church that suits their particular needs; many families attend church in more than one car; more and more Americans are looking for large churches that can offer specialized ministries."[2] However, if they make the drive, they must have parking.

Often a church can solve its building space problems by adding additional services—for example, multiple Sunday School classes and multiple worship services. Indeed, with the baby boomers and baby busters accustomed to options in all phases of their lives, church service options are beneficial even if adequate space is still available. Yet many churches will choose multiple services without considering parking needs. For example, a church that has two worship services and one Sunday School will still have most of the people using the parking lots during Sunday School. If the church opts for two Sunday Schools and two worship services running simultaneously, no parking problems are solved.

---

[1]For example, see William M. Easum, *The Church Growth Handbook* (Nashville: Abingdon, 1990), 79, where he states "Growth Principle Twelve: When 80 Percent of Any Space Is in Use, It Is Time to Start Making Plans for More."
[2]Ibid., 83.

Some churches are attempting innovative parking approaches such as shuttle parking or valet parking. We used shuttle parking before completing our new parking lot. It helped, but the shuttle was at best an interim solution.

For those churches wanting to reach young families, adequate preschool space is a must. Today's discerning parents hesitate to leave their children in a room with wall-to-wall preschoolers. Easum suggests at least thirty square feet for each child in first grade and younger. Twenty square feet is a minimum for an older child, youth, or adult.[3] (See Easum's "ministry audit" on the next pages for space guidelines.)

Creating new space is not the only answer to grow a church. If a church builds well over its present needs, the excess of space creates what social psychologists call the "psycho-spatial dynamics." The excitement of a crowd is replaced by a sense that decline is taking place, even when it is not.[4] Such is the case for both education and worship space.

James Emery White recalls a church experiencing rapid growth that exceeded the capacity of its 300-seat sanctuary. A decision was made to build an 1800-seat auditorium. When the people moved into the new facility, their mood changed from excitement and expectancy to discouragement and defeat. The growth stopped within months.[5] From a viewpoint of growth needs, multiple services are the best option, followed by building which is slightly ahead of projected growth.

Ministry Audit

1. What level of commitment do we expect from our members—high, medium, low?   _____

2. In the past, has our church missed any windows of opportunity?   _____

3. Does our church understand that we can use only 80% of our space?   _____

Ministry Audit from *The Church Growth Handbook*. Copyright © 1990 by Abingdon Press. Excerpted by permission. (Can be ordered through Cokesbury, 1-800-672-1789, ISBN # 0-687-08161-0 @ $14.95)
[3]Ibid, 81.
[4]C. Kirk Hadaway, *Church Growth Principles: Separating Fact from Fiction* (Nashville: Broadman, 1991), 59.
[5]James Emery White, *Opening the Front Door: Worship and Church Growth* (Nashville: Convention, 1992), 50-51.

Ministry Audit
(continued)

4. What is the total and individual square feet of
all our facilities, excluding the sanctuary?
(Measure each class separately, as well as
sanctuary and nursery. Keep records of the
square feet of each to answer #10.)

    _____

    _____

    _____

5. Do we need more worship space?   _____
(Do not estimate or take an architect's word.
Have several people sit down on a pew and
measure what is comfortable, then compute
throughout the sanctuary. Or measure actual
pew lengths and divide by 22 inches.)
  a. Sanctuary capacity: _____
  b. 80% of capacity: _____
  c. Average main attendance: _____
  (If (c) is larger than (b), the answer to #5 is yes.)

6. Is worship capacity more than 50% larger than
Sunday school capacity?   _____

7. Do we need more choir space?   _____
  a. Choir capacity: _____
  b. 80% of capacity: _____
  c. Average main attendance: _____
  (If (c) is larger than (b), the answer to #8 is yes.)

8. Do we need more nursery space?   _____
  a. Nursery capacity: _____
  b. 80% of capacity: _____
  c. Average main attendance: _____
  (If (c) is larger than (b), the answer to #8 is yes.)
  How many personnel at main attendance?   _____
  Is there a nursery for all events?   _____
  Are infants and toddlers separated?   _____
  Are any nursery policies given to mothers?   _____

9. Do we need more education space?   _____
  a. Education capacity from #4:   _____
  b. 80% of capacity: _____
  c. Average main attendance: _____
  (If (c) is larger than (b), the answer to #9 is yes.)

10. Is each Sunday school class under 80%?   _____
(Allow 30 square feet per person for kindergarten
and under; 20 square feet per person for first
grade and up. Draw a floor plan for each level of
each building and show the capacity of each
room and the average attendance of the class.)

Ministry Audit
(continued)

11. Which classes are over 80% or near it? _____
    Do we need to rearrange any of these classes? _____

12. Number of classrooms available: _____
    Number of classrooms presently used: _____

13. Sunday school average attendance for last 20 years including percentage over previous year:

    _____ _____%   _____ _____%
    _____ _____%   _____ _____%
    _____ _____%   _____ _____%
    _____ _____%   _____ _____%
    _____ _____%   _____ _____%
    _____ _____%   _____ _____%
    _____ _____%   _____ _____%
    _____ _____%   _____ _____%
    _____ _____%   _____ _____%
    _____ _____%   _____ _____%

    Sunday School attendance has increased/decreased _____% over the past ten years.

14. Do we have more than one session of Sunday School? _____
    Attendance at each: _____

15. According to the 80% rule, does our church
    need to add space? _____
    If so, where? _____

16. Conclusion: _____
    _____
    _____

1. Does our church own enough land? If less than
   8 acres, is there adjacent property for sale? _____
   We own: _____
   We need: _____

2. Does our congregation understand the radical
   changes in parking needs during the last twenty years? _____

3. Average attendance of largest service: _____
   (If Sunday school and worship occur at the same hour,
   count the total number at that hour.) _____

4. Average number of people per car: _____

5. Paved off-street parking spaces available: _____
   (please count)

6. 80% of the total parking spaces: _____

7. Number of spaces needed to accommodate

attendance: (divide #4 into #3).   _____

8. How many spaces do we need to add?   _____
    (If #7 is larger than #6, more spaces are needed. If #6 is larger than #7, no more
    spaces are needed. Remember—this is an immediate need and does not
    consider future growth. [Note: March 1987 survey reported 2.66 people per
    household. This compares to 2.76 in 1980 and 3.58 in 1970. Source: Bureau of
    the Census, P-20, No. 417])

9. Do people have trouble finding a parking space
    on Sunday morning?   _____

10. Conclusion: _____
    _____
    _____
    _____

Appearance

Every six months I ask a person who has never seen our church to walk inside and outside our church campus. If possible, this person will not be active in a church so that he or she can give us a perspective that a non-Christian may have. I ask the person to take notes; give first impressions; be critical where necessary; and give favorable comments where applicable. My concern is that our church exude quality. A lost person should be able to walk into our church and see that Christians care about their facilities. An unkempt church may convey a lackadaisical attitude about other matters to the unchurched.

The church should take note of its cleanliness in all areas. One church growth consultant told me that he can discover a great deal about a church just by going into the restrooms! Look at the church daily through the eyes of a guest. We who are in the church week after week grow accustomed to the frayed carpet and peeling wallpaper—but it may be the first thing a guest notices.

Lighting and sound can make all the difference in the church, especially in the worship service. The mood and emotions of a service are affected either positively or negatively by sound and lighting. The church should view expenses associated with either as an investment in outreach. Quality in this area often encourages our guests to return.

The comfort of the people attending should be another consideration. We have the most important message in the universe to communicate. Yet our message may not be heard if the temperature and the seating cause discomfort. I like what James White said about most church pews: "Growing up in the church, I often felt that God had nothing to do with the creation of the average pew. Surely it was an invention of the devil to distract me physically so that I could not concentrate on the sermon."[6]

A church that wants to reach the unchurched will have a facility that speaks a friendly welcome to them. The best parking places, other than those reserved for the handicapped, are reserved for guests. When someone parks in a guest parking place, our greeters place a card on the windshield. The card has a schedule of activities on one side and four mints attached on the other side. On the "mint" side, the card reads: "Hoping that your visit at Green Valley Baptist Church leaves a sweet taste" (see the card on the next page). Our staff is asked to park in those places furthest from the building as our example to the members that we care about the lost and the unchurched. Conspicuous signs and friendly greeters meet the guests as they come to our church. In everything we do, we try to put ourselves in the place of first-time guests and ask ourselves if we are really a friendly, welcoming church.

Evaluation

There is a positive correlation, albeit a slight one, between guest-friendly facilities and church growth. Plateaued or declining churches may blame poor facilities, but it is unlikely that improving those facilities will lead a declining church toward growth. "But it should be stressed that any tendency to put hope in the ability of a building to attract people is dangerous. . . .There is no reason why church facilities should not be attractive and well-constructed, but space should be viewed as space which will only be filled through the actions of church members, not through its mere existence."[7]

[6]Ibid., 47.
[7]Hadaway, 131-132.

Card placed on windshield
of cars in guest parking

Hoping that your visit at

Green Valley
Baptist Church

leaves a sweet taste.

GREEN VALLEY
BAPTIST CHURCH
1815 Patton Chapel Road
Birmingham (Hoover), Alabama 35526
822-2173

SUNDAY
Sunday School ....9:15 A.M.
Morning Worship................10:30 A.M.
Discipleship Training ....6:00 P.M.
Evening Worship...................7:00 P.M.

WEDNESDAY
Family Dinner ....5:00 P.M.
Solid Rock (Youth).................6:00 P.M.
Prayer-Bible Study ....6:15 P.M.
Missions and Music .....from 5:45 P.M.

CHOIRS FOR ALL AGES

Sanctuary Choir	Wed.......7:15-8:45 PM	
(Adult)		
Celebration Singers	Sun ....5:30-6:30 PM	
(7th-12th Grade)		
Children's Choirs	Wed ....5:45-6:35 PM	
(1st-6th Grade)		
Preschool Choirs	Wed ......6:00-6:45 PM	
(Age 4 and 5)		

*We were happy to have you
visit with us today and hope
that you will join us again.*

(See Back For Schedule Of Activities)

Another factor that must be considered is small groups; a topic we examine in chapter 29. Momentum is building among American churches that reflects a trend in other nations: rapid growth of small groups that meet outside the church. If such groups become common in American churches, how will that affect the building plans of these churches? Southern Baptist churches will probably continue to emphasize Sunday School, and this will require on-site education space. What will be the shape of those churches that use off-campus small groups in place of Sunday School? For the Southern Baptist churches who opt for a dual Sunday School/small group emphasis: What affect will this approach have on the needs for building space?

The church is experiencing its most rapid changes since the Reformation, and these changes create as many questions as they answer. The shape of church buildings, parking, and other facilities may change significantly in the twenty-first century. This trend bears watching.

Suggested Reading for Chapter 27

Easum, William M. *The Church Growth Handbook.* Nashville: Abingdon, 1990. Easum's "ministry audit" at the end of the book is especially helpful.

Hadaway, C. Kirk. *Church Growth Principles: Separating Fact from Fiction.* Nashville: Broadman, 1991.

White, James Emery. *Opening the Front Door: Worship and Church Growth.* Nashville: Convention, 1992.

28

Assimilation, Reclamation, and Church Growth

Paul and Melissa joined our church with great enthusiasm. They became friends with another young couple in their Sunday School class. They could not say enough good things about their church. Yet after nine months they stopped attending. Sunday School members were diligent in keeping in contact with Paul and Melissa, but their absenteeism continued. Six months after they stopped attending, we received notice that they had joined another Baptist church in our area.

I must admit that I am hurt each time we lose a member to inactivity or another church. I feel like the shepherd who has seen his sheep stray, perhaps never to be found again. In the case of Paul and Melissa, I am grateful that they are active in another church. Most drop-outs leave all church activity for years, perhaps forever.

Later I learned that Paul, who had ambitious career goals, had not been accepted into graduate school. He was embarrassed and did not want to face his peers in Sunday School. The members of the class had certainly done their jobs. What could we have done differently? Was there anything we could have done to keep them?

When churches seek to get people into their fellowship, they are attempting to open "the front door." Keeping those members in the church, active and fulfilled, is called "closing the backdoor." Keeping the backdoor closed is a major problem in most churches today. A church with half of its membership in attendance is considered successful by most standards. Would Jesus be content with half of His followers missing at a given moment? Even if we allow absenteeism for sickness, far too many members are AWOL each week. What can we do to regain the spirit of the early church where Christians "devoted themselves to the . . . fellowship" and where "*all* the believers were together" (Acts 2:42, 44, emphases added)? How can we assimilate new members, and how can we reclaim inactive members? Those are the two "backdoor" questions.

Assimilating New Members

Gary McIntosh and Glen Martin, in their book *Finding Them, Keeping Them,* identify five strategies for assimilation.[1] Friendship with other church members is the first step toward a new member's assimilating into the church. Lyle Schaller says that "there is considerable evidence which suggests that at least one-third, and perhaps as many as one-half, of all Protestant church members do not feel a sense of belonging to the congregation of which they are members. They have been received into membership, but have never felt they have been accepted into the fellowship circle."[2]

Church members obviously need to develop relationships with new members. This is rarely successful with programs. Instead regular emphasis on friendliness and openness motivates members to welcome newcomers into their friendship circles. One family in a church that I pastored in Louisville, Kentucky, invited most new members to a meal in their home. As church leaders encourage and applaud such actions, other members will follow their example.

An even more successful approach is for the relationship with the new member to begin before the new member comes into the church. If we as leaders are succcessful in motivating church members to invite and bring their friends to church, evangelism and assimilation can become one victorious step.

As important as relationships are in closing the backdoor it is important that new members become involved in ministry in

[1]Gary McIntosh and Glen Martin, *Finding Them, Keeping Them: Effective Strategies for Evangelism and Assimilation in the Local Church* (Nashville: Broadman, 1992).

[2]Lyle E. Schaller, *Assimilating New Members* (Nashville: Abingdon, 1978), 16.

the church. A review of chapter 20 might help at this point. Are we as church leaders giving our laity "permission" to start and become involved in ministries? Or is involvement in the church limited to redundant committees, where the committee members are chosen by a select group? Do we encourage or require spiritual gift assessments to involve people in ministry according to their giftedness? Or are we choosing June or John for the kitchen committee because they are not doing anything else? Do we teach, preach, and show that ministry is done by the people of God, rather than by some artificial ecclesiological hierarchy? Ministry involvement, real ministry involvement, is a key to assimilation.

In the next chapter we examine the impact of small groups on various factors, including assimilation. For now it is important to note the beauty of small groups in creating a sense of belonging. What is "small"? Most studies indicate that ten is a maximum size where everyone can have the opportunity to interact with the rest of the group. Sunday School, therefore, can operate within the dynamics of a small group, but only if the class is small. Church members in classes of twenty, thirty, forty, or more are not reaping the benefits of a small group. Though I am not aware of any studies in this area, I sense that small group dynamics may operate better in a non-church location.

The importance of vision has been mentioned frequently in this book, but it cannot be overstated. A clear, Great Commission vision creates a sense of "being on the team." Who has not identified with a sports team that has a vision for being the best? You see fans wearing their hats, displaying their bumper stickers, and naming their children after the stars. A similar dynamic can happen with a church that has a clear, challenging, and exciting vision. New members are assimilated because they identify with the "team" and its vision.

The final key to assimilation, say McIntosh and Martin, is spiritual growth. Such is the discipleship thrust of the Church Growth Movement. The deeper the level of discipleship, the more likely assimilation is to take place. Church leaders must seek innovative and challenging ways for all members to have opportunities to grow in Christ.

Reclamation

If churches effectively integrated all new members, reclamation would not need to be addressed. In a given year a church will lose up to two percent of its attendance due to death, three percent to transfer, and six percent to reversion.[3] For a church of two hundred in attendance, up to twelve people will simply "walk away." Though we will focus in this section on reclaiming those who have drifted away from the church, we must recognize that reclamation is the most difficult type of outreach. Something negative usually preceded their leaving. The negative factor may have been a singular event such as a dispute with another church member. Most dropouts, however, simply became bored with church because they never felt like they were part of the body.[4] Convincing these people that the church still cares for them and has a place for them is difficult at best.

Often reclamation begins with a systematic effort to visit every inactive member. I once thought this would be impossible. Then, in anticipation of a building program, we assembled a large group of church members who visited nearly every home of our members. It was amazing what we could do when we had a financial need! What if we had used those same people to visit the inactives simply to minister?

A word of caution: those who go into the homes of the inactive must be fully trained and prepared. New Christians are best suited for other tasks. Many of these visits will be painful, and the worst perceptions of the church may be conveyed. Church members who make these visits must be prepared to encounter anger, pain, and indifference. They must be willing to listen more than talk. They must keep the perspective that the church is not really so bad as they are hearing; and they must have a Christ-like attitude that conveys to these inactives: "We do care for you."

The best opportunity for reclamation will be reclaiming those who express indifference toward the church. They

---

[3]McIntosh,10.

[4]See for example Carl S. Dudley, *Where Have All Our People Gone?: New Choices for Old Churches* (New York: Pilgrim, 1979).

have no barrier of hostility and hurt to overcome. The inactive person simply does not believe that church is that important. Other areas of life have higher priorities.

Loss of Members Illustration

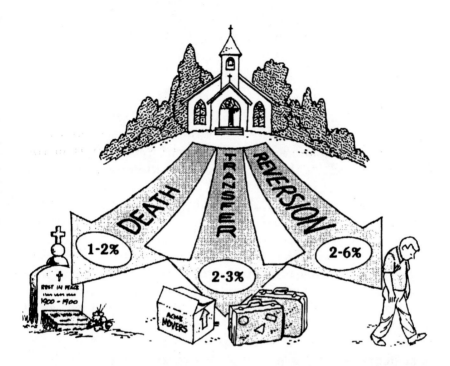

The key to reclamation here is finding some area of the church toward which the inactive may not feel indifferent. For example, some area of the children's ministry may attract the inactive. They may decide to send their sons or daughters to children's choirs, Vacation Bible School, or Sunday School. Baby boomers especially are concerned about the welfare of their children. If the children get involved in the church, the parents may soon follow.

Though evidence is sketchy at this point, there are some indications that small groups may be good re-entry points for the inactive, especially if the small group meets off the church campus. We in our church are looking at the possibility of giving the name of one inactive family to each of our small groups. If a few families come back into the church as a result of this effort, it will be a greater success than anything previously attempted.

One final point to be considered in the attempt to reclaim inactive members: inactive members may not be Christians. Church membership is not the final certification for the Lamb's book of life. If our church members attempt to visit inactives, they should ever be aware of evangelistic opportunities.

Evaluation

If I understand Jesus' parable of the prodigal son correctly, our Lord rejoices when one of His children returns "home." (Luke 15:11-32). When we seek to assimilate new members, we are attempting to keep the "children" from leaving. When we seek to reclaim the inactive, we are attempting to get the "children" to return.

Though inactive members should never be forgotten, prevention is much easier than reclamation. A multilevel ministry of assimilation from the day a person expresses interest in our churches will reduce dramatically our inactive roles. Sadly, most churches today are cumbered with a bureaucracy that hinders assimilation and excludes newcomers.

Also, leaders must accept the fact that they will lose some church members to other churches. Once a vision becomes clear and a style of ministry established, membership transfers are inevitable. Rather than becoming burdened over the loss, we must learn to praise God that His children are in another church with which they identify and can best make a contribution. Yet some members will leave because a clearly cast vision shakes them from their comfort zones and the status quo. Such losses are reasons for sorrow, for those people have considered the cost of discipleship and decided that the cross was too heavy to carry (Mark 8:34).

Suggested Reading for Chapter 28

Hadaway, C. Kirk. *Church Growth Principles: Separating Fact from Fiction.* Nashville: Broadman, 1991. See chapter 8.

Hadaway, C. Kirk. *What Can We Do about Church Dropouts?* Nashville: Abingdon, 1990.

McIntosh, Gary and Glen Martin. *Finding Them, Keeping Them: Effective Strategies for Evangelism and Assimilation in the Local Church.* Nashville: Broadman, 1992.

Schaller, Lyle E. *Assimilating New Members.* Nashville: Abingdon, 1978.

29

Small Groups
and Church Growth

The first Christian church met in the homes of the believers, where they broke bread "and ate together with glad and sincere hearts" (Acts 2:46). Such was the pattern of the church of the past. Carl F. George predicts that the church of the future may return to a structure very similar to that first church at Jerusalem: large enough to win thousands but small enough to have a personal touch. "It is my contention," said George, "that our present models for doing ministry are ineffective and inadequate for the opportunities that are coming our way. If Christian churches are to receive the harvest of souls that we believe God is calling to enter His kingdom, it will happen only because churches have reorganized their structures. They must be large enough to make a difference and yet small enough to care."[1]

The small group concept is one of the most discussed topics in American church growth today. For years it was seen as a strategy best suited for churches in other lands, but the small group concept is spreading rapidly in the United States. It is no longer viewed as the successful aberration of Paul Yonggi Cho's church in South Korea. Many pastors and church growth leaders consider small groups a return to the basics of the early church.

A modern-day model of the power of small groups is the church in China. The Communists seized power in the 1950s, expelling all missionaries and persecuting the Chinese Christians who numbered about one million. Most observers feared that Communists had nearly eliminated

[1]Carl F. George, *Prepare Your Church for the Future* (Tarrytown, NY: Fleming H. Revell, 1991), 23.

the Christian presence. To the surprise of many, Christians in China thirty years later numbered between thirty and one hundred million! The church had multiplied as much as one hundred times! The Chinese Christians had no church buildings, few trained pastors, and few Bibles. The Chinese Christians testified about their life of persecution over thirty years and attributed their survival to prayer and the spread of the gospel through house churches—small groups.

A form of small groups has dominated the American church scene for most of the twentieth century: the Sunday School. Though Sunday School is not always viewed as a small group, the two ministries have enough similarities to be considered part of the same family. Yet Sunday School is largely an *on-campus* small group, while the term "small group" usually refers to gatherings *off campus.*

Sunday School

A brief historical overview

The Sunday School movement originated in England in the late 1700s. Robert Raikes, editor of the *Gloucester Journal,* hired teachers for impoverished children. The movement quickly moved to the United States and was aided by other movements pushing for social reform. Just before the beginning of the nineteenth century, Sunday Schools had spread to Massachusetts, New York, Pennsylvania, Rhode Island, and New Jersey. Their primary role was educating children, especially those employed in factories.

After 1800 the purpose of Sunday School expanded to both education and evangelism. The first national Sunday School effort began in 1824. The American Sunday-School Union's stated purpose was to organize, evangelize, and civilize. The Union trained leadership, published literature, and formed thousands of Sunday Schools by 1880.

Though the Sunday School movement began by educating children, in America, it became the teaching, nurturing, and evangelizing arm of the church for all ages as the nineteenth century closed. Sunday School outreach was especially effective. By 1900, about eighty percent of all new church members first came to the church through Sunday School.[2]

Though many denominations and churches have used Sunday School effectively in their churches, no body has been so consistently successful at applying Sunday School principles as the Southern Baptist Convention. Early in the twentieth century, Arthur Flake and J. N. Barnett led the Sunday School focus. As the century comes to a close, Andy Anderson and Harry Piland are among the modern prophets of Sunday School. A recognized leader outside of the Southern Baptist ranks, Elmer Towns continues to be a leader promoting the Sunday School message today.

Many consider Sunday School the teaching, nuturing, *and* evangelizing arm of the church. Because of its versatility and strength, it has been the "front door" through which people have been introduced to a church. James Emery White notes, however, that the "front door" has shifted from Sunday School to worship. No longer are most new members introduced to the church through the Sunday School; their first encounter is the worship service. In Southern Baptist churches, average worship attendance now exceeds average Sunday School attendance by over twenty-six percent. The gap is even wider in many other denominations.[3]

The future of Sunday School

What are the implications for the future of Sunday School? Some predict the eventual demise of Sunday School. Others assert that no significant change will take place, that Sunday School will be as dominant and healthy as ever. Neither of these scenarios is likely. Though the shape of Sunday School may change in the twenty-first century, it will continue in many of our fastest-growing and strongest churches.

Sunday School should continue because it is still the best way to teach the Bible on a regular and systematic basis.

[2]J. L. Seymour, "Sunday-School Movement," in *Dictionary of Christianity in America,* ed. Daniel G. Reid, (Downers Grove, IL: InterVarsity, 1990), 1146-1147.

[3]James Emery White, *Opening the Front Door: Worship and Church Growth* (Nashville: Convention, 1992), 16-18.

While Bible studies are available in off-campus small groups, Sunday School still offers the most consistent model for *all* age groups. Children especially benefit from Sunday School.

The Sunday School model is still an outstanding tool for church growth. Flake's fivefold method of growth continues to be effective: (1) find the people; (2) provide the space; (3) equip leadership; (4) enlarge the organization; and (5) divide and multiply. Ken Hemphill's discovery of the church growth value of Sunday School came as a revelation to him: "Why should I create all sorts of new organizations when I have an exciting organization that already embraces acknowledged church-growth principles: Sunday School?"[4]

One of the challenges facing Sunday School in the twenty-first century is the need for space. Education space can limit growth while building for additional space is expensive. Unlike off-campus small groups, which have no space restrictions, Sunday School cannot grow any faster than the space allows. Multiple Sunday Schools are an option; but even then a saturation point is inevitable in rapid growth. An alternative is to have some Sunday School classes off-campus and on days other than Sunday. In such cases, the Sunday School begins to look much like off-campus small groups.

Another challenge facing Sunday School is its ability to be the evangelistic arm of the church. The unchurched are apparently more willing to try a church initially in the comfort and anonymity of a large worship service rather than a Sunday School class. Those unchurched who are willing to enter a small group often prefer the less-threatening environment of a home or other non-church site.

Is it possible then that the role of Sunday School may be shifting to retention more than outreach? Or to use church growth vernacular, will Sunday School become a method of closing the "back door" instead of opening the "front door"? The strength of the Sunday School movement for two centuries has been its ability to adjust to the changing world while remaining true to God's Word. From a movement designed to educate impoverished children to a multipurpose

---

[4]Ken Hemphill and R. Wayne Jones, *Growing an Evangelistic Sunday School* (Nashville: Broadman, 1989), 16.

group system for all ages, Sunday School has been a dynamic factor in church growth. With off-campus small groups growing exponentially across the United States, it will be interesting to see how the two movements will relate to each other in the twenty-first century.

Small Groups

Carl F. George, director of the Charles E. Fuller Institute of Evangelism and Church Growth, is one of America's most outspoken proponents of small groups. In his book *Prepare Your Church for the Future,* he states his case:

> I believe that the smaller group within the whole—called by dozens of terms, including the *small group* or the *cell group*—is a crucial but underdeveloped resource in most churches. It is, I contend, the most strategically significant foundation for spiritual formation and assimilation, for evangelism and leadership development, for the most essential functions that God has called for in the church . . . . It's so important that everything else is to be considered secondary to its promotion and preservation.[5]

Advantages of small groups

What strengths do small groups have that may not be present in other church groups such as Sunday School? One decided advantage is the lack of space restrictions. Small groups meet in homes, offices, schools, or anywhere people gather. Related to that advantage is the freedom expressed by many participants of being away from the church campus. The very presence of the church edifice can be uncomfortable, especially to the unchurched.

Small groups also help develop deeper levels of trust that help participants share. Much of what takes place in Sunday School tends to be abstract. We can study the authorship of Hebrews and the rebellion of the Israelites without ever seriously considering where we are with Jesus. The small

[5]George, 41.

group has us developing intimacy and sharing; this can be life changing.

How many church leaders have searched in vain for a way to assimilate new members or prospects? We are told that involvement in ministry and the development of relationships are critical for a person to develop a sense of belonging. Both ministry and relationship development takes place in the small group. Often before declaring official church membership, a person is well assimilated into the church through a small group.

Another issue is pastoral care. For almost a decade, C. Peter Wagner and Lyle Schaller have been teaching that pastors must become "ranchers" looking after "shepherds" who, in turn, look after "sheep."[6] The sheep are shepherded, but the rancher does not do it—he sees that the ministry gets done. Many pastors have enthusiastically endorsed this shepherding ministry, but they have had little success in finding shepherds. The small group method can provide more pastoral care than most churches and leaders ever thought possible.

The New Hope example

Some small groups have explosive evangelistic potential. One of the most effective small group ministries for evangelism is that of the New Hope Community Church in Portland, Oregon.[7] Begun by pastor Dale Galloway in 1972, the church grew to five thousand members. The most rapid growth came *after* the tenth anniversary of the church. From 1982 to 1990 membership increased by four thousand members. The key to the growth has been the outreach of about five hundred small groups.

New Hope's groups are TLC cells, which means "tender loving care" groups. The stated threefold purpose of the TLC group is discipling, evangelizing, and shepherding.

---

[6]See C. Peter Wagner, *Leading Your Church to Growth* (Ventura, CA: Regal, 1984), 58-60, and Lyle E. Schaller, *Survival Tactics in the Parish* (Nashville: Abingdon, 1977), 53.

[7]This information on New Hope Community Church came from Elmer Towns, *Ten of Today's Most Innovative Churches* (Ventura, CA: Regal, 1990), 71-88.

Each group is given the goal of bringing a new family to Christ every six months. Galloway regularly motivates them to give priority to evangelism. The cell group system began with one group for every ten members. By 1990, 4,800 persons were in weekly attendance in 485 groups. The one-to-ten ratio has remained constant for nearly 20 years.

Early in this book we examined three types of growth: transfer, biological, and conversion. It is fascinating to see the type of church growth New Hope has experienced. Approximately eighty percent of the people now at New Hope have never before been in church. Most of them were lost. Small groups have made New Hope Community Church one of the most evangelistic churches in the nation! The key is not a confrontational soul-winning method, but "side-door evangelism." Small groups are a "point of entry" where an attempt is made to "win a hearing" first. Only after the group has won the trust and perhaps met a need of the individual does a verbal presentation of the gospel take place.

New Hope Community Church has grown through small groups but has also kept the Sunday School in place. The Sunday School meets at the same time as both morning services. The emphasis is placed on a strong children's Sunday School, although many adult elective and ongoing classes are offered.

The structure of small groups

Churches with successful small groups tend to have strong leadership, organization, and accountability. Some churches follow the *Jethro model.*[8] In Exodus 18:13-23, Moses' father-in-law helped him establish an organization to meet needs of the Israelites. Jethro organized each of the two million Israelites into groups of ten with a leader placed over each group. A leader of fifty then would be over five group leaders. Next were leaders of one hundred, then finally leaders of one thousand.

Churches with trained leadership, an organization similar to the Jethro model, and a report system for accountability

[8]See for example, Robert E. Logan, *Beyond Church Growth* (Old Tappan, NJ: Fleming M. Revell, 1989), 133-135.

are today's most effective small-group models. New Hope Community Church uses five levels: lay people, lay pastors, lay pastor leaders, district pastors, and the senior pastor. All leaders complete a weekly report on their ministry. This promotes a unified ministry. No lay pastor can remain a lay pastor without submitting to this level of accountability through weekly reports.

The future of small groups

Small groups are fast becoming the norm. Carl F. George calls this model the "Meta-Church system." (The word "meta" means "change" and is not to be confused with megachurch.) The Meta-Church model is applicable to any congregation, large or small. The requisites, says George, are willingness to have "both a *change of mind* about how ministry is to be done and a *change of form* in the infrastructure of the church."[9]

Small groups will continue to grow worldwide well into the twenty-first century. The small group phenomenon largely results from our highly impersonal society. In the early church, people caring for one another, eating in each other's homes, and giving out of love was the norm. Today city-dwellers do not know even the names of the family living three houses down the street.

My wife Jo was raised on a farm in rural Alabama. I was amazed how well her family knew neighbors who lived several miles away. Those neighbors would walk into the home of my in-laws, Arthur Clyde and Nell King, without announcement. There was intimacy between neighbors despite the distance that separated them. Neighbor was always available to help neighbor.

Findley Edge describes today's American life-style in contrast with our rural heritage:

> Today, however, in our urban setting with our urban life-style, we are exceedingly close physically, but we are miles apart emotionally and relationally. In our cities with their bumper-to-bumper traffic, with office and apartment

[9]George, 57, emphasis in original.

buildings towering overhead seemingly about to engulf all that is below, we are like worms in the can, crawling all over each other but never touching one another. A family in a high-rise apartment scarcely knows the family living in the next apartment and certainly does not know (and does not care to know) the ones who live on the floor above or below. And, so we move closer to a society in which we are just a number. But eventually our very nature rebels against this. We were not made to be a number; we were made for community. Thus, in a society that is becoming increasingly impersonal, the small group provides a setting in which I can be a *human* being in a relationship and not merely an animal who simply exists. I can know and be known. I can love and be loved.[10]

Evaluation

It is difficult, if not impossible, to discern one particular type of church organization from Scripture. The pattern of a healthy church, however, can be gleaned from several passages of Scripture. Acts 2:42-47 is often cited as an example of a healthy church. Characteristics include teaching, fellowship, prayer, miracles, giving, meeting needs, praise, evangelism, and assimilation. Romans 12:10, Ephesians 4:2, and Ephesians 4:32 add to the list devotion, self-sacrifice, humility, gentleness, patience, love, kindness, compassion, and forgiveness. Galatians 6:2 includes the characteristic of caring for each other's burdens: "Carry each other's burdens, and in this way you will fulfill the law of Christ." First Thessalonians 5:11 adds to the functions encouragement and edification: "Therefore encourage one another and build each other up, just as in fact you are doing."

These are a few of the passages that direct the body of believers toward their God-given roles. As you scan the characteristics of the church above, it is difficult to see how any structure other than small groups can best fulfill these needs. They allow for the ministry to a few by a few, rather than one or a few staff members attempting to meet the

[10]Findley B. Edge, "Introduction," in William Clemmons and Harvey Hester, *Growth through Groups* (Nashville: Broadman, 1974), 14, emphasis in original.

needs of hundreds or thousands. Christ Himself limited His immediate ministry group to the twelve. This is a pattern for Christians today.

When we speak of small groups, we still must resolve the issue of the type of small group. The two broad areas mentioned at the onset of this chapter were on-campus small groups (usually the Sunday School) and off-campus small groups. Apparently off-campus groups best meet the needs of nurturing, pastoral care, and discipleship; Sunday School is the best educational arm of the church, especially for children. Though it cannot be stated with certainty, the church of the future may experience explosive growth through off-campus small groups while providing systematic Bible education through on-campus units, which many churches will continue to call Sunday School. An unanswered question concerns space. If unrestricted growth takes place off-campus, how will the church of the future handle on-campus space needs for worship and education? The church has met other challenges for two thousand years. There is no reason to believe Spirit-led innovations will not meet the challenges of the twenty-first century.

Suggested Reading for Chapter 29

Arnold, Jeffrey. *The Big Book on Small Groups.* Downers Grove, IL: InterVarsity, 1992.

Clemmons, William and Harvey Hester. *Growth through Groups.* Nashville: Broadman, 1974. See also the introduction by Findley B. Edge.

Easum, William M. *The Church Growth Handbook.* Nashville: Abingdon, 1990. See especially his material on "growth principle two," where he speaks of choices and growth in Sunday School.

George, Carl F. *Prepare Your Church for the Future.* Tarrytown, NY: Fleming H. Revell, 1991.

Hemphill, Ken and R. Wayne Jones. *Growing an Evangelistic Sunday School.* Nashville: Broadman, 1989.

Jones, R. Wayne. *Overcoming Barriers to Sunday School Growth.* Nashville: Broadman, 1987.

Logan, Robert E. *Beyond Church Growth.* Old Tappan, NJ: Fleming H. Revell, 1989.

Neighbour, Ralph W. *Where Do We Go from Here?: A Guidebook for the Cell Group Church.* Houston: Touch, 1990.

Peace, Richard. *Small Group Evangelism.* Downers Grove, IL: InterVarsity, 1985.

Seymour, J. L. "Sunday School Movement," in *Dictionary of Christianity in America.* Ed. Daniel G. Reid. Downers Grove, IL: InterVarsity, 1990.

Towns, Elmer L. *How to Grow an Effective Sunday School.* Lynchburg, VA: Church Growth Institute, 1987.

Towns, Elmer L. *Ten of Today's Most Innovative Churches.* Ventura, CA: Regal, 1990.

30

Signs and Wonders
and Church Growth

A similar story has been repeated several times by signs-and-wonders enthusiasts. This particular story took place in the early 1980s in Mexico City. The parents of a twelve-year-old boy asked evangelist and church planter Ausencio Gonzalez to go with them to the hospital to pray for their child. The boy was paralyzed, deaf, and dumb. The hospital staff would not allow Gonzalez to pray in the hospital because other Pentecostals had disturbed patients earlier. The evangelist decided that the child should be put in a wheelchair and taken outside.

A crowd gathered at a busy subway station as Gonzalez proclaimed that God would heal the boy. The evangelist prayed. Quietly he spoke to the child, "Stand up." The father reminded Gonzalez that the child was deaf and could not hear the admonition to rise. Much to the shock of the crowd, the boy got up from the wheelchair and began to walk. Next the child spoke: "Mama, Papa"; then he began singing, *"Cristo viene muy pronto."*

Many the onlookers received Christ as Lord and Savior immediately in the presence of the large crowd. Others rushed into the hospital to bring out their sick relatives and friends. Many others were healed. With each healing the crowd began to cheer. And many more came to Christ.[1]

This event and many other testimonies like it describe what is now called "signs-and-wonders evangelism" or "power evangelism." Healings, exorcisms, or other miracles are demonstrated with the credit and glory given to Jesus Christ.

[1]C. Peter Wagner, *Spiritual Power and Church Growth* (Altamonte Springs, FL: Creation House, 1986), 119-120. Wagner received this information from a personal interview with Ausencio Gonzalez, September 6, 1984.

Consequently, many people, either those directly affected by miracles or onlookers, received Christ on the spot.

Such scenes are often described as similar to Pentecost in Acts 2 or other early church events. Peter and John prayed for such miracles: "Now, Lord, consider their threats and enable your servants to speak your word with great boldness. Stretch out your hand to heal and perform *miraculous signs and wonders* through the name of your holy servant Jesus," (Acts 4:29-30, emphasis added). In Acts 5:12, "the apostles performed many *miraculous signs and wonders* among the people" (emphasis added). The result? "Nevertheless, more and more men and women believed in the Lord and were added to their number" (Acts 5:14).

In chapter 6 of this book, we looked at C. Peter Wagner's signs-and-wonders pilgrimage and the influence his paradigm shift has had on the Church Growth Movement. We now look beyond Wagner to determine why some leaders of church growth look to power evangelism as God's anointed method to reach the most people for Christ in this century and the next.

The Latin American Phenomenon

"Never before in human history has a voluntary movement grown as rapidly as Christianity is growing today. Without the aid of political or military forces the message of the kingdom of God is breaking frontiers in vast areas of Asia, Africa and Latin America with extraordinary church growth following . . . . Among Pentecostals, the most rapid growth has taken place in Latin America."[2] This phenomenon has not escaped the Church Growth Movement's notice. Much time and effort has been expended in studying the growth of the church in Latin America.

The statistics of church growth in Latin America reveal that this movement has seen more new growth than any similar movement in church history. The growth started slowly at the beginning of the twentieth century, but its momentum has been phenomenal:[3]

[2]Ibid., 11-12.
[3]Ibid., 26-27.

Number of Protestants in Latin America

1900..50,000
1930...1,000,000
1950...5,000,000
1960...10,000,000
1970...20,000,000
1980...50,000,000
2000 (estimated)..137,000,000

Most of the growth has come from the Pentecostals. At the turn of the century there were no Pentecostals in Latin America. In 1950 about twenty-five percent of the five million Protestants were Pentecostals. Today, with the Protestant population approaching one hundred million, seventy-five percent are Pentecostals. In Chile that proportion is over ninety percent.[4]

The rapid growth of Pentecostalism in Latin America is cited because of the manner in which the movement is growing. With few exceptions the great numbers are coming to Christ because of power evangelism. Testimonies of healings, exorcisms, and miracles abound. As a result, many have accepted Christ.

The late Donald A. McGavran believed that the most skeptical of Christians could be convinced of the reality of power evangelism in Latin America and other areas of the world:

> Some hard-headed Christians, who would normally be highly skeptical about divine healing, have gradually come to accept healing campaigns upon seeing the great numbers who throw away crutches, plus those healed of deafness and blindness and cured of heart disease. They have seen large numbers of recent nonbelievers rejoicing at Christ's power, singing his praises, hearing his word, and praying to him. The facts overwhelm the hard-headed. Finally, some Christians believe that God has called them to engage actively in healing the sick, exorcising evil spirits and multiplying churches. They deliberately used the virogous expressed faith in Christ which abounds in a healing campaign to multiply sound churches of responsible

[4]Ibid., 27.

Christians. All Christians ought to think their way
through this matter and realize that here is a power which
a great many of us have not sufficiently used.[5]

McGavran's words would be prophetic. Not only has
signs-and-wonders evangelism grown in other countries, it is
becoming increasingly active and accepted in the United
States. One of the milestones that drew attention to power
evangelism in the United States took place at the school
where McGavran was dean, Fuller Theological Seminary in
Pasadena, California.

The Legacy of MC510

"'I know of only two seminary courses which have become
famous,' said Robert Mege, Dean of the Fuller Seminary
School of Theology, at a joint faculty meeting. 'One was the
course on dogmatics taught at Basel by Karl Barth and the
other is MC510 taught by John Wimber here at Fuller.'"[6]

In chapter 6 we looked at a seminary course called "Signs,
Wonders, and Church Growth"—MC510, which became one
of the most controversial and publicized classes in history.
Christian Life magazine devoted its entire October 1982
issue to cover the class; this was soon known as "the sold-
out issue."[7] Wagner's book *Signs and Wonders Today* was
written about the class.[8] The publicity that mounted caused
many to worry that Fuller had "gone charismatic." Some
Fuller faculty members publically disagreed with the
content of the course, adding to the mounting controversy.
As a consequence, MC510 was discontinued after four years.
Several months later a new course appeared in the catalog

---

[5]Donald A. McGavran, "Divine Healing and Church Growth," in *Signs and
Wonders Today,* ed. C. Peter Wagner (Altamonte Springs, FL: Creation House,
1987), 78, emphasis in original. This quote originally came from McGavran's
lecture on healing which he presented to his Fuller Theological Seminary students
during the final years of his teaching ministry

[6]C. Peter Wagner, *The Third Wave of the Holy Spirit* (Ann Arbor, MI: Vine,
1988), 25.

[7]Ibid.

[8]C. Peter Wagner, ed., *Signs and Wonders Today* (Altamonte Springs, FL:
Creation House, 1987).

to replace MC510. The new course was called "The Ministry of Healing and World Evangelization."

MC510 was taught by C. Peter Wagner and his friend, John Wimber, an adjunct professor in the church growth program. The class was taught on ten consecutive Monday nights for one quarter. Wimber lectured for three hours as he related the phenomenon of power evangelism to his students. Wimber also used vivid personal illustrations from his own experiences.

The primary source of controversy took place after class. Wimber called for a voluntary "ministry time." Students were allowed to stay or to leave. Few left. In fact the ministry time often attracted others not enrolled in the course. During this time Wimber might speak "words of knowledge." Sometimes students who needed physical, emotional, or spiritual healing would come to the front of the class as Wimber prayed for them. On other occasions small prayer groups would form spontaneously in different parts of the classroom.

The widespread publicity of the class, especially the ministry time, caused many faculty members to receive telephone calls and letters of concern. Supporters of Fuller Seminary began to question the direction of the school. The pressures increased during the four-year period the course was taught. Those who were only informed about MC510 by hearsay imagined that the class had degenerated to something like a television faith healer's program.

Tension peaked when the theology school decided to discontinue giving theology students credit for MC510, though the material was offered in the School of World Mission. As a way to diffuse the tension, the provost at Fuller created a task force to study MC510 and bring a recommendation. The dean of the School of World Mission withdrew the course for the 1985-86 academic year while the task force met.

The twelve professors who comprised the task force were from each of the three Fuller schools: Theology, World Mission, and Psychology. After eight months the group presented an eighty-two-page document that affirmed the miraculous; stated that all spiritual gifts operate in the body

of Christ today; and clearly stated that Fuller Seminary was
not anti-charismatic. The new course was begun, and the
controversy ended.

MC510 was significant in that an evangelical seminary
was offering a class that advocated the evangelization of the
world through power evangelism. Not only were many
students affected by this thesis, outside observers were
influenced by MC510 as well. Signs-and-wonders
evangelism gained credibility in many evangelical circles. In
fact the acceptance of power evangelism by many
evangelicals is another example of gains the movement has
made. Those evangelicals who accept the tenets of power
evangelism are now called "the third wave."

The American Scene: The Third Wave

The "first wave" of power evangelism acceptance in the
United States was known as the Pentecostal movement. For
many years evangelical Christianity looked at
Pentecostalism as a movement on the fringe of the faith.
Some evangelicals declared the movement heresy. Early
twentieth-century evangelical books often included
Pentecostalism in the listing of cults, alongside Mormons,
Jehovah's Witnesses, and Christian Scientists.[9]

The emotional excesses of the Pentecostals were as difficult
for evangelicals to accept as baptisms in the Holy Spirit,
speaking in tongues, healing the sick, and casting out demons.
Pentecostals were labled "holy rollers," and the Pentecostal
manifestations were sometimes attributed to the devil.

The "second wave" of signs and wonders is called the
charismatic movement. While the Pentecostals had, for the
most part, started their own churches and denominations, the
charismatics took the same beliefs into mainline
denominations. The movement made significant advances
into the Catholic Church, as well as the Episcopal, Lutheran,
Presbyterian, and United Methodist denominations.[10]
Evangelicals still had difficulty accepting the movement's
emphasis of baptism in the Holy Spirit and speaking in

[9]Wagner, *The Third Wave of the Holy Spirit,* 16.
[10]Ibid., 17.

tongues. Unfortunately a charismatic presence in some evangelical churches resulted in a purging or a church split.

By 1980 the "third wave" terminology began to stick to certain evangelicals who were open to the manifestation of all of the gifts of the Spirit. The point of departure for these evangelicals from the two previous "waves" was over the baptism of the Holy Spirit and tongues as a sign of authentication. Evangelical "third wavers" believe that the baptism of the Holy Spirit is a one-time event that takes place at salvation, when believers are incorporated into the body of Christ (1 Cor. 12:13). Third wave evangelicals do not dismiss the manifestation of tongues for today, as do those who hold to the cessation of tongues at the conclusion of the apostolic era. They do have differences with Pentecostals and charismatics who make tongues the necessary evidence for either salvation or the baptism of the Holy Spirit.

For essentially those two reasons, third wave evangelicals refuse to be labeled either Pentecostal or charismatic. C. Peter Wagner represents this sentiment: "I myself, for example, would rather not have people call me a charismatic. I do not consider myself a charismatic. I am simply an evangelical Congregationalist who is open to the Holy Spirit working through me and my church in anyway he chooses."[11]

Churches that consider themselves part of the third wave are not monolithic in the way they practice their beliefs. In 1987, Wagner published a book entitled *How To Have a Healing Ministry without Making Your Church Sick.*[12] The theme of the book was the implementation of third wave beliefs without dividing a church. Wagner covered a variety of issues, but his main thrust was healing ministries. Indeed most third wave churches have a healing ministry of some type. It may be within the main worship service accompanied by outpourings of emotion. Or the healing ministry may take place quietly in a back room at the conclusion of a service. Some churches have healing

[11]Ibid., 18-19.
[12]C. Peter Wagner, *How To Have a Healing Ministry without Making Your Church Sick* (Ventura, CA: Regal, 1987).

ministry teams or elders who go to the afflicted, pray for them, and possibly anoint them with oil (Jas 5:14).

Is signs-and-wonders church growth biblical? Is power evangelism a God-anointed approach to reach people for Christ? In the final section of this chapter we will examine what for many has become an emotional issue.

Evaluation

We must take power evangelism and its accompanying church growth seriously. Because millions of people worldwide are claiming to accept Christ through this movement, it can not be ignored. Some claim that it is a new outpouring of the power of the Holy Spirit, one of the greatest developments in church history. Others see it as heretical and cultic, a movement leading millions of vulnerable people astray.

One group of evangelicals, often identified with dispensationalism, believes that the "sign" gifts (tongues, interpretation, prophecy, etc.) ceased at the end of the apostolic age, or at the end of the earliest centuries of the Christian church. These evangelicals believe that 1 Corinthians 13:8-10 refers to the end of the manifestation of these gifts: "Love never fails. But where there are prophecies they will cease; where there are tongues, they will be stilled; where there is knowledge, it will pass away. For we know in part and we prophesy in part, but when the perfection comes, the imperfect disappears." These evangelicals teach that "perfection" refers to the completion and closure of the New Testament. The "imperfect" then refers to the "sign" gifts that have "disappeared" or ceased. Such a hermeneutic then does not allow for any of the elements of power evangelism.

A second perspective looks at 1 Corinthians 13:8-10 differently, but still believes the historical and theological evidence for power evangelism today is weak. John MacArthur admits that the "perfect" must be something other than the completion of the New Testament: "But it seems that the perfect thing Paul has in mind must be the eternal state—'face to face' in verse 12 can best be explained as being with God in the new heavens and new earth. It is only in glory that we will know as we are known (v. 12)."[13]

MacArthur, however, finds various problems with power evangelism. Signs, wonders, and miracles are for a different age when authentication was necessary. Now we have the revelation of Scripture. "Nothing in Scripture," he says, "indicates that the miracles of the apostolic age were meant to be continuous in subsequent ages."[14] The apostles were authenticated by miraculous signs, but the apostles were unique. They were the eyewitnesses to the resurrection personally chosen by Jesus Christ.[15] Power evangelism "is hardly evangelism at all"[16] He adds: "Third wave methodology seriously blunts the force of the gospel. Many Third Wavers are even guilty of omitting or badly corrupting the saving message."[17] Finally he says: "Third wave evangelistic strategy itself undermines the gospel message. The emphasis is on signs and wonders, and not on preaching the Word of God."[18]

John Wimber is the American spokesperson and advocate of the third wave. He contends that most of the Western world has a worldview that refuses to see signs and wonders.[19] A worldview is the way we see reality; it takes into account our beliefs, experiences, and prejudices. Christians in non-Western lands have no problem with power evangelism, which explains the explosive growth of the church in Latin America, Africa, China, and South Korea. Says Wimber: "We have, it seems, excluded God and his power from our theology and thus from our churches.

[13]John F. MacArthur, Jr., *Charismatic Chaos* (Grand Rapids, MI: Zondervan, 1992), 230-231. This quote is in footnote 20.

[14]Ibid., 117.

[15]Ibid., 123-124.

[16]Ibid., 136.

[17]Ibid.

[18]Ibid., 137.

[19]John Wimber, "Signs and Wonders in the Growth of the Church," in C. Peter Wagner, ed., with Win Arn and Elmer Towns, *Church Growth: State of the Art* (Wheaton, IL: Tyndale, 1986), 217. The complete treatment of Wimber's perspective is: John Wimber with Kevin Springer, *Power Evangelism* (San Francisco: Harper & Row, 1986) and its sequels: John Wimber with Kevin Springer, *Power Healing* (San Francisco: Harper & Row, 1987); and John Wimber and Kevin Springer, *Power Points* (San Francisco: Harper & Row, 1991).

Fearing that which we could not control or understand, we have thrown the baby out with the bathwater. We have said, 'It simply does not exist.' When confronted with manifestations of God's power, we have rejected such things with the excuse that they are too divisive!"[20]

Wimber believes the scriptural testimony supports signs and wonders today. "Signs" is found seventy-seven times in the Bible; and "wonders" occurs sixteen times in connection with "signs."[21] The Book of Acts, he demonstrates, is replete with references to signs and wonders such as tongues (Acts 2:4, 41); raising the dead (Acts 9:40-42; 20:7-12); visions (Acts 10:1, 9, 47); miracles (Acts 28:3-10); healings (Acts 9:32-43); and angelic visitations (Acts 8:26-40).[22]

The testimony of signs-and-wonders evangelism is not limited to the Book of Acts, says Wimber. After Paul argued persuasively at the Areopagus, only "a *few* men became followers of Paul and believed" (Acts 17:34, emphasis added). At Corinth, the next stop, "*many* of the Corinthians who heard him believed and were baptized" (Acts 18:8, emphasis added). What was the difference between the two evangelistic visits? The answer can be found in Paul's first Letter to the Corinthians: "When I came to you brothers, I did not come with eloquence or superior wisdom as I proclaimed to you the testimony about God . . . . My message and my preaching were not with wise and persuasive words, but with a *demonstration of the Spirit's power,* so that your faith might not rest on men's wisdom, but on God's power" (1 Cor. 2:1, 4-5, emphasis added). Thus concludes Wimber: "It appears that in Corinth Paul combined proclamation with demonstration, as Christ had done throughout his ministry. The word and works of God were coupled in an expression of God's divine will and mercy, culminating in the conversion of individuals as well as groups."[23]

[20]Ibid., 218.

[21]Ibid., 219.

[22]John Wimber with Kevin Springer, *Power Evangelism* (San Francisco: Harper & Row, 1986), 117-118.

[23]John Wimber and Kevin Springer, *Power Points* (San Francisco: Harper & Row, 1991), 172.

MacArthur is unfair in his criticism that third wave evangelistic strategy undermines the gospel message and fails to emphasize the preaching of the Word of God. Wimber emphasizes that

> signs and wonders do not save; only Jesus saves. The power for salvation in power evangelism is through the gospel alone. "I am not ashamed of the gospel," Paul writes in Romans 1:16, "because it is the power of God for the salvation of everyone who believes." The content of the gospel, Paul writes elsewhere, is "that Christ died for our sins according to the Scriptures, that he was buried, that he was raised on the third day according to the Scriptures" (1 Cor. 15:3-4).[24]

The role of power evangelism, contends Wimber, *never* includes adding to the gospel.

> In power evangelism we do not add to the gospel, nor do we even seek to add power to the gospel. But we do turn to the Third Person of the triune God in our evangelistic efforts, *consciously* cooperating with his anointing, gifting, and leading. Preaching and demonstrating the gospel are not mutually exclusive activities; they work together, reinforcing each other.[25]

It is difficult if not foolish to write off the most explosive Christian movement in history (all three "waves") as something that "undermines the Word of God."[26] Such a vitriolic spirit might be palatable if a clear scriptural case against the movement could be made. One evangelical reviewer of *Charismatic Chaos,* after finding significant theological weaknesses in MacArthur's arguments, concluded that

> while MacArthur claims otherwise, his style does not reflect one speaking to a wide audience, but only to his "amen" corner. His less than irenic spirit and preachy tone will preclude a wide hearing. Rather than fostering the

---

[24]Ibid., 173
[25]Ibid., emphasis in original.
[26]MacArthur, 137.

theological integrity he longs for, his books may serve to deepen existing divisions within the evangelical family.[27]

Certainly excesses can be found in all of the "waves" of power evangelism. The warning from Jesus that we must not demand signs (Matt. 12:38-39; 16:1-4; Mark 8:11-12; Luke 11:16, 29; 23:8-9; John 4:48) should be heeded. Yet one of the most damaging weaknesses of Western Christianity is our skepticism about the supernatural. God *is* at work in our midst, but we fail to see Him and, thus, fail to acknowledge Him. The countries of the Third World have, for the most part, not been affected by our skepticism about the supernatural. As a consequence, church growth has been phenomenal; millions of lives have been eternally changed.

Neither mindless emotion nor dead orthodoxy is the pattern of New Testament Christianity today. Nor should either be our model today. On the one side, some argue for a faith firmly grounded in the Word—the Bible as the final authority on all matters. On the other side, some argue for freedom of the Spirit, freedom of expression, an openness to the supernatural that believes in God's miracles for today. Why must we choose one over the other? Why not both orthodoxy *and* power? Such seems to be the way of the early church. May God grant us their same evangelistic successes: "Everyone was filled with awe, and many wonders and miraculous signs were done by the apostles . . . . And the Lord added to their number daily those who were being saved" (Acts 2:43, 47).

Suggested Reading for Chapter 30

Geisler, Norman. *Signs and Wonders.* Wheaton, IL: Tyndale, 1988. Geisler's position is similar to MacArthur's.

MacArthur, John F., Jr. *Charismatic Chaos.* Grand Rapids, MI: Zondervan, 1992.

---

[27]Robert W. Patterson, review of *Charismatic Chaos* by John F. MacArthur, Jr., *Christianity Today,* 36 (May 18, 1992), 70-75. Patterson is the former associate to the executive director of the National Association of Evangelicals.

Springer, Kevin, ed. *Power Encounters.* San Francisco: Harper & Row, 1988.

Wagner, C. Peter, ed. *Engaging the Enemy.* Ventura, CA: Regal, 1991.

Wagner, C. Peter. *How To Have a Healing Ministry without Making Your Church Sick.* Ventura, CA: Regal, 1987.

Wagner, C. Peter, ed. *Signs & Wonders Today.* Altamonte Springs, FL: Creation House, 1987.

Wagner, C. Peter. *Spiritual Power and Church Growth.* Altamonte Springs, FL: Cration House, 1986.

Wagner, C. Peter. *The Third Wave of the Holy Spirit.* Ann Arbor, MI: Vine, 1988.

Wagner, C. Peter. *Warfare Prayer.* Ventura, CA: Regal, 1992.

Wagner, C. Peter, ed., with Win Arn and Elmer Towns. *Church Growth: State of the Art.* Wheaton, IL: Tyndale, 1986.

Wagner, C. Peter and F. Douglas Pennoyer, eds. *Wrestling with Dark Angels.* Ventura, CA: Regal, 1990.

Wimber, John with Kevin Springer. *Power Evangelism.* San Francisco: Harper & Row, 1986.

Wimber, John with Kevin Springer. *Power Healing.* San Francisco: Harper & Row, 1987.

Wimber, John and Kevin Springer. *Power Points.* San Francisco: Harper & Row, 1991.

Part IV

Concluding Matters

31

The Church Growth Movement: A Postscript

The Church Growth Movement began with one man asking the question: "Why do some churches grow and some churches don't?" Business as usual was not acceptable to Donald McGavran. He knew that his Lord had commanded him to make disciples of all nations. He knew that the churches in India where he served as a missionary were doing little to fulfill the Great Commission.

Donald McGavran, Peter Wagner, and other church growth leaders have made many Christians uncomfortable. Pioneers and trailblazers will always have their critics; some of the criticisms have strengthened the movement. Peter Wagner especially has listened carefully, made adjustments where necessary, and maintained an irenic spirit.

When the homogeneous unit principle was the lightning rod of criticism, it was Wagner for whom the issue was most personal. After all, the principle had been the subject of his doctoral dissertation, which also became a full-length book. With some valid points made by the critics, the principle was acknowledged as being descriptive rather than prescriptive. Little is said today about the homogeneous unit principle.

Other critics took issue with the principle of receptivity, the quantitative emphasis of the movement, and the overemphasis of evangelism above social ministries. Today the focus of the critics seems to be on the power evangelism segment of the movement, the effectiveness of church growth principles, and the ever-present issue of pragmatism. It would seem that the more reasonable critics are asking for *balance* in these controversial areas.

For example, D. A. Carson offers a much more balanced perspective of the signs-and-wonders movement than the fierce dogmatism of John MacArthur. After a thoroughly biblical study of power evangelism, especially examining John Wimber's Vineyard movement, Carson concludes: "Even though the problem is largely one of balance and proportion, it is not incidental. We may gratefully concur with the Vineyard movement that genuine signs and wonders (in the generic sense) *sometimes* in the New Testament became occasional causes of belief, and that they may do so today as well. But on the evidence of Scripture, it is doubtful this theme is anywhere near as central as some think."[1]

Bill Hull argues that the Church Growth Movement is not "really working." He supports his thesis with statistics of declining church attendance and eroding evangelistic effectiveness. Perhaps Hull's point would be valid if the church growth had *complete* responsibility for evangelical Christianity in America. One also wonders if the discouraging statistics might have been more dismal without the efforts of the Church Growth Movement. Yet Hull is willing to concede that the movement has given hope to many church leaders and has been a catalyst for renewal. Hull's concern is really for balance. He fears the "danger of having an entire generation of pastors committed to clever programming instead of Scripture."[2]

Hull is on target when he cries for the balanced use of church growth "tools."

> The need to reach out to a hurting world, and the need to use tools invented by the world in order to do so, cannot be denied. The trouble comes when we employ those tools uncritically, without careful biblical scrutiny. The more the church *accomodates* the culture, the more it becomes secularized itself and, therefore, incapable of offering solutions as a hand *outside* a ruined culture, reaching into the pit to pull the captives to freedom. A secularized

[1]D. A. Carson, "The Purpose of Signs and Wonders in the New Testament," in *Power Religion: The Selling Out of the Evangelical Church,* ed. Michael Scott Horton (Chicago: Moody, 1992), 117, emphasis in original.

[2]Bill Hull, "Is the Church Growth Movement Really Working?" in *Power Religion: The Selling Out of the Evangelical Church,* ed. Michael Scott Horton (Chicago: Moody, 1992), 147.

church cannot *make* disciples because it is not itself a
faithful servant of its risen King.[3]

A similar concern is voiced over the movement's
pragmatism. We must not view pragmatism as an
inherently evil approach. Christians make decisions daily
based on "what best works" without violating scriptural
truths. The danger, rather, is replacing theology with
pragmatism. *Methods* must always be subservient to the
message. Again the call is for biblical balance.

As a church growth proponent, I appreciate the concerns
of even-handed and Christ-like critics. No human
movement is above scrutiny and correction. Indeed critics of
church growth do a great service in keeping the movement
biblically faithful and balanced.

In the midst of the verbiage and concerns, however, we
need to remember what the Church Growth Movement *has*
done for evangelical Christianity. It has caused us to refocus
on kingdom building, on making disciples, and on winning
the lost to Jesus Christ. It has made us evaluate again the
question: What *is* the true mission of the church? Such
introspection has been healthy for evangelical Christianity.
The inward examination has given us a more outward
concern for making disciples of all nations.

My mentor Lewis Drummond once responded to one of my
fellow students who was finding fault with every
evangelistic method mentioned in class. Finally the
professor said, "Brother, I like the way they *do* evangelism a
lot more than the way most people *don't* do evangelism." I
like the way the Church Growth Movement reaches out in
the name of our Savior a lot more than the way most people
don't reach out at all. To God be the glory.

Suggested Reading for Chapter 31

Horton, Michael Scott. *Power Religion: The Selling Out of
the Evangelical Church?* Chicago: Moody, 1992.

[3]Ibid., 145, emphasis in original.

Church Growth Bibliography

Approximately two hundred church growth books are included in the following pages. All of the books have church growth material, even if it is not the primary topic. I have attempted to include most of the American church growth books of which I am aware. I am certain, however, that some omissions have occurred. If the reader knows of any oversights, please write me and I will include them in a future edition.

Allen, Roland. *Essential Missionary Principles.* New York: Revell, 1913.

_____. *Missionary Methods: St. Paul's or Ours?* Grand Rapids, MI: Eerdmans, 1962.

_____. *The Case for Voluntary Clergy.* London: Eyre and Spottisworde, 1930.

_____. *The Spontaneous Expansion of the Church and the Causes Which Hinder It.* 2nd ed. London: World Dominion, 1927.

Amberson, Talmadge R., ed. *The Birth of Churches: A Biblical Basis for Church Planting.* Nashville: Broadman, 1979.

Anderson, Andy with Linda Lawson. *Effective Methods of Church Growth.* Nashville: Broadman, 1985.

Anderson, Leith. *Dying for Change.* Minneapolis, MN: Bethany, 1990.

Annan, Nelson. *More People! Is Church Growth Worth It?* Wheaton, IL: Harold Shaw, 1987.

Appleby, Jerry L. *Missions Have Come Home to America.* Kansas City, MO: Beacon Hill, 1986.

Arn, Charles, Donald McGavran, and Win Arn. *Growth: A New Vision for the Sunday School.* Pasadena, CA: Church Growth, 1980.

Arn, Win. *Church Growth Ratio Book.* Pasadena, CA: Church Growth, 1979.

_____, ed. *The Pastor's Church Growth Handbook.* Pasadena, CA: Church Growth, 1979.

_____, ed. *The Pastor's Church Growth Handbook,* Vol. II. Pasadena, CA: Church Growth, 1982.

Arn, Win, and Charles Arn. *The Master's Plan for Making Disciples.* Pasadena, CA: Church Growth, 1979.

Arn, Win, and Donald McGavran. *Back to Basics in Church Growth.* Wheaton, IL: Tyndale, 1981.

Arn, Win, Carrol Nyquist, and Charles Arn. *Who Cares About Love?* Pasadena, CA: Church Growth, 1986.

Arnold, Jeffrey. *The Big Book on Small Groups.* Downers Grove, IL: InterVarsity, 1992.

Barna, George. *Marketing the Church.* Colorado Springs, CO: NavPress, 1988.

_____. *The Frog in the Kettle.* Ventura, CA: Regal, 1990.

_____. *The Power of Vision.* Ventura, CA: Regal, 1992.

_____. *User Friendly Churches.* Ventura, CA: Regal, 1991.

_____. *What Americans Believe.* Ventura, CA: Regal, 1991.

_____. *Without a Vision, the People Perish.* Glendale, CA: Barna Research, 1991.

Bartel, Floyd G. *A New Look at Church Growth.* Newton, KS: Faith and Life, 1979.

Bassham, Rodger C. *Mission Theology: 1948-1975, Years of Worldwide Creative Tension: Ecumenical, Evangelical, and Roman Catholic.* Pasadena, CA: William Carey, 1979.

Beasley-Murray, Paul and Alan Wilkinson. *Turning the Tide: An Assessment of Baptist Church Growth in England.* Swindon, England: British Bible, 1981.

Belew, M. Wendell. *Churches and How They Grow.* Nashville: Broadman, 1971.

Benjamin, Paul. *The Growing Congregation.* Lincoln, IL: Lincoln Christian College, 1972.

Bontrager, G. Edwin and Nathan D. Showalter. *It Can Happen Today! Principles of Church Growth from the Book of Acts.* Scottdale, PA: Herald, 1986.

Brock, Charles. *The Principles and Practices of Indigenous Church Planting.* Nashville: Broadman, 1981.

Brown, Jr., J. Truman, ed. *Visionary Leadership for Church Growth.* Nashville: Convention, 1991.

Brown, Lowell E. *Grow: Your Sunday School Can Grow.* Glendale, CA: Regal, 1974.

Callahan, Kennon L. *Twelve Keys to an Effective Church.* San Francisco: Harper & Row, 1983.

Carroll, Jackson W. *Small Churches Are Beautiful.* San Francisco: Harper & Row, 1977.

Chandler, Russell. *Racing Toward 2001: The Forces Shaping America's Religious Future.* Grand Rapids, MI: Zondervan and Harper, 1992.

Chaney, Charles L. *Church Planting at the End of the Twentieth Century.* Wheaton, IL: Tyndale, 1982.

Chaney, Charles L., and Ron S. Lewis. *Design for Church Growth.* Nashville: Broadman, 1977.

Cho, Paul Y. *More Than Numbers.* Waco, TX: Word, 1984.

Clemmons, William and Harvey Hester. *Growth through Groups.* Nashville: Broadman, 1974.

Conn, Harvie M. *Theological Perspectives of Church Growth.* Nutley, NJ: Presbyterian and Reformed, 1976.

Cook, Harold R. *Historic Patterns of Church Growth.* Chicago: Moody, 1971.

Costas, Orlando. *The Church and Its Mission: A Shattering Critique from the Third World.* Wheaton, IL: Tyndale, 1974.

Crawford, Dan R. *Church Growth Words from the Risen Lord.* Nashville: Broadman, 1990.

Dale, Robert D. *To Dream Again.* Nashville: Broadman, 1981.

Dodd, C. H. *The Apostolic Preaching and Its Developments.* Grand Rapids, MI: Baker, 1980.

Drummond, Lewis A. *The Awakening That Must Come.* Nashville: Broadman, 1978.

DuBose, Francis M. *How Churches Grow in an Urban World.* Nashville: Broadman, 1978.

Dudley, Carl S. *Making the Small Church Effective.* Nashville: Abingdon, 1978.

Dudley, Roger L. and Des Cummings, Jr. *Adventures in Church Growth.* Washington, D. C.: Review and Herald, 1983.

Easum, William M. *The Church Growth Handbook.* Nashville: Abingdon, 1990.

Elliot, Ralph. *Church Growth That Counts.* Valley Forge, PA: Judson, 1982.

Ellis, Joe S. *The Church on Target: Achieving Your Congregation's Highest Potential.* Cincinnati, OH: Standard, 1986.

Engel, James F., and Wilbert H. Norton. *What's Gone Wrong with the Harvest? A Communication Strategy for the Church and World Evangelism.* Grand Rapids, MI: Zondervan, 1975.

Exman, Gary W. *Get Ready . . . Get Set . . . Grow! Church Growth for Town and Country Congregations.* Lima, OH: CSS, 1987.

Faircloth, Samuel D. *Church Planting for Reproduction.* Grand Rapids, MI: Baker, 1991.

Falwell, Jerry and Elmer Towns. *Stepping Out on Faith.* Wheaton, IL: Tyndale, 1984.

Fickett, Harold L. *Hope for Your Church: Ten Principles of Church Growth.* Glendale, CA: Regal, 1972.

George, Carl F. *Prepare Your Church for the Future.* Tarrytown, NY: Revell, 1991.

George, Carl F., and Robert E. Logan. *Leading and Managing Your Church.* Old Tappan, NJ: Revell, 1987.

Gerber, Vergil. *God's Way to Keep a Church Going and Growing.* Glendale, CA: Regal, 1973.

Gibbs, Eddie. *I Believe in Church Growth.* London: Hodder & Stoughton, 1985.

_____. *Ten Growing Churches.* London: MARC Europe, 1984.

Glasser, Arthur F. and Donald A. McGavran. *Contemporary Theologies of Mission.* Grand Rapids, MI: Baker, 1983.

Green, Hollis. *Why Churches Die.* Minneapolis, MN: Bethany, 1972.

Green, Michael. *Evangelism in the Early Church.* Grand Rapids, MI: Eerdmans, 1970.

Griswold, Roland E. *The Winning Church.* Wheaton, IL: Victor, 1986.

Hadaway, C. Kirk. *Church Growth Principles: Separating Fact from Fiction.* Nashville: Broadman, 1991.

_____. *What Can We Do about Church Dropouts?* Nashville: Abingdon, 1990.

Hale, J. Russell. *The Unchurched: Who They Are and Why They Stay Away.* San Francisco: Harper & Row, 1980.

Hemphill, Ken. *The Bonsai Theory of Church Growth.* Nashville: Broadman, 1991.

Hemphill, Ken, and R. Wayne Jones. *Growing an Evangelistic Sunday School.* Nashville: Broadman, 1989.

Hesselgrave, David J. *Planting Churches Cross-Culturally: A Guide for Home and Foreign Missions.* Grand Rapids, MI: Baker, 1980.

Hoge, Dean R. and David A. Rouzen, eds. *Understanding Church Growth and Decline: 1950-1978.* New York: Pilgrim, 1979.

Horton, Michael Scott, ed. *Power Religion: The Selling Out of the Evangelical Church?* Chicago: Moody, 1992.

Hundnut, Robert K. *Church Growth Is Not the Point.* New York: Harper & Row, 1975.

Hunter, III, George G. *The Contagious Congregation: Frontiers in Evangelism and Church Growth.* Nashville: Abingdon, 1979.

_____. *To Spread the Power: Church Growth in the Wesleyan Spirit.* Nashville: Abingdon, 1987.

Hunter, Kent R. *Foundations For Church Growth.* New Haven, MO: Leader, 1983.

_____. *The Road to Church Growth.* Corunna, IN: Church Growth, 1986.

_____. *Your Church Has Doors: How to Open the Front and Close the Back.* New Haven, MO: Leader, 1983.

Jackson, Jr., Neil E. *100 Great Growth Ideas.* Nashville: Broadman, 1990.

Jenson, Ron and Jim Stevens. *Dynamics of Church Growth.* Grand Rapids, MI: Baker, 1982.

Johnson, Douglas W. *Vitality Means Church Growth.* Nashville: Abingdon, 1989.

Jones, R. Wayne. *Overcoming Barriers to Sunday School Growth.* Nashville: Broadman, 1987.

Kane, J. Herbert. *Understanding Christian Missions.* Grand Rapids: Baker, 1978.

Kelley, Dean M. *Why Conservative Churches Are Growing.* Rev. ed. Macon, GA: Mercer University, 1986.

Kraus, C. Norman, ed. *Missions, Evangelism, and Church Growth.* Scottdale, PA: Herald, 1980.

Lawson, E. LeRoy and Tetsunao Yamamori. *Church Growth: Everybody's Business.* Cincinnati: New Life, n.d..

Lewis, Larry L. *Organize to Evangelize.* Nashville: Broadman, 1977.

Lewis, Ron S. *Design for Church Growth.* Nashville: Broadman, 1977.

Logan, Robert E. *Beyond Church Growth.* Old Tappan, NJ: Revell, 1989.

McCoury, D. G. and Bill May. *The Southern Baptist Church Growth Plan.* Nashville: Convention, 1991.

McGavran, Donald A. *The Bridges of God.* Rev. ed. New York: Friendship, 1981.

_____. *Church Growth and Group Conversion.* South Pasadena, CA: William Carey, 1973.

_____. *Church Growth Bulletin: Second Consolidated Volume.* South Pasadena, CA: William Carey, 1977.

_____. *Effective Evangelism: A Theological Mandate.* Phillipsburg, NJ: Presbyterian and Reformed, 1988.

_____. *How Churches Grow.* London: World Dominion, 1959.

_____. *Understanding Church Growth.* 2nd rev. ed. by C. Peter Wagner. Grand Rapids, MI: Eerdmans, 1990.

_____, ed. *Church Growth and Christian Mission.* South Pasadena, CA: William Carey, 1976.

_____, ed. *Church Growth Bulletin: First Consolidated Volume.* Palo Alto, CA: Overseas Crusades, 1969.

McGavran, Donald A., and Win Arn. *How to Grow a Church.* Ventura, CA: Regal, 1973.

_____. *Ten Steps for Church Growth.* San Francisco: Harper & Row, 1977.

McGavran Donald A., and George G. Hunter, III. *Church Growth: Strategies That Work.* Nashville: Abingdon, 1980.

McIntosh, Gary and Glen Martin. *Finding Them, Keeping Them: Effective Strategies for Evangelism and Assimilation in the Local Church.* Nashville: Broadman, 1992.

McQuilkin, J. Robertson. *Measuring the Church Growth Movement: How Biblical Is It?* Chicago: Moody, 1974.

Miles, Delos. *Church Growth: A Mighty River.* Nashville: Broadman, 1981.

Miller, Herb. *How to Build a Magnetic Church.* Nashville: Abingdon, 1987.

Murren, Doug. *The Baby Boomerang.* Ventura, CA: Regal, 1990.

Mylander, Charles. *Secrets for Growing Churches.* San Francisco: Harper & Row, 1979.

Neighbour, Ralph W. *Where Do We Go from Here?: A Guidebook for the Cell Group Church.* Houston: Touch, 1990.

Ogden, Greg. *The New Reformation.* Grand Rapids, MI: Zondervan, 1990.

Padilla, C. Rene, ed. *The New Face of Evangelicalism: An International Symposium on the Lausanne Covenant.* Downers Grove, IL: InterVarsity, 1976.

Palmer, Donald C. *Explosion of People Evangelism.* Chicago: Moody, 1974.

Paton, David and Charles H. Long, eds. *A Roland Allen Reader: The Compulsion of the Spirit.* Grand Rapids, MI: Eerdmans, 1983.

Peace, Richard. *Small Group Evangelism.* Downers Grove, IL: InterVarsity, 1985.

Pentecost, Edward C. *Reaching the Unreached.* South Pasadena, CA: William Carey, 1974.

Peters, George W. *A Theology of Church Growth.* Grand Rapids, MI: Zondervan, 1981.

Peterson, Jim. *Church without Walls.* Colorado Springs, CO: NavPress, 1992.

Pickett, J. Waskom. *Christian Mass Movements in India.* New York: Abingdon, 1933.

_____. *The Dynamics of Church Growth.* Nashville: Abingdon, 1963.

Pickett, J. Waskom, A. L. Warnshuis, G. H. Singh, and D. A. McGavran. *Church Growth and Group Conversion.* 5th ed. South Pasadena, CA: William Carey, 1973.

Piland, Harry M. and Arthur D. Burcham. *Evangelism through the Sunday School.* Nashville: Convention, 1981.

Powell, Paul W. *The Nuts and Bolts of Church Growth.* Nashville: Broadman, 1982.

Rainer, Thom S. "An Assessment of C. Peter Wagner's Contributions to the Theology of Church Growth," The Southern Baptist Theological Seminary, Louisville, KY, Ph.D. Dissertation, 1988.

_____. *The Book of Church Growth: History, Theology, and Principles.* Nashville: Broadman, 1993.

_____, ed. *Evangelism in the Twenty-First Century.* Wheaton, IL: Harold Shaw, 1989.

Ratz, Calvin, Frank Tillapaugh, and Myron Augsburger. *Mastering Outreach and Evangelism.* Portland, OR: Christianity Today and Multnomah, 1990.

Redford, Jack. *Planting New Churches.* Nashville: Broadman, 1978.

Schaller, Lyle E. *Activating the Passive Church: Diagnosis and Treatment.* Nashville: Abingdon, 1981.

_____. *Assimilating New Members.* Nashville: Abingdon, 1978.

_____. *Choices for Churches.* Nashville: Abingdon, 1990.

_____. *Effective Church Planning.* Nashville: Abingdon, 1979.

_____. *44 Questions for Church Planters.* Nashville: Abingdon, 1991.

_____. *44 Ways To Increase Church Attendance.* Nashville: Abingdon, 1988.

_____. *Growing Plans.* Nashville: Abingdon, 1983.

_____. *Hey, That's Our Church!* Nashville: Abingdon, 1975.

_____. *It's a Different World.* Nashville: Abingdon, 1987.

_____. *Looking in the Mirror.* Nashville: Abingdon, 1984.

_____. *The Middle-Sized Church.* Nashville: Abingdon, 1985.

_____. *The Multiple Staff and the Larger Church.* Nashville: Abingdon, 1980.

_____. *The Pastor and the People.* Rev. ed. Nashville: Abingdon, 1986.

_____. *Reflections of a Contrarian.* Nashville: Abingdon, 1989.

_____. *The Senior Minister.* Nashville: Abingdon, 1988.

_____. *The Seven-Day-a-Week Church.* Nashville: Abingdon, 1992.

_____. *Survival Tactics in the Parish.* Nashville: Abingdon, 1977.

Schuller, Robert H. *Your Church Has Real Possibilities.* Ventura, CA: Regal, 1975.

Shenk, Wilbert R., ed. *The Challenge of Church Growth: A Symposium.* Scottdale, PA: Herald, 1973.

_____, ed. *Exploring Church Growth.* Grand Rapids, MI: Eerdmans, 1983.

_____, ed. *Mission Focus: Current Issues.* Scottdale, PA: Herald, 1980.

Sisemore, John T. *Church Growth through the Sunday School.* Nashville: Broadman, 1983.

Slocum, Robert E. *Maximize Your Ministry.* Colorado Springs, CO: NavPress, 1990.

Smith, Ebbie C. *Balanced Church Growth.* Nashville: Broadman, 1984.

_____. *A Manual for Church Growth Survey.* South Pasadena, CA: William Carey, 1976.

Spader, Dan and Gary Mayes. *Growing a Healthy Church.* Chicago: Moody, 1991.

Springer, Kevin, ed. *Power Encounters.* San Francisco: Harper & Row, 1988.

Stevens, R. Paul. *Liberating the Laity.* Downers Grove, IL: InterVarsity, 1985.

Sullivan, Bill M. *Ten Steps to Breaking the 200 Barrier.* Kansas City, MO: Beacon Hill, 1988.

Taylor, Richard S. *Dimensions of Church Growth.* Grand Rapids, MI: Francis Asbury, 1989.

Tillapaugh, Frank R. *The Church Unleashed.* Ventura, CA: Regal, 1982.

Tippett, Alan R. *Church Growth and the Word of God: The Biblical Basis of the Church Growth Viewpoint.* Grand Rapids, MI: Eerdmans, 1970.

_____, ed. *God, Man, and Church Growth.* Grand Rapids, MI: Eerdmans, 1973.

_____, ed. *Verdict Theology in Missionary Theory.* South Pasadena, CA: William Carey, 1973.

Towns, Elmer L. *How to Grow an Effective Sunday School.* Lynchburg, VA: Church Growth Institute, 1987.

_____. *154 Steps to Revitalize Your Sunday School.* Wheaton, IL: Victor, 1988.

_____. *Ten of Today's Most Innovative Churches.* Ventura, CA: Regal, 1990.

_____. *Winning the Winnable.* Lynchburg, VA: Church Growth Institute, 1987.

Towns, Elmer L., John N. Vaughan, and David J. Seifert. *The Complete Book of Church Growth.* Wheaton, IL: Tyndale, 1981.

Vaughan, John N. *The Large Church: A Twentieth Century Expression of the First Century Church.* Grand Rapids, MI: Baker, 1985.

_____. *The World's Twenty Largest Churches.* Grand Rapids, MI: Baker, 1984.

Verkuyl, J. *Contemporary Missiology: An Introduction.* Grand Rapids, MI: Eerdmans, 1978.

Vines, Jerry. *Wanted: Church Growers.* Nashville: Broadman, 1990.

Wagner, C. Peter. *Church Growth and the Whole Gospel: A Biblical Mandate.* San Francisco: Harper & Row, 1981.

_____. *Church Planting for a Greater Harvest.* Ventura, CA: Regal, 1990.

_____. *Engaging the Enemy.* Ventura, CA: Regal, 1991.

_____. *Frontiers in Missionary Strategy.* Chicago: Moody, 1971.

_____. *How to Have a Healing Ministry without Making Your Church Sick.* Ventura, CA: Regal, 1988.

_____. *Leading Your Church to Growth.* Ventura, CA: Regal, 1984.

_____. *On the Crest of the Wave.* Ventura, CA: Regal, 1983.

_____. *Our Kind of People: The Ethical Dimensions of Church Growth in America.* Atlanta: John Knox, 1979.

_____. *Spiritual Power and Church Growth.* Altamonte Springs, FL: Creation House, 1986.

_____. *Stop the World! I Want to Get On.* Glendale, CA: Regal, 1974.

_____. *Strategies for Church Growth.* Ventura, CA: Regal, 1987.

_____. *The Third Wave of the Holy Spirit.* Ann Arbor, MI: Vine, 1988.

_____. *A Turned-On Church in an Uptight World.* Grand Rapids, MI: Zondervan, 1971.

_____. *Warfare Prayer.* Ventura, CA: Regal, 1992.

_____. *Your Church Can Be Healthy.* Nashville: Abingdon, 1979.

_____. *Your Spiritual Gifts Can Help Your Church Grow.* Glendale, CA: Regal, 1979.

_____, ed. *Church/Mission Tensions Today.* Chicago: Moody, 1972.

_____, ed. *Signs & Wonders Today.* Altamonte Springs, FL: Creation House, 1987.

_____, ed. with Win Arn, and Elmer Towns. *Church Growth: State of the Art*. Wheaton, IL: Tyndale, 1986.

Wagner, C. Peter, and F. Douglas Pennoyer, eds. *Wrestling with Dark Angels*. Ventura, CA: Regal, 1990.

Wagner, C. Peter, and Bob Waymire. *The Church Growth Survey Handbook*. 3rd ed. Milpitas, CA: Global Church Growth, 1983.

Warren, Max. *I Believe in the Great Commission*. Grand Rapids, MI: Eerdmans, 1976.

Weese, Carolyn. *Eagles in Tall Steeples*. Nashville: Oliver Nelson, 1991.

Werning, Waldo J. *Vision and Strategy for Church Growth*. Rev. ed. Grand Rapids, MI: Baker, 1983.

White, James Emery. *Opening the Front Door: Worship and Church Growth*. Nashville: Convention, 1992.

Wilkie, Richard B. *And Are We Yet Alive?* Nashville: Abingdon, 1986.

Wimber, John with Kevin Springer. *Power Evangelism*. San Francisco: Harper & Row, 1986.

Wimber, John with Kevin Springer. *Power Healing*. San Francisco: Harper & Row, 1987.

_____. *Power Points*. San Francisco: Harper & Row, 1991.

Yamamori, Tetsunao and E. LeRoy Lawson. *Introducing Church Growth: A Textbook in Missions*. Cincinnati: New Life, 1975.

Yeakley, Flavil R., Jr. *Why Churches Grow*. Nashville: Anderson's, 1977.

Zunkel, C. Wayne. *Church Growth Under Fire*. Scottdale, PA: Herald, 1987.

_____. *Strategies for Growing Your Church*. Elgin, IL: David C. Cook, 1986.

Name and Subject Index

Abelard 137
accident theory 137
Adams, Arthur 267
administration/leadership, gift of 118
adoption 140
adoption method of church planting 210-211
adultery 131, 190
All Souls Church 152
Allen, Roland 28-29
altar call 225
Altizer, Thomas 137
American Sunday-School Union 290
amillennialism 164
Anderson, Rufus 28, 151
Andes Evangelical Mission 52
angelology 121-127
angels
   church growth and 121-126
   fallen 121, 123-125
   guardian 122
   unfallen 121
Anselm 137
anthropological, anthropology 129-130
apartheid 259
apostle, gift of 114
Apostolic Preaching and Its Developments, The 102
appearance of church building 271, 276-277
archangel 122, 163
Arius 111
Arn, Win 38, 41, 44, 57
Assemblies of God 205, 208
assimilation 281-286, 293, 294, 297
atheism 133
atheistic evolution 133
atonement 106, 135-139
Azalea Baptist Church 200

baby boomers 64, 67, 222, 232, 233, 234, 272, 285
baby busters 64, 222, 272
backdoor 281, 282, 292
Balanced Church Growth 75
Barna, George 64, 65, 177, 183, 188, 189, 216, 219, 241, 242
Barnabas 212
Barnette, J. N. 291
Barth, Karl 304
Bassham, Rodger 48, 150
Bavnick, Herman 97
Bear Valley Baptist Church 240
behaviorial sciences 20, 21, 87, 89
Benjamin, Paul 43, 44
Berkhof, Louis 97
Berlin Congress of 1966 151
Bible
   authority of 74, 76, 87, 88
   inspiration of 87-88, 89, 112
   original autographs of 88
   power of 76, 89
   translation 80
Bible Institute of Los Angeles, see Biola College
biblical theology 73
bibliology 20, 75, 87-91
Billy Graham Evangelistic Association 42
Biola College 52
biological growth 22, 24, 295
bishop 147
Black Power and White Protestants 258
body of Christ 112, 145
Bolivian Indian Mission 52
bride of Christ 145
Bridges of God, The 21, 25, 31, 34-36, 38, 53, 149, 254
bridging growth 23, 43
Buddhist 68

Bushnell, Horace 137
business meetings 67, 222

Campbell, J. McLeod 137
Campus Crusade for Christ 42
Cannon, Kim 241
Carey, William 27
Carson, D. A. 317, 318
Carter, Chuck 65, 178, 200
caste system 259
Chandler, Russell 209, 226
Chaney, Charles 41
charismatic 306, 307
Charismatic Chaos 311
Charles E. Fuller Institute of
   Evangelism and Church Growth 38,
   41, 56, 65, 293
cherubim 122
children's ministries 285
Cho, Paul Yonggi 269-270, 289
Christ, see Jesus Christ
Christian Life 304
Christian Mass Movements in India 29
Christian Missions in Mid-India 33
Christian Scientists 306
Christological heresies 104-105
Christology 101-109
church
   government of 146-147
   images of 145-146
   purpose of 147-158
church growth
   angels and 121-126
   anthropology and 129-130
   assimilation and 281-286
   bibliology and 87-91
   Christology and 101-109
   church planting and, see church
      planting
   conferences 20, 24, 64, 66, 68
   consultation 20, 64, 65
   criticisms of 44-49, 57-58
   definitions of 20-22
   demons and, see demons
   ecclesiology and 145-158, 173-174
   ecumenism and 42, 66
   eschatology and 161-167
   evangelism and 22-24, 215-223
   goal setting and, see goal setting
   hamartiology and 129-133
   in China 289-290

   in Latin America 302-304
   influences on 42-43
   laity and, see lay ministry
   leadership and, see leadership
   methodology of 29, 39, 98, 126, 176,
      177, 319
   numerical emphasis of 20, 35, 46, 91,
      102, 142, 153, 167, 203, 250, 268,
      269, 317
   Pasadena influence on 38
   physical facilities and 271-279
   planning and 253, 265-270
   pneumatology and 111-119
   prayer and 126, 175-184
   principles of 65, 169-312
   prospects and, see prospects
   publications and other media 24, 65-66
   reclamation and 281-286
   receptivity and, see receptivity
   Satan and, see Satan
   signs and wonders and, see sign and
      wonders
   small groups and, see small groups
   soteriology and 135-143
   spiritual warfare and, see spiritual
      warfare
   theology of 38, 47, 48, 69, 71-168
   theology proper and 93-99
   types of 22-23
   worship and 66, 225-236
Church Growth and Group Conversion
   29, 33
Church Growth and the Whole Gospel
   54, 58, 59, 153, 154, 155, 259, 262
Church Growth Book Club 38
Church Growth Bulletin 37
Church Growth Center 41
Church Growth Institute 209
Church Growth Movement 19, 21, 25,
   27, 29, 30, 31, 34, 36, 37, 38, 39, 41,
   42, 43, 44, 47, 48, 49, 51, 52, 54, 55,
   57, 58, 59, 61, 62, 64, 66, 67, 68, 69,
   87, 90, 91, 101, 102, 112, 113, 114,
   121, 123, 126, 133, 142, 149, 150,
   153, 157, 166, 167, 171, 175, 176,
   189, 195, 196, 215, 218, 227, 246,
   249, 253, 254, 259, 262, 283, 302,
   317, 318, 319
*Church Growth Principles: Separating
   Fact from Fiction* 65, 172
Church Growth Series 37
Church Growth: State of the Art 59

Church Growth Visions 65
Church of the Nazarene 205
Church on the Way, The 212
church planting 98, 114, 205-213
church splits 211
civil rights movement 257, 258
Clarke, Samuel 137
classical mission 150
cold call evangelism 215, 216, 222
colonization 210
Columbia University 33
commercial theory 106, 137
committees 67, 200, 222, 283
community presence 239-240
confrontational evangelism 215, 216
congregational form of government
    146-147
Continuing Witness Training 216, 222,
    245
consultation, church growth, see church
    growth, consultation
Consultation on World Evangelization
    156
Contemporary Theologies of Mission 75
contemporary theology 73
conversion 29, 116, 167, 310
conversion growth 22, 24, 206, 295
Costas, Orlando 47, 152, 155, 156
Council of Nicaea 111
creation, creationism 129-130
Crystal Cathedral 173
cultural mandate 151, 152, 153, 154,
    155, 156, 157, 158, 260

David 103, 192
day-age theory 129
Dayton, Edward R. 56, 251
deacon 201
demographics, demography 21, 64, 65,
    90, 98, 126, 186, 187, 235
demon possession 124
demonic, demons (also see fallen angels)
    81, 121, 123-124, 132, 150, 306
denominations 66, 67, 68, 158, 180,
    197, 291, 306
Design for Church Growth 41
direct mail 242
discerning spirits, see distinguishing
    spirits
disciple, disciple-making, discipleship
    20, 22, 28, 35, 66, 78, 82, 91, 108,

109, 116, 119, 130, 133, 140, 142,
    148, 151, 167, 201, 216, 223, 250,
    251, 283, 286, 298, 317, 319
discipling 34, 35, 36
Disciples of Christ 33
discrimination 259, 260
dispensationalism 114, 215, 308
distinguishing spirits, gift of 114, 116
divorce 220
Docetists 105
Dodd, C. H. 102, 103, 105
Doerksen, Vernon D. 95
Dorris, Charles 178
drama 233, 241
dramatic theory 106
dreams 94
Drummond, Lewis A. 24, 319
drunkenness 131

E-0 22
E-1 22-23
E-2 23
E-3 23
Easum, William 272, 273
Ebionites 105
ecclesiocentricity 28
ecclesiology 145-158, 161
Edge, Findley 296
Enns, Paul 105, 124, 135
elder 147
elect, election 99, 140
Elliot, Ralph H. 253
Engel, James 218
Engel scale 218-219
episcopal form of church government 147
Episcopalians 306
Erickson, Millard J. 96, 131, 139, 146,
    162
eschatology
    church growth and, see church
        growth, eschatology and
    cosmic 161, 162-165
    individual 161-162
Escobar, Samuel 152
ethical theory 106
ethnocentrism 256
Eubank, Marion 178
evangelical, evangelicalism 150, 151,
    152, 153, 155, 156, 157, 158, 164,
    166, 197, 306, 307, 308, 311, 312,
    318, 319

evangelism, evangelization
and church growth 215-223
approaches 76-77
church and 79, 148, 149
cooperation in 79-80
life-style 245-246
nature of 77-78
priority of 27, 79, 149, 155-158, 256,
295, 317
relationship 247
training, see Evangelism Explosion III
and Continuing Witness Training
Evangelism Explosion III 42, 215, 216,
222, 245
evangelism, gift of 116
evangelistic mandate 152, 153, 156,
157, 158, 254, 260
event evangelism 216
evolution 129, 130
example theory 106
exhortation, gift of 117
exorcisms 303
expansion growth 23, 43
extension growth 23, 43

faith 77, 78, 79, 83, 124, 126, 138, 150,
154, 174, 215, 218, 245, 261, 267,
270, 303
Faith at Work 43
faith, gift of 117, 118
fall 130
fellowship 282, 297
fiat creation 130
Finding Them, Keeping Them 282
Finney, Charles 25
First Baptist Church of Leesburg,
Florida 239
first wave 306
Flake, Arthur 291, 292
flesh 131-132
flock 146
forgiveness 130, 135, 138, 218
fornication 131
Foundations of Church Growth 75
Friends 147
Frog in the Kettle, The 65
front door 220, 225, 228, 249, 281, 291,
292
Frontiers in Missionary Strategy 46, 152
fruit of the Holy Spirit, see Holy Spirit
Full Gospel Business Men's Fellowship 43

Fuller Theological Seminary 37, 38, 41,
51, 52, 53, 54, 55, 56, 63, 304, 305, 306

Galloway, Dale 294, 295
Gallup, George 64
gap theory 129
Gehenna 162
general revelation 77, 88, 94
geographical expanded parish church 209
George, Carl F. 64, 289, 293, 296
Gibbs, Eddie 75
gifts of the Holy Spirit 113-119
giving, gift of 118
Glasser, Arthur 41, 75, 153
Global Church Growth 37
Gloucester Journal 290
gluttony 131
goal setting 98, 265, 270
God
attributes of 95-97
existence of 93-94, 97
glory of 74, 97
holiness of 95, 96, 97, 137
image of 108, 124, 130
immanence of 95
immutability of 95, 97
infinity of 95, 97
love of 95, 96, 97, 130, 139
omnipotence of 95, 97, 98, 123
omnipresence of 95, 97, 123
omniscience of 95, 123
revelation of 94
righteousness of 95, 96, 97
sovereignty of 74, 98-99, 253, 265
Trinity of 95
Gonzalez, Ausencio 301
gospel 148, 152, 176, 218, 219, 223,
236, 250, 251, 252, 253, 255, 257,
261, 309, 311
governmental theory 136
grace
common 141
efficacious 141
irresistible 141
prevenient 141
special 141
sufficient 141
Graham, Billy 197
Great Commission 21, 28, 35, 66, 88,
101, 102, 108, 116, 122, 124, 152,
185, 209, 210, 212, 213, 216, 239,

246, 252, 283, 317
Great Reversal 153
great tribulation, see tribulation
Green Valley Baptist Church 178, 181,
    182, 202, 208, 210, 229, 230, 231,
    235, 243, 244, 272, 277, 278
Grotius 137
Growing Churches 65, 68
Growing Congregation, The 34
Grubb, Sir Kenneth 34

Hadaway, C. Kirk 65, 172-173, 183,
    186, 192, 203, 241, 245, 265, 266
Hades 162
hamartiology 129-133
Hayford, Jack 212
healing 61, 62, 63, 303, 305, 306, 307, 310
healing, gift of 114, 115
heaven 163, 164, 166-167
hell 157, 161, 166
helps, gift of 117, 118, 201
Hemphill, Ken 292
hermeneutic, church growth 47, 48, 59,
    75, 87, 90-91
Hindu 68
historical theology 73
Hodge, Charles 97
Hoekstra, Harvey 150
holiness of God, see God, holiness of
holistic evangelism 152-153, 155, 156
Holy Spirit
    baptism by 112
    filling with 118-119
    fruit of 118-119, 142
    gifts of, see gifts of the Holy Spirit
    in the birth of Jesus 112
    in the writing of Scripture 112
    indwelling by 112
    ministry of 112-113
    person of 111-112
    power of 83
    sealing with 113
Home Mission Board 68, 205
homogeneous unit principle 35, 45, 54,
    57, 246, 249, 254-262, 317
Hough, Joseph 258
How Churches Grow 149
How to Grow a Church 44
*How to Have a Healing Ministry
    without Making Your Church Sick*
    51, 63, 176, 307

Hundnutt, Robert K. 46
Hull, Bill 318
humanism 68
Hunter, George 211, 249
Hunter, Kent R. 41, 75
Hybels, Bill 64, 65

I Believe in Church Growth 75
Iberville Consultation of 1963 37
Irenaeus 137
indigeneous 28, 82
inerrancy 94, 112
infinity of God, see God infinity of
Institute for Church Renewal 43
Institute for American Church Growth
    38, 41, 57
Institute of Church Growth (Eugene,
    Oregon) 36, 37
integration 258
internal growth 23
International Review of Missions 37
International Congress on World
    Evangelization, see Lausanne
invitation 242, 245

Jehovah's Witnessses 68, 111, 306
Jesus Christ
    ascension of 103, 107, 122, 162, 166
    birthplace of 103
    death of 102, 103, 105, 107
    deity of 105, 106
    earthly ministry of 107
    eternality of 102, 105, 108
    exclusiveness of salvation through
        74, 101-102, 108-109
    fulfillment of prophecy 102-103, 106-
        107
    future ministry of 107-108
    glorification of 107
    immutability of 105
    incarnation and humanity of 102,
        103-104, 105
    infancy of 122
    intercessory ministry of 77, 107
    lineage of 102-103
    lordship of 74
    offices of 103
    omnipotence of 105
    omnipresence of 105
    omniscience of 105

present ministry of 107
resurrection of 102, 106-107, 108, 122
return of (second coming) 84, 103, 107, 108, 109, 122, 162-167
suffering of 104
temptation of 122
uniqueness and universality of 76
virgin birth of 102, 103, 104, 105, 122
Jethro 200, 295
Jethro model, 295
Jewish 68
John the Baptist 103, 150
Joshua 192
judgment 163, 166
justice 158
justification 106, 138

Kelley, Dean 44
kerygma 102, 103, 106
Keswick Movement 43
Kilian, Sabbas J. 46, 47
King, Arthur Clyde 296
King, Nell 296
kingdom, kingdom of God 74, 76, 78, 89, 141, 150, 154, 166, 192, 205, 206, 260, 289, 319
Kingdom beyond Caste, The 258
kingdom growth 205-206, 207
knowledge, gift of 114, 116
Kraft, Charles 41
Krass, Alfred C. 47, 155

Ladd, George 165
Laity Lodge 43
Large Church, The 211
Latourette, Kenneth Scott 34
Lausanne Covenant 42, 74, 75-85, 93, 101, 105, 107, 149, 152, 155, 156, 166
Lausanne (International Congress on World Evangelization) 42, 55, 56, 66, 74, 75, 151, 152, 155, 156, 197, 259
Lausanne Committee for World Evangelization 42, 55
Lausanne Strategy Working Group 55, 251
lay ministry 43, 66, 113, 167, 195-203, 283
leadership 126, 167, 177-178, 180, 185-193, 266, 293

leadership, gift of, see administration
Leading Your Church to Growth 185
Lewis, Gordon R. 96
Lewis, Ron 41, 65
liberalism 91, 105, 156, 158
Look Out! The Pentecostals Are Coming! 45
Lord's Supper 148
lordship of Christ, see Jesus Christ, lordship of
Lucifer, see Satan
Luther, Martin 89, 195, 232
Lutherans 306

MacArthur, John 308, 309, 311, 318
Mackintosh, H. R. 137
mainline denominations 24, 68
marketing 90, 241-242
Marketing the Church 241
marriage 219-220
Martin, Glen 282, 283
Martyn, Henry 27
mass movements 29, 30
Maxwell, Aulene 181
Maxwell, John 64
MC510 63, 304
MC550 63
McGavran, Donald A. 20, 21, 22, 25, 27, 28, 29, 30, 31, 33-39, 41, 43, 44, 45, 46, 47, 48, 51, 52-53, 54, 55, 57, 58, 62, 75, 98, 142, 149, 211, 252, 254, 255, 256, 257, 303, 304, 317
McGavran, Helen Anderson 33
McGavran, John Grafton 33
McIntosh, Gary 282, 283
megachurches (superchurches) 42, 67
mercy, gift of 117-118
Messiah 137
meta-church 296
Meye, Robert 304
Michael 122
Miles, Delos 38, 42, 43
millenialism 163
Miller, Tim 178
miracles 62, 105, 297, 303, 309, 310, 311
miracles, gift of 114, 115, 118
missiology, missiologist 27, 34, 35, 38, 47, 48, 49, 55, 261
missionary 27, 28, 30, 31, 34, 36, 52, 80, 81, 157, 317
mission, missions 28, 36, 47, 48, 76, 79,

80, 82, 98, 107, 149, 150-155, 167,
  207, 319
Missions Advanced Research and
  Communications Center (MARC) 38
modernity 91
moral influence theory 137
Mormans 68, 306
Moses 192, 200
Mott, John 28
Mount Paran Church of God 212
multicampus 207, 212
multicongregational 212
Murren, Doug 64
Muslim 68
mysticism 68

National Church Growth Research
  Center 44
National Council of Churches 44, 46
naturalism 68
Nehemiah 192
Neo-Pentecostal 43
New Age 68
New Hope Community Church 294-295
New Orleans Baptist Theological
  Seminary 68
new pagans 217, 222
*New Reformation: Returning the
  Ministry to the People of God, The* 195
new residents 242-243
Ninety-Five Theses 89
North American Society for Church
  Growth 20, 57
Northwest Christian College 36, 37
numbers, church growth emphasis on, see
  church growth, numerical emphasis of

Ogden, Greg 195, 196, 197, 198
omnipotence of God, see God,
  omnipotence of
omnipresence of God, see God,
  omnipresence of
omniscience of God, see God,
  omniscience of
*Opening the Front Door: Worship and
  Church Growth* 225
Origen 137
Our Kind of People 57, 256-262

Padilla, Rene 152, 155, 261, 262
paradigm, paradigm shift 62, 176, 196,

197, 199, 215, 217
parking 232, 271, 272, 273, 275, 276,
  277, 279
passive media 242
pastor
  as equipper 198—203
  leadership of 186-193
  tenure of 192-193, 199
Pastor's Update, The
pastor-teacher, gift of 116
penal-substitution theory, see
  substitutionary
Pentecostal, Pentecostalism 62, 63,
  303, 306, 307
people movements 30, 34, 35
people of God 145
perfecting 34, 36
perimeter church 210
phenomenological hermeneutics 90
Philadelphia Baptist Church 210
physical facilities 271-279
Pickett, J. Waskom 29-30, 33, 37
Piland, Harry 291
PIPPs (Pastor's Intercessory Prayer
  Partners) 182
planning, see church growth, planning
  and
Plymouth Brethen 147
pneumatology 111-119
pope 147
Pope, Liston 258
postmillennialism 163
posttribulationalism 165
power evangelism, see signs and
  wonders
practical dispensationalists 114
practioners 63-64
pragmatic, pragmatism 29, 30, 35, 87,
  89, 101, 196, 250, 251, 253, 256, 266,
  268, 269, 317, 319
prayer
  church growth and, see church
    growth and prayer
  intercessory 181
  spiritual warfare and 126, 179-180
  vision and 177-179, 188
prayer cards 181
prayer chains 181
prayer emphases 182
prayer groups 182
prayer ministry 180-183
prayer room 181

preaching 99, 148, 152, 166, 309, 310, 311
predestination 99, 140
premillenialism 164
Prepare Your Church for the Future 293
presbyterian form of government 147
Presbyterians 306
preschool space 272, 273
pretribulationalism 164-165
pre-wrath rapture view 165-166
priesthood 146
Princeton Theological Seminary 53
professors, professorships 24, 59
progressive creationism 129
progressive revelation 73
prophecy, gift of 114, 115
propitiation 106, 136
prospects 239-247, 294
psycho-spatial dynamics 273
PTL 43

Quakers 147
quantitative growth, see church
     growth, numerical emphasis of

racism 254, 259, 260, 261
Raikes, Robert 290
Rainer, Jo 296
Rainer, Thom S. 19, 181, 244
Ramm, Bernard 90
ranchers 188-189, 294
ransom 137
ransom theory 106, 137
rapture 164, 165, 166
recapitulation theory 137
receptivity 30, 80, 246, 249-254, 317
reclamation 281-286
reconciliation 106, 130, 133, 135, 138
redemption 106, 138
Reformation 67, 89, 195, 203, 279
regeneration 141
relevancy 91, 220-221, 222, 223, 234,
     236
repentance 24, 77, 137, 150, 154, 156,
     218
resistance-receptivity axis 251
resistance-receptivity theory 250
response evangelism 216
responsible church membership 20, 21,
     22, 69, 142, 151, 167
Revivalism and Social Reform 157

revivals 234
righteousness 126, 130, 133, 138, 164
Ritschl, Albrecht 137
Roesel, Charles 239-240
Roman Catholic Church 147, 306
Rutgers, Herman 28
Rutgers University 52

Saddleback model 191
saint 141
sanctification 140
Satan 121, 123, 124-125, 132, 179
satellite churches 179, 207, 209, 211-
     212, 235
satisfaction theory 137
Schaller, Lyle 64, 67, 179, 188, 192,
     208, 282, 294
schedule, church 221-222
Scherer, James 46
Schleiermacher, Friedrich 137
School of World Mission and Institute
     of Church Growth 38, 41, 52, 54
Schweitzer, A. 137
scientism 68
Scofield Bible 62
Scripture, see Bible
Second Great Awakening 232-233
second wave 306
seminaries 24, 59, 67, 68
seraphim 122
sermons, see preaching
service, gift of 117, 118
Seven-Day-a-Week Church, The 67
700 Club 43
Shades Mountain Independent Church
     241
Shedd, William G. T. 97
sign gifts 61, 62, 114, 215, 308
signs and wonders 61-63, 114, 115,
     116, 176, 301-312, 317, 318
Signs and Wonders Today 304
sin 74, 81, 105, 106, 107, 108, 118, 129-
     133, 135-139, 218, 223, 234
slothfulness 131
small groups 180, 189, 196, 200, 221,
     242, 245, 278, 279, 283, 285, 289-
     298
Smith, Ebbie 75
Smith, Kenneth L. 45
Smith, Timothy L. 157
Snyder, Howard 153

social action 154, 156
social concerns, social responsibility,
    social ministry 58, 78-79, 148-149,
    151, 152, 153, 154, 155, 157-158,
    173, 317
Social Conscience of the Evangelical 157
social gospel 151
social sciences 20, 21, 47, 65, 67, 87,
    89, 90, 91, 98, 126
social service 154
Socinian view of atonement 136
Socinius 137
sociologist 64
sociology, see social sciences
sodality models 212
sola scriptura 89
soteriology 135-143, 161
sound and lighting 276
South American Mission 52
Southern Baptist Convention 25, 41, 42,
    43, 65, 68, 146, 192-193, 201, 205,
    209, 210, 216, 226, 240, 278, 279, 291
sovereignty of God, see God,
    sovereignty of
special events 240-241
special revelation 88, 94
specialty churches 67
Speer, Robert 28
spiritual awakenings 25
spiritual gifts 107, 113-118, 148, 187,
    196, 283, 305
spiritual warfare 82, 121, 122, 123,
    126, 192, 200-201
*Spontaneous Expansion of the Church and
    the Causes Which Hinder It, The* 28-29
Spurgeon, Charles 25
staffing 67
Stott, John R. W. 152
strategies 266
Strategies for Church Growth 59
Strong, A. H. 95
Student Volunteer Movement 28, 158
substitutionary death of Christ 106,
    108, 136, 138-142
Sudan Interior Mission 52
Sullivan, Bill 266
Sunday School 25, 41, 43, 68, 216, 226,
    272, 274, 275, 278, 279, 281, 283,
    285, 290-293, 295, 298
Surburban Captivity of the Church, The
    258
surveys 187, 243-244

syncretism 68, 101
systematic theology 73-75

teacher, gift of 116-117, 201
telemarketing 242
TELL 42
Temple, Archbishop William 45
temple of the Holy Spirit 146
theism 68
theological education 80, 82
theology proper 93-99
theophanies 94
Thiessen, Henry C. 95
third wave 306, 307, 309
Tillapaugh, Frank 201-202
Tippett, Allen 37, 41
tongues, gift of speaking in 61, 62, 114,
    115, 306-307, 308
tongues, gift of interpretation of 61,
    115-116, 308
Towns, Elmer 41, 209, 226, 291
tradition 268
traditional churches 67
traditional model of church planting 210
traditionalism 268
transfer growth 22, 295
tribulation 123, 164, 165, 166
Trinity, see God, Trinity of

U. S. Center for World Mission 38
Understanding Church Growth 38, 39,
    43, 45, 46, 47, 149, 254
Unitarianism, Unitarians 111, 137
United Christian Missionary Society
    31, 33, 37
United Methodists 306
Universal Declaration of Human
    Rights, The 83
University of Southern California 54, 257
Unleashing the Church 201
Unreached Peoples 56
user friendly 66, 90, 132
User Friendly Churches 177, 216

Vacation Bible School 285
Vaughan, John 211
Venn, Henry 28
verbal plenary 88
Vicedom, George F. 34

Vineyard Christian Fellowship 56, 62, 318
vision 65, 177-179, 186-188, 265, 266, 268, 283, 286

Wagner, C. Graham 51
Wagner, C. Peter 21, 22, 23, 35, 41, 45, 46, 48, 49, 51-59, 61-63, 74, 90, 113, 116, 121, 123, 126, 149, 150, 151, 152, 153, 154, 155, 156, 157, 158, 172, 176, 185, 188, 192, 195, 200, 205, 206, 207, 208, 211, 212, 215, 228, 249, 250, 251, 252, 253, 254, 255, 256-262, 265, 266, 267, 269, 270, 294, 302, 305, 307, 317
Wagner, Doris Mueller 52
Wagner, Mary Lewis 51
Walker, Paul 212
Warren, Rick 64
Watson, Richard 137
Weese, Carolyn 190
Wesley, John 25
Wheaton College 218
Whitby, Daniel 137
White, James Emery 225, 236, 273, 277, 291
Whitefield, George 25
Why Conservative Churches Are Growing 44
William Carey Library 38
Willow Creek Community Church 65
Willow Creek model 191
Wimber, John 41, 56, 62, 63, 304, 305, 307, 310, 318
WIN 42
Winter, Gibson 258
Winter, Ralph D. 38, 41, 259
Wirt, Sherwood 157
wisdom, gift of 118
Without a Vision the People Perish 65, 186
Wittenberg 89
Women Aglow 43
words of knowledge 305
world 131
World Congress on Evangelism 42
worldview 310
worship 79, 115, 171, 172, 174, 225-236
worship services
   atmosphere of 228-230
   day of 236

music and 172, 226, 232-233
quality of 228
sermons and 233-234
variety in and scheduling of 233, 271, 272
welcoming guests in 172, 230-232

Yoido Full Gospel Church 269
Yokefellows 43
Young, Ed 64
Your Church Can Grow 57
Your Spiritual Gifts Can Help Your Church Grow 57

Scripture Index

Genesis
1:1...129
1:2.......................................112, 129
1:26...130
1:26-27 ....79, 108
1:27...94
1:28...131
2:16-17 130
2:17...133
2:21...22
3...108, 130
3:16...130
3:17-18 130
3:17-19 130
3:24...122
4:21-22 81
9:6...94
12:2...102
18:25...79
49:10...102

Exodus
3:14...93
15:13...146
18:13-23 295
18:13-27 200

Leviticus
4:1...88
4:35...136
19:18...79

Numbers
24:17...103

Deuteronomy
18:15-18 103

2 Samuel
7:12-16 103

1 Kings
19:5-7 122

Esther
4:14...187

Psalms
2:6...103
16:10....................................103, 107
19:1-6 94
22:1...103
22:7-8 103
22:8...103
22:16...103
22:17...103
22:24...103
22:48...103
34:7...122
45:7...79
67:1-3 84
68:18...103
85:4-7 84
110:4...103
148:2-5 121

Proverbs
6:16-17 133

Isaiah
1:10...88
1:17...79
6:2-3 122
7:14...103
40:3...103
40:28...76
52:14...103
53:4-6 136
53:5...103
55:11...76

58:6-7 8

Jeremiah
1:11...88

Ezekiel
1...122
28:12...125
28:15...125

Daniel
10:13..122

Micah
5:2...103

Zechariah
8:17..133

Malachi
3:1...103

Matthew
1:1-2 103
1:18..112
1:20..104, 108
1:23..103
2:6..103
2:13..112
3:2..150
3:3..103
4:1..125
4:2..104
4:3..125
4:4...88
4:7...88
4:10...88, 124, 125
4:11..122
4:24..124
5:10-12 83
5:13-14 91
5:17-18 ....76, 88
5:20...79
6:33...79
7:3..133
7:7-11 131
7:16...142
8:16..123, 124
8:23-27 105
8:28..124
8:33..124
9:18-20 105

9:27-31 105
9:35-38 81
9:36..104
9:37-38 251
10:7-8 150
10:11-14 251
10:28..157, 161
11:28..77
12:22...124
12:24...125
12:26...124
12:38-39 312
13:1-23 250
13:28...125
14:15-21 105
14:26...105
15:22...124
16:1-4 312
16:18...101
19:28...141
20:18-19 105
21:5..103
21:22...181
21:42..88
22:44..88, 105
23:37...104
24:30...163
25:13...165
25:31...122
25:31-46 ....81, 148, 163
25:32...163
25:40...240
25:41...123
25:41-46 133
25:46..163, 167
26:1-2 105
26:39...103
27:39...103
27:43...103
27:46...103
28:5-7 122
28:9..236
28:15...105
28:18..84, 166
28:18-20 20
28:19.......................36, 76, 88, 101,
    109, 119, 130, 133, 140, 148, 167,
    185, 209, 239
28:19-20 ....79, 116, 148
28:20..84, 166

Mark

1:13	124
1:32	124
2:1-12	105
3:23	124
3:26	124
4:15	124
5:15	124
5:16	124
5:18	124
7:8-9	81
7:13	81
8:11-12	312
8:34	78, 286
9:43	162
9:48	162
10:42-45	82
10:43-45	78
13:10	84, 166
13:21-23	84, 166
13:32-33	163
14:62	84, 166
15:34	103
16:6-7	122
16:15	81
16:19	107

Luke

1:26-38	122
1:35	104, 108
2:52	104
4:18	83
5:1-11	105
6:27	79
6:35	79
8:11	250
8:31	123
8:36	124
10:17	123
10:25-37	148
11:16	312
11:18	124
11:29	312
12:32	84, 166
14:25-33	78
15:11-24	135
15:11-32	286
19:14	104
19:46	181
22:3	124
22:43	122
23:8-9	312

23:43	162
24:4-7	122
24:13	236
24:50-53	103
24:51	107

John

1:1	88, 102, 105, 108, 112
1:14	88, 104
2:1-11	105
2:18	84, 166
3:3	79, 141
3:5	79
3:6-8	84
3:16	130, 133
3:16-18	140
3:16-19	77
4:1-3	84, 166
4:6	104
4:35	250
4:36-37	250
4:42	77
4:46-54	105
4:48	312
5:1-18	105
5:25	105
7:37-39	84, 112
8:44	125
8:58	101
9:4	81
10:11	116
10:14	116
10:16	116, 146
10:21	123, 124
10:27-28	141
10:34	88
10:35	76
11:1-44	105
11:34-35	104
12:31	125
13:27	124
13:35	80
14:6	101, 108, 112
14:12	145
14:16	112
14:26	111
15:18-21	83
15:26	111
15:26-27	84
16:7	107
16:8-11	84
16:13	111, 146

16:17......................................107
16:30......................................105
17:6..76
17:11-23 80
17:15...............................83, 125
17:18................................76, 79
17:21..80
17:23..80
19:1.................................103, 104
19:18...............................103, 104
19:24......................................103
19:28......................................104
19:33-36 103
20:12-13 122
20:19......................................236
20:21................................78, 79
20:25......................................103
20:28......................................105

Acts
1:8.........................79, 84, 148
1:8-11 ....84, 166
1:9..107
1:9-11 103
1:10..122
1:11..163
1:14..175
1:15-26 147
2................................236, 302
2:4..310
2:16..106
2:27-28 103
2:32-39 78
2:40..78
2:41..310
2:42....................116, 175, 282
2:42-47 297
2:43..312
2:44..282
2:44-45 ....81, 148
2:46..289
2:47....................78, 119, 312
3:22-23 103
4:2..116
4:12.................................77, 101
4:18..175
4:19..83
4:24-26 148
4:28..140
4:29-30 302
4:31.................................146, 175
4:33..146

4:34-35 81
5:12................................115, 302
5:14................................115, 302
5:19..122
5:29..83
5:42..116
6:1-6 147
6:3-4 199
6:7..199
8:1-4 209
8:26-40 310
9:32-43 310
9:40-42 310
10:1..310
10:3-6 122
10:9..310
10:47......................................310
11:11......................................176
11:23......................................176
11:26......................................116
12:5....................122, 148, 175
12:7-11 122
13:1..116
13:1-3 80
13:2..112
13:2-3 212
14:23................................82, 147
15:14..76
15:28......................................236
15:35......................................117
16:7..111
16:13..99
16:30......................................247
17:26..79
17:31..79
17:34......................................310
18:8..310
18:11......................................117
18:26......................................148
19:13-16 124
20:7-12 310
20:27..79
28:3-10 310

Romans
1:1..99
1:8..80
1:16................................76, 311
1:18-21 94
1:18-32 77
1:20..94
3:22..138

3:24..138
3:25..106
5:1...106
5:5...142
5:9...138
5:12....................................108, 130
5:17-18.....................................133
6:23..133
7:21-25.....................................132
8:5-6...132
8:9...112
8:19-21.....................................108
8:26..112
8:29-30.....................................140
8:30...99
8:34..107
9:1-3...81
9:11...99
10:9...105
10:14-15.....................................99
12:2...76
12:3-8...84
12:6..115
12:7..117
12:8....................................117, 118
12:10...297
14:5..236

1 Corinthians
1:2..89, 140
1:21...76
1:23.......................................77, 78
2:1...310
2:4...84
2:4-5..310
2:6...118
2:7...140
2:11...111
2:16..142
3:12-15.......................................270
3:18-19.......................................178
5:10...76
6:3...122
6:19..112
6:20....................................108, 138
7:23....................................106, 138
9:16...99
9:19-23..81
9:22...90
11:23-26.....................................148
12..148
12:1..113

12:3...84
12:4-31..84
12:8..116
12:9....................................115, 117
12:10...................................115, 116
12:11..112
12:12...145
12:13....................................112, 307
12:28.........................115, 117, 118
12:30...................................115, 116
13:8..114
13:8-10................................114, 308
13:10...114
13:12...308
14:3..115
14:3-4..148
14:18...115
14:22...115
14:23-25......................................225
14:28-29......................................115
14:37..88
15:3-4...................................78, 311
15:17...106
15:51-58......................................108
15:56-57...............................108, 161
16:2..148

2 Corinthians
1:1...140
1:22..113
2:17...83
3:18.......................................79, 84
4:2...83
4:3-4...83
4:4..124, 125
4:5..78, 81
4:7...76
5:8..162
5:11...78
5:17..142
5:18-20......................................106
5:20...78
5:21..136
6:3-4...79
6:15..125
6:16..146
6:20..106
10:3-5..83
10:4...91
11:3..124

Galatians
1:6-9 ....77, 83
3:13...................................106
4:5.............................106, 140
4:8....................................236
5:11....................................83
5:22-23 ....84, 118, 142
6:2....................................297
6:10...................................154
6:14....................................79
6:17....................................79

Ephesians
1:1....................................140
1:4..............................140, 141
1:4-5 98
1:5..............................140, 141
1:5-11 99
1:7....................................138
1:9-10 79
1:11.........................76, 98, 140
1:13..........................112, 113
1:17-18 76
1:20-21 77
1:22-23 145
2:2....................................125
2:8....................................117
2:21...................................146
2:22...................................146
3:9-11 79
3:10............................76, 122
3:17...................................105
3:18....................................76
4:2....................................297
4:3-4 80
4:8....................................107
4:11............................115, 116
4:11-12 ....82, 188
4:11-13 ....107, 115, 167
4:12.............76, 114, 188, 196, 199
4:24...................................142
4:30...................................111
4:32...................................297
5:18...................................118
5:19...................................148
5:23...................................145
5:27...................................141
6:10-18 ....123, 132, 192
6:11....................................83
6:11-18 179
6:12.............83, 112, 126, 179
6:13...................................126

6:13-18 83
6:14-16 126
6:17...................................126
6:18............................126, 179

Philippians
1:5....................................80
1:23...................................162
1:27.............................79, 80
2:3-5 133
2:5-7 81
2:7-8 ....104, 108
2:8....................................135
2:9-11 ....77, 105
4:7....................................133
4:13...................................192
4:14...................................188
4:15....................................80

Colossians
1:16...................................121
1:17...................................102
1:18............................107, 145
1:27...................................105
1:27-28 82
2:16...................................236
3:24....................................83

1 Thessalonians
1:6-8 80
3:5....................................124
4......................................161
4:13-18 108
4:15-16 163
4:17...................................165
5:4-10 109
5:9....................................165
5:11...................................297
5:17...................................181
5:19....................................84

2 Thessalonians
1:7-9 77

1 Timothy
1:1-4 83
2:5-6 77
3:5....................................190
3:6....................................104
4:2....................................133
5:8....................................154

2 Timothy
1:9...98
2:19-21 79
3:15...88
3:16..................................76, 87, 88
4:5...116

Titus
1:5...82
1:9...82
2:13...105
3:5.......................................112, 141

Hebrews
1:8...102
1:14...122
2:7...122
2:17...136
4:12.....................................88, 89
4:14...107
4:14-16 146
5:6-10 103
5:7...103
7:25....................................107, 141
9...138
9:27...161
9:28.....................84, 136, 138, 166
10...138
10:1..138
10:25..148
12:22..122
13:1-3 83
13:8.....................................105, 236
13:20..116

James
1:27...81
2:1-9 81
2:14-26 79
2:15-17 148
2:20...79
3:9...79
4:7...132
4:7-8 180
5:14...308
5:16...181

1 Peter
1:15...141
2:9...146
2:24.................................106, 108, 136
2:25...116

3:22
3:22...107
5:8...125

2 Peter
1:4...142
1:16-21 88
1:21...............................76, 88, 112
2:4...123
3:9...77
3:13.....................................84, 166

1 John
1:5-10 133
1:9...118
2:1...107
2:15...131
2:16...131
2:18-26 83
3:5.....................................104, 137
3:11...................................235, 247
4:1...116
4:1-3 83
4:2...104
4:3...116
4:7...133
4:10...139
4:19...141

Jude
3..76
9..122

Revelation
5:9...138
9:2...123
9:3-11 123
9:11...125
12:3...125
12:7...................................123, 125
12:9...125
12:10..125
20..164
20:1-6 163
20:15..123
20:13-15 162
21:1-5 ....84, 166